Savor it!

Credit: Traverse City Record Eagle

FAVORITE RECIPES® OF
THE MICHIGAN 4-H FAMILY

EDITORIAL STAFF

Editorial Manager	Mary Jane Blount
Cookbook Editors	Georgia Brazil
	Mary Cummings
	Jane Hinshaw
	LaNita Stout
Book Design and Typography	Shirley Edmondson

EDITOR'S NOTE

The editors and publishers have attempted to present these tried-and-true family recipes in a form that allows approximate nutritional values to be computed. Persons with dietary or health problems or whose diets require close monitoring should not rely on the nutritional information provided. They should consult their physicians or a registered dietitian.

ABBREVIATIONS FOR NUTRITIONAL ANALYSIS

Cal	Calories	Sod	Sodium
Car	Carbohydrates	T Fat	Total Fat
Chl	Cholesterol	g	gram
Pot	Potassium	mg	milligram
Prot	Protein		

Michigan State University, the Michigan 4-H Foundation, and Favorite Recipes Press are not responsible for the nutritional analysis provided at the end of each recipe if ingredients are substituted. Nor can they be held responsible for the mistaken identity of any plant or animal listed in this book. The recipes are home-tested and are not endorsed by Michigan State University or the Michigan 4-H Foundation.

Published by Great American Opportunities, Inc.
P. O. Box 77, Nashville, Tennessee 37202

First Printing: 20,000 Editions

©Michigan 4-H Foundation MCMLXXXV
1407 South Harrison Avenue, East Lansing, Michigan 48823
Library of Congress Cataloging-in-Publication Data
Main entry under title:

Savor it!

Edited under the supervision of the Michigan 4-H
Foundation.
Includes index.
1. Cookery. 2. Cookery—Michigan. I. Michigan
4-H Foundation.
TX715.S2735   1985   641.5   85-21877
ISBN 0-87197-204-2

Contents

Acknowledgements

SAVOR IT! From Michigan's lake shores and woodlands, rich fruit belts, the upper peninsula hills, agricultural lands and urban centers, comes a collection of recipes special to our Michigan 4-H family.

Chosen from over 1200 recipes contributed, these selections represent our multi-cultural people. With gratitude to the many county Extension 4-H Youth Agents, state 4-H staff, volunteers, 4-H members and families who contributed to this project, the Michigan 4-H Foundation is proud to present the first Michigan 4-H cookbook.

Our special thanks to the SAVOR IT! Cookbook Committee: Donald Jost, Theresa Silm, Pat Hammerschmidt, Dean Keisling, Ruth Eggert, Earl Threadgould, and to Jane Taylor, Project Coordinator. Other persons who have been especially helpful include: Marian Reiter, Sharon Fritz, Edward Poole, and Rhonda Walker-Buckingham.

PHOTOGRAPHY CREDITS

Cover photo provided courtesy of Ed Appleyard, Appleyards Studio, South Haven, Michigan. The photo was taken at the Liberty Hyde Bailey Birthsite Museum, a National and State Historic Site in South Haven, Michigan. The cover photo depicts Van Buren County 4-H'ers with their projects.

Many black and white photographs were taken at 4-H Exploration Days on the Michigan State University campus by the following 1985 district photography delegates: Michael Barnovitz, Lynne Brooks, Julie Easler, Caryn Groleau, Jim Hawthorn, Craig McDowell, Susan Peterson, Kathy Roggenbuck, James Rund, and Patty Strange. Other photos by Jack H. Worthington, Shelly Noodle, Nancy Victorson Kipling, Linda Buddemeir, and Mark McDowell.

Savor it!

The Michigan 4-H Story

Credit: L. H. Bailey Hortorium, Cornell University

America's 4-H clubs did not start at any one time or place, but developed gradually across the nation, and in diverse situations over a period of years. However, one early pioneer in youth education, Liberty Hyde Bailey (1858-1954) can be called the father of the 4-H organization's ideals and aims. His early writings and ideas on nature study and education, and eventual publication of his Nature Study Leaflets in 1896, set the pattern for the 4-H youth education program.

Liberty Hyde Bailey was born March 15, 1858, in South Haven, Michigan. In 1877 he entered Michigan Agricultural College (MAC), − or Michigan State University as it is presently called. Bailey studied botany and horticulture and, during his sophomore year in 1878-1879, spent five months teaching in a rural East Lansing one-room school. He was greatly admired by the students to whom he taught nature study during recess and on Saturdays. In an early application of a fundamental insight into education for rural youth, Bailey brought grafting stock from the MAC campus and taught his students how to graft apple trees to improve fruit quality.

As one former student recalled, "He showed us things we'd never thought to look at before. Knowledge learned from him was useful when we grew up and had families of our own."

In 1881, as the first editor of the MAC newspaper, **The Speculum**, Bailey's first and last editorials stressed the importance of practical agricultural education, and identified this need in the education of young farmers: "The farmer has taken no pains to develop his head and heart . . . "

Upon his graduation in 1882, Bailey worked and studied at Harvard University and in 1885 returned to the MAC campus to head the Department of Horticulture. In 1888, he left for Cornell University where he later became the Dean of the College of Agriculture.

President Theodore Roosevelt called upon Bailey to act as chairman of the Commission on Country Life in America in 1908. This national committee was to make recommendations on rural problems. This resulted in the subsequent establishment of a nationwide federal extension service, the Cooperative Extension Service, created by passage of the Smith-Lever Act in 1914.

Throughout his long, distinguished career, Bailey advocated teaching practical skills to youth, skills that were learned by doing. He noted that scholarship begins in your own backyard and encouraged educators to teach rural girls and boys to meet the challenge of life around them. His main objective was to "open a child's mind by direct observation to a knowledge and love of the common things in his environment."

4-H Exploration Days

4-H Exploration Days

4-H club work in Michigan began in 1908 with the organization of boys and girls in agricultural clubs. The first corn-growing contests were initiated in western Michigan counties by J. C. McLaughlin. E. C. Lindeman was appointed the first 4-H director in 1914.

In 1925, A. G. Kettunen began his 31 year career as state 4-H club director. By the end of the 1930's, yearly enrollments surpassed 50,000. In 1952, Kettunen was responsible for establishing one of the first state 4-H foundations.

During the 1940's, the State 4-H Show began on the Michigan State University campus, a three-day event attracting 4-H'ers from all over the state. Russell Mawby became the new state director in 1956. By this time, state membership was over 70,000. Project expansion began, and projects beyond home economics and agriculture were added. The first leader training conference, Leadermete, was held in 1957, attracting volunteer leaders to the campus for training.

4-H expanded into the urban areas during the 1960s, and was no longer a program just for rural youth. Enrollments exceeded 100,000 with over 10,000 volunteer leaders. Many new projects and activities were added. Kettunen Center, the 4-H leadership training facility near Tustin, Michigan was opened in 1961.

In 1970, Michigan 4-H Youth Programs celebrated the opening in June of the first annual Exploration Days event in which the State 4-H Show was combined with 4-H Club Week. This event continues to attract approximately 4,000 youths each summer. Exploration Days is known as the largest 4-H event of its kind in the world.

Through the 1970s and continuing into the '80s, 4-H programs are expanding — and Michigan has been in the forefront of state youth programs with projects for urban youth in gardening and expanded nutrition programs. Michigan 4-H has also been a leader in the establishment of programs for the handicapped, proving that "4-H is for everyone." Special grants make possible the development of programs such as Horseback Riding for Handicappers, and the leader dog training project.

From the publication of the first club bulletin in 1915 listing 12 projects, Michigan 4-H now has over 150 projects from which to choose, an enrollment of 200,000 youth, over 30,000 volunteer leaders, and is the largest youth program in Michigan.

Michigan 4-H members receive opportunities to attend county, state and national events and conferences. Many 4-H'ers are involved in international travel adventures. Thousands of 4-H'ers receive scholarships for college, trips, and awards. These funds are received from the private sector at the local, state and national levels.

The Michigan 4-H Foundation's mission is to obtain private financial support and to use these funds to enhance the Michigan 4-H program. The Foundation obtains gifts from hundreds of individuals and organizations to provide continuing cash support for 4-H programming. In addition, the Foundation owns and operates Kettunen Center.

4-H is the youth component of the Cooperative Extension Service and is supported by each county, the State of Michigan, and the U.S. Department of Agriculture through Michigan State University. 4-H participation is open to all youth regardless of race, color, sex, creed, national origin or handicap.

After more than a century, the aims and ideals of Liberty Hyde Bailey are still in use "Learning by Doing" and "To Make the Best Better," to produce responsible and productive citizens.

The 4-H pledge reflects this aim:

I PLEDGE

My HEAD to clearer thinking,
My HEART to greater loyalty,
My HANDS to larger service, and
My HEALTH to better living
for my Club, my Community, my Country, and my World.

Michigan Grown Fruits & Vegetables Guide

These charts are a buyer's guide for fruits and vegetables commonly grown in Michigan. It shows a wide range of availability because the peak seasons for any fruit or vegetable often vary slightly from year to year and from one area of the state to another.

The solid bars indicate the usual, expected seasons of peak supply. The lighter-tinted bars represent the phasing in and out of harvest, and times when locally grown supplies are coming to market from storage.

This is a general guide and may need to be adjusted to compensate for locality and current weather.

Fruit Availability Chart

FRUIT	JAN	FEB	MAR	APR	MAY	JUN	JUL	AUG	SEP	OCT	NOV	DEC
APPLES (fall)	░	░	░	░				░	█	█	█	█
APPLES (summer)							█	█				
BLACKBERRIES							█	█				
BLUEBERRIES							█	█	░			
CANTALOUPE								█	░			
CHERRIES (tart)							█	░				
CHERRIES (sweet)							█					
CURRANTS							█	░				
GRAPES									█	█		
PEACHES								█	█			
PEARS									█	█	█	
PLUMS								░	█			
RASPBERRIES							█					
RHUBARB (field)					█	░						
STRAWBERRIES						█						

This information was developed by Consumer Marketing Information, Cooperative Extensive Service, Michigan State University.

Vegetable Availability Chart

VEGETABLE	JAN	FEB	MAR	APR	MAY	JUN	JUL	AUG	SEP	OCT	NOV	DEC
ASPARAGUS					▓	▓						
BEANS (green & snap)							▓	▓	▓	▓		
BEETS								▓	▓	▓		
BROCCOLI							▓	▓	▓	▓		
CABBAGE						▓	▓	▓	▓	▓		
CARROTS							▓	▓	▓	▓		
CAULIFLOWER							▓	▓	▓	▓		
CELERY							▓	▓	▓	▓		
COLLARDS					▓	▓	▓	▓	▓			
CORN							▓	▓	▓			
CUCUMBERS (pickling)							▓	▓				
CUCUMBERS (slicers)							▓	▓	▓			
LETTUCE (field)						▓	▓	▓	▓	▓		
ONIONS	▓	▓	▓	▓					▓	▓	▓	▓
PEPPERS (green)								▓	▓	▓		
POTATOES	▓	▓	▓	▓			▓	▓	▓	▓	▓	▓
RUTABAGAS	▓								▓	▓	▓	▓
SPINACH						▓	▓			▓		
SQUASH (summer)							▓	▓	▓	▓		
SQUASH (winter)	▓								▓	▓	▓	▓
TOMATOES (field)								▓	▓	▓		
TURNIPS									▓	▓	▓	

This information was developed by Consumer Marketing Information, Cooperative Extensive Service, Michigan State University.

Appetizers, Soups & Beverages

KIM'S CHEESE BALLS

2 8-oz. packages cream cheese, softened
2 5-oz. jars Old English cheese spread
1 5-oz. jar Roka blue cheese spread
1 tbsp. white vinegar
2 tbsp. chopped olives
1/2 tsp. (about) garlic salt
1 1/2 c. chopped pecans (opt.)

Combine cheeses, vinegar, olives and garlic salt to taste in bowl; mix well. Shape into 2 balls. Coat with pecans. Place on serving plate.
Yield: 33 one-tablespoon servings.

Kim Smith, Muskegon

PEGGY'S CHEESE BALL

1 8-oz. package cream cheese, softened
1 4-oz. jar Old English cheese spread
1 4-oz. jar Roka bleu cheese spread
1 tsp. Worcestershire sauce
1 tsp. minced onion
1 c. chopped walnuts

Combine cheeses, Worcestershire sauce and onion in bowl; mix well. Shape into ball. Coat with walnuts. Chill in refrigerator. Serve with snack crackers. Yield: 20 servings.
NOTE: May be stored, covered, in refrigerator for several days.

Approx per serv: Cal 118; Prot 4.0 g; T Fat 10.8 g; Chl 20.8 mg; Car 2.1 g; Sod 211.9 mg; Pot 63.6 mg.

Peggy Vogt, Jackson

SALMON PARTY LOG

1 16-oz. can salmon, drained, flaked
1 tbsp. lemon juice
1 8-oz. package cream cheese, softened
2 tsp. grated onion
1 tsp. horseradish
1/4 tsp. salt
1/4 tsp. liquid smoke
3/4 c. chopped pecans
1/4 c. chopped parsley

Combine first 7 ingredients in bowl; mix well. Shape into log. Coat with pecans and parsley. Chill until firm. Serve with butter crackers.
Yield: 10 servings.

Approx per serv: Cal 225; Prot 11.9 g; T Fat 19.1 g; Chl 41.1 mg; Car 2.1 g; Sod 348.0 mg; Pot 241.8 mg.

Connie Byers, Berrien

HAM AND CHEESE LOG

2 3-oz. packages cream cheese, softened
1 4-oz. can deviled ham
1 tsp. prepared mustard
2 c. shredded Cheddar cheese
2 tbsp. chopped chives
1/2 c. chopped cashews

Combine first 3 ingredients in bowl; mix well. Stir in Cheddar cheese and chives. Chill, covered, in refrigerator. Shape into log. Coat with cashews. Store, wrapped in plastic wrap, in refrigerator. Serve at room temperature with assorted crackers.
Yield: 50 one-tablespoon servings.
NOTE: May substitute macadamia nuts for cashews.

Approx per serv: Cal 52; Prot 2.1 g; T Fat 4.5 g; Chl 9.9 mg; Car 0.8 g; Sod 73.3 mg; Pot 22.1 mg.

Mrs. Martin Rubingh, Antrim

CHEESE WITH PEPPERS DIP

1/2 c. melted margarine
1/2 c. flour
2 c. milk
4 4-oz. jars Old English cheese
     spread, chopped
1/2 c. chopped seeded hot chili peppers
Hot sauce to taste

Blend margarine and flour in saucepan until smooth. Stir in milk and cheese. Bring to a boil, stirring constantly. Add peppers and hot sauce; mix well. Serve hot with fresh vegetables or chips. Yield: 64 one-tablespoon servings.

Approx per serv: Cal 27; Prot 0.7 g; T Fat 2.1 g; Chl 2.3 mg; Car 1.3 g; Sod 49.7 mg; Pot 17.9 mg.

Fred Lindholm, Wayne

CORNED BEEF DIP

1 15-oz. can corned beef, chopped
1 c. sour cream
1 env. dry onion soup mix
1 8-oz. package cream cheese, softened

Combine all ingredients in bowl; mix well. Spoon into serving dish. Chill for 1 hour. Serve with snack crackers.
Yield: 32 one-tablespoon servings.

Approx per serv: Cal 60; Prot 2.6 g; T Fat 5.1 g; Chl 18.9 mg; Car 1.2 g; Sod 170.2 mg; Pot 26.8 mg.

Amy Oomen, Oceana

SPINACH DIP

1 10-oz. package frozen chopped
   spinach, thawed
1 1/2 c. sour cream
1 c. mayonnaise
1 pkg. dry vegetable soup mix
1 8-oz. can water chestnuts,
   drained, chopped
3 green onions, chopped
1 round loaf pumpernickel bread

Squeeze spinach dry. Combine with sour cream, mayonnaise, soup mix, water chestnuts and green onions in bowl; mix well. Chill, covered, for 2 hours. Hollow out bread to make shell; serve with bread pieces. Stir spinach mixture; spoon into bread shell. Serve with reserved bread pieces.

Pat Engel, Livingston

TACO DIP DISH

1 8-oz. package cream cheese, softened
1/2 c. sour cream
2 tbsp. salad dressing
6 tbsp. mild taco sauce
1 bunch green onions, chopped
1 green pepper, chopped
1 6-oz. jar green olives, drained, sliced
2 tomatoes, chopped
1 8-oz. package shredded Cheddar cheese
2 tbsp. sliced black olives (opt.)
1 8-oz. package taco chips

Blend first 4 ingredients in bowl. Spread on serving tray, leaving border. Layer green onions, green pepper, green olives and tomatoes over cream cheese layer. Sprinkle cheese and black olives over top. Arrange taco chips around edge. Yield: 10 servings.

NOTE: The finished tray should resemble a sunflower.

Greg Weidmayer, Washtenaw

VEGETABLE DIP

2/3 c. salad dressing
1 c. sour cream
1 tbsp. onion flakes
1 tbsp. parsley flakes
1 tsp. seasoned salt
1 tsp. dillweed
1/2 tsp. dried chives
1/2 env. dry garlic-cheese salad
   dressing mix
1 tsp. seasoned salt
1 tsp. dillweed

Combine all ingredients in bowl; mix well. Spoon into serving bowl. Serve with fresh vegetables. Yield: 32 servings.

Donna M. Johnson, Calhoun

HARD SALAMI

6 lb. ground beef or venison
18 drops of liquid smoke
10 tsp. curing salt
6 tsp. garlic salt
6 tsp. mustard seed
6 tsp. pepper
1/2 tsp. crushed red pepper
1/2 tsp. MSG

Combine all ingredients in bowl; mix well. Chill, covered, for 4 days. Shape into rolls. Place on wire racks in baking pans. Bake at 150 degrees for 10 hours. Drain. Cool. Cut into 1/8-inch slices. Serve with crackers. Yield: 18 servings.

Shirley Merriman, Calhoun

ZESTY WINGS

Chicken wings
Corn oil for deep frying
White vinegar
Hot sauce
1 c. sour cream
1 c. mayonnaise
1 pkg. ranch-style dressing mix
4 oz. blue cheese, crumbled

Remove and discard chicken wing tips. Deep-fry chicken wings for 20 minutes. Drain on paper towel. Marinate in mixture of equal parts white vinegar and hot sauce. Combine remaining ingredients in bowl. Serve wings with blue cheese dip, celery sticks and French bread.

Dr. Garry J. Fedore, Cass

SCANDINAVIAN SANDWICH WHEEL

1 pkg. refrigerator crescent dinner rolls
1 8-oz. package cream cheese, softened
1/4 c. mayonnaise
1 tbsp. milk
1/8 tsp. dried dillweed
1 16-oz. can salmon, drained, flaked
1 tsp. lemon juice
1 hard-boiled egg, sliced
1/2 c. sliced ripe olives
1/2 c. chopped green pepper
1 lg. tomato, seeded, chopped

Fit crescent rolls into greased 12-inch pizza pan; seal edges. Bake at 375 degrees for 10 to 12 minutes or until browned. Cool. Place on serving tray. Beat cream cheese, mayonnaise and milk in bowl until light and fluffy. Reserve 3/4 cup mixture. Stir dillweed into remaining cream cheese. Spread over cooled crust. Mound salmon in center. Sprinkle with lemon juice. Arrange egg slices on salmon. Arrange olives, green pepper and tomato in rings around salmon. Pipe reserved cream cheese mixture around edge. Chill, covered, in refrigerator. Cut into wedges. Yield: 12 servings.

Approx per serv: Cal 254; Prot 12.1 g; T Fat 16.8 g; Chl 59.4 mg; Car 13.5 g; Sod 441.2 mg; Pot 218.0 mg.

Katherine Whybrew, Delta

STEAK BITES

1/2 c. dry red wine
1 clove of garlic, crushed
1 2-lb. top round 1-in. thick beef steak
2 tbsp. butter, melted
1 1/2 tsp. Worcestershire sauce
1/4 tsp. salt
1/8 tsp. hot pepper sauce
1 1/2 tsp. dry mustard

Combine wine and garlic in 9 x 13-inch dish. Add steak, coating well. Marinate, covered, in refrigerator for 1 1/2 hours, turning once. Drain, reserving marinade. Broil 5 inches from heat source for 10 minutes; turn steak. Broil for 8 minutes longer or to desired degree of doneness. Cut into 1-inch cubes. Blend remaining ingredients and 2 tablespoons reserved marinade in saucepan. Cook until heated through. Combine with steak bites in chafing dish. Serve with toothpicks. Yield: 20 servings.

Approx per serv: Cal 105; Prot 9.2 g; T Fat 6.7 g; Chl 34.4 mg; Car 0.4 g; Sod 76.9 mg; Pot 156.4 mg.

Sherry Jonckheere, Livingston

CHESTNUT APPETIZERS

36 whole chestnuts, peeled
12 slices bacon, cut into thirds
1/2 c. catsup
1/2 c. sugar

Wrap each chestnut with bacon piece; secure with toothpick. Place in baking pan. Bake at 350 degrees for 30 minutes. Drain. Add mixture of catsup and sugar. Bake for 20 minutes longer. Yield: 36 servings.

NOTE: This recipe uses real chestnuts not water chestnuts.

Approx per serv: Cal 117; Prot 2.0 g; T Fat 2.0 g; Chl 2.2 mg; Car 22.8 g; Sod 63.0 mg; Pot 224.0 mg.

Kelly Leach, Kalamazoo

SAUERKRAUT BALLS

8 oz. pork sausage
1/4 c. chopped onion
1 14-oz. can sauerkraut, drained,
*   finely chopped*
2 tbsp. fine bread crumbs
1 3-oz. package cream cheese, softened

2 tbsp. chopped parsley
1 tsp. mustard
1/4 tsp. garlic salt
1/2 c. flour
2 eggs, well beaten
1/4 c. milk
3/4 c. dry bread crumbs
Oil for deep frying

Brown sausage with onion in skillet, stirring until crumbly; drain. Add sauerkraut and 2 tablespoons bread crumbs; mix well. Combine cream cheese, parsley, mustard and garlic salt in bowl; mix well. Add to sausage mixture; mix well. Shape into balls. Coat with flour, mixture of eggs and milk and 3/4 cup bread crumbs in order listed. Deep-fry at 375 degrees for 1 to 2 minutes or until brown. Drain on paper towels.
NOTE: May be frozen and reheated in 425-degree oven for 15 minutes.

Barbara Vogel, Muskegon

SPINACH QUICHE BALLS

2   10-oz. packages frozen spinach, thawed
2 c. herb-flavored stuffing mix
1 stick margarine, softened
1 c. Parmesan cheese
1/8 tsp. salt
Pepper and nutmeg to taste
5 eggs, beaten

Squeeze excess moisture from spinach; dry with paper toweling. Combine stuffing mix, margarine, cheese and seasonings in bowl; mix well. Add eggs; mix well. Stir in spinach. Shape into 1-inch balls. Place on baking sheet. Bake at 350 degrees for 10 minutes. Yield: 48 servings.
NOTE: May store unbaked Spinach Quiche Balls in freezer.

Approx per serv: Cal 49; Prot 2.3 g; T Fat 3.3 g; Chl 28.8 mg; Car 2.7 g; Sod 99.2 mg; Pot 57.9 mg.

Vicki Lee Sylvester, Bay

4-H is investing in youth.

ZUCCHINI APPETIZERS

1 c. buttermilk baking mix
1/2 c. finely chopped onion

1/2 c. Parmesan cheese
2 tbsp. chopped parsley
1/2 tsp. salt
Pepper to taste
1/2 tsp. oregano
1 clove of garlic, finely chopped
1/2 tsp. seasoned salt
1/2 c. oil
4 eggs, lightly beaten
3 c. thinly sliced zucchini

Combine first 9 ingredients in bowl. Add oil and eggs; mix well. Add zucchini; stir to coat. Spread in greased 9 x 13-inch baking pan. Bake at 350 degrees for 25 minutes or until golden brown. Cut into 1 x 2-inch bars. Serve warm. Yield: 48 servings.

Approx per serv: Cal 45; Prot 1.3 g; T Fat 3.4 g; Chl 22.2 mg; Car 2.3 g; Sod 91.4 mg; Pot 29.8 mg.

Carolyn Haske, Presque Isle

Soups

MEATBALL SOUP

1 lb. stew beef
6 bouillon cubes
5 whole allspice
5 whole peppercorns
2 c. chopped cauliflower
2 c. chopped carrot
1/4 to 1/2 lb. fresh spinach
2 to 3 leeks, chopped
8 oz. vermicelli
1 lb. ground chuck
1/2 tsp. allspice

Combine stew beef, bouillon cubes, whole allspice, peppercorns and 8 cups water in saucepan. Simmer for 2 1/2 to 3 hours or until tender. Add vegetables. Cook until tender. Add vermicelli. Combine ground chuck, 1/2 teaspoon allspice and salt to taste in bowl. Shape into marble-sized meatballs. Drop into hot soup. Remove from heat. Let stand until vermicelli is tender and meatballs are cooked through. Yield: 8 servings.

Approx per serv: Cal 460; Prot 34.0 g; T Fat 19.9 g; Chl 94.1 mg; Car 35.7 g; Sod 833.9 mg; Pot 821.1 mg.

Melissa Peters, Van Buren

HEARTY OVEN-BAKED BEEF SOUP

1 1/2 lb. stew beef, cut into sm. cubes
1 c. chopped onion
1 tsp. minced garlic
1 1/2 tsp. salt
1 tsp. freshly ground pepper
2 tbsp. oil
3 cans condensed beef broth
1 to 2 16-oz. cans tomatoes
1/4 c. barley
1/4 c. brown rice
1 1/2 c. pitted ripe olives
1 1/2 c. thinly sliced carrots
2 c. sliced zucchini
1/2 c. chopped celery
1 can kidney beans (opt.)
Chopped parsnips (opt.)
Chopped rutabaga (opt.)
1 1/2 tsp. Italian seasoning
2 tbsp. chopped parsley

Combine first 6 ingredients in large casserole; mix well. Bake at 400 degrees for 40 minutes, stirring several times. Reduce temperature to 325 degrees. Add broth, 2 cups water and 1 can tomatoes. Bake, covered, for 1 hour. Add remaining ingredients. Bake for 40 to 45 minutes. Serve with Parmesan cheese.

Lois A. Stuart, Wayne

VEGETABLE-BEEF SOUP

3 lb. beef shank
1 18-oz. can tomato juice
1/3 c. chopped onion
4 tsp. salt
2 tbsp. Worcestershire sauce
2 bay leaves
1/4 tsp. chili powder
1 16-oz. can tomatoes
1 c. chopped celery
1 8-oz. can whole kernel corn
1 c. sliced carrots
1 c. chopped potatoes
1 10-oz. package frozen lima beans

Combine beef shank, tomato juice, onion, seasonings and 6 cups water in saucepan. Simmer, covered, for 2 hours. Skim and strain broth. Cut meat from bones. Combine strained broth, beef and remaining ingredients. Simmer, covered, for 1 hour.

Yvette Smith, Wayne

NEW ENGLAND CLAM CHOWDER

2 oz. bacon, finely chopped
2 med. onions, finely chopped
3 med. potatoes, chopped
1 pt. clam juice
1/2 tsp. thyme
3 6-oz. cans minced clams
2 c. milk
5 tbsp. flour

Brown bacon in saucepan. Add onions. Saute until tender. Add potatoes, clam juice and thyme. Simmer until potatoes are just tender. Add clams with liquid and milk. Simmer for 10 minutes. Blend flour with enough water to make of pouring consistency. Stir into simmering soup gradually. Simmer for 3 minutes, stirring constantly. Yield: 8 servings.

Approx per serv: Cal 217; Prot 12.0 g; T Fat 7.7 g; Chl 40.9 mg; Car 24.7 g; Sod 716.0 mg; Pot 534.1 mg.

Gaylia Anger, Midland

BROCCOLI SOUP

2 to 3 c. finely chopped broccoli
1 med. onion, chopped
2 to 3 tbsp. margarine
2 to 3 tbsp. flour
1 lg. can evaporated milk
2 c. (about) milk
1/2 c. shredded Cheddar cheese (opt.)

Cook broccoli in a small amount of water in saucepan until tender-crisp. Do not drain. Saute onion in margarine in saucepan. Stir in flour, evaporated milk and milk gradually. Cook over low heat until thickened, stirring constantly. Add broccoli and cooking liquid. Season with salt and pepper to taste. Add cheese.
Yield: 4 servings.

Approx per serv: Cal 407; Prot 18.3 g; T Fat 26.0 g; Chl 63.7 mg; Car 27.1 g; Sod 400.8 mg; Pot 778.3 mg.

Carolyn Worth, Barry

CANADIAN CHEESE SOUP

1/2 c. finely chopped onion
1/4 c. butter
1/2 c. flour
4 c. milk
4 c. chicken broth

1/2 c. finely chopped carrots, cooked
1/2 c. finely chopped celery, cooked
2 c. (or more) chopped sharp
   Cheddar cheese
Paprika to taste

Saute onion in butter in saucepan until tender. Add flour; mix well. Stir in milk and broth. Cook until thickened, stirring constantly. Add carrots and celery. Reduce heat. Add cheese. Simmer for 15 minutes. Season with paprika and salt to taste. Ladle into soup bowls. Yield: 8 servings.

Approx per serv: Cal 393; Prot 19.8 g; T Fat 28.4 g; Chl 91.5 mg; Car 15.1 g; Sod 780.5 mg; Pot 297.8 mg.

Robyn Staelgraeve, Monroe

MICHIGAN NAVY BEAN SOUP

2 c. dried navy beans
1 c. chopped onion
2 c. chopped peeled potatoes
1/2 c. shredded carrot
1 c. (or more) chopped ham (opt.)
1 tbsp. catsup
2 1/2 tsp. salt
1/8 tsp. pepper

Soak beans in water to cover in saucepan overnight. Bring to a boil. Cook over medium heat for 2 hours. Add 5 cups water and remaining ingredients. Return to a boil; reduce heat. Simmer for 1 1/2 hours. Yield: 8 servings.

Approx per serv: Cal 266; Prot 16.3 g; T Fat 4.8 g; Chl 15.6 mg; Car 40.8 g; Sod 832.8 mg; Pot 870.2 mg.

Irene L. Johnson, Bay

CREAM OF MUSHROOM SOUP

8 oz. mushrooms, finely chopped
2 tbsp. butter
4 c. hot chicken broth
2 tbsp. melted butter
2 tbsp. flour
1 c. light cream

Saute mushrooms in 2 tablespoons butter in saucepan for 5 minutes, stirring constantly. Add broth. Simmer for 5 minutes. Blend melted butter and flour in saucepan. Stir in 2/3 of the broth mixture. Cook until thickened, stirring constantly. Add with cream to remaining broth mixture. Season with salt and pepper to taste. Heat to serving temperature. Spoon into soup bowls. Garnish with paprika and parsley. Yield: 4 servings.

Approx per serv: Cal 316; Prot 4.3 g; T Fat 30.5 g; Chl 104.9 mg; Car 8.0 g; Sod 1130.2 mg; Pot 306.8 mg.

Kay Ringel, Monroe

POTATO SOUP

3 c. chopped potatoes
1/2 c. chopped celery
1/4 c. chopped onion
1 chicken bouillon cube
1 tsp. parsley flakes
1/4 tsp. salt
2 tbsp. flour
1 1/2 c. milk
8 oz. Velveeta cheese, chopped

Combine first 6 ingredients and 1 1/4 cups water in saucepan. Cook until vegetables are tender. Stir in mixture of flour and milk. Cook until thickened, stirring constantly. Add cheese. Cook until cheese melts, stirring constantly. Yield: 6 servings.

Approx per serv: Cal 234; Prot 11.8 g; T Fat 11.3 g; Chl 36.3 mg; Car 21.6 g; Sod 1164.7 mg; Pot 528.1 mg.

Louise Feldpausch, Clinton

CREAM OF TOMATO SOUP

2 tbsp. finely chopped onion
2 tbsp. butter
3 tbsp. flour
2 tsp. sugar
1 tsp. salt
1/8 tsp. pepper
2 c. tomato juice
2 c. milk

Saute onion in butter in saucepan until tender. Stir in flour, sugar and seasonings. Cook until bubbly, stirring constantly. Remove from heat. Stir in tomato juice gradually. Bring to a boil, stirring constantly. Boil for 1 minute. Stir hot mixture into cold milk. Return to saucepan. Heat to serving temperature. Serve immediately. Yield: 4 servings.

Approx per serv: Cal 185; Prot 6.1 g; T Fat 10.2 g; Chl 34.8 mg; Car 18.2 g; Sod 907.7 mg; Pot 467.5 mg.

Mandy Winkler, Washtenaw

Beverages

CELEBRATION PUNCH

3 pkg. lemon-lime drink mix
2 c. sugar
1 46-oz. can pineapple-grapefruit juice
2/3 c. lemon juice
1 qt. lime sherbet
1 64-oz. bottle of 7-Up, chilled

Combine drink mix, sugar and 2 quarts ice water in punch bowl; mix well. Add juices. Add sherbet and 7-Up just before serving.
Yield: 30 servings.

Approx per serv: Cal 134; Prot 0.4 g; T Fat 0.3 g; Chl 0.0 mg; Car 33.5 g; Sod 2.8 mg; Pot 43.4 mg.

Amy Smith, Gratiot

KOOL-AID PUNCH

2 pkg. cherry drink mix
Sugar
1 12-oz. can frozen orange juice concentrate, thawed
1 qt. ginger ale

Combine drink mix and sugar according to package directions. Add 2 quarts water. Prepare orange juice using package directions. Combine with cherry drink in punch bowl. Stir in ginger ale. Add ice or ice ring.
Yield: 64 six-ounce servings.

Carol Marenger, Delta

SEVEN-UP-APRICOT AND ORANGE PUNCH

1 6-oz. can frozen orange juice concentrate
1 46-oz. can apricot nectar, chilled
3 28-oz. bottles of 7-Up, chilled
1 qt. lemon sherbet

Combine orange juice concentrate and apricot nectar in punch bowl; mix well. Add 7-Up gently. Spoon in sherbet.
Yield: 34 four-ounce servings.

Brenda Guenther, Washtenaw

HOLIDAY PUNCH

1 6-oz. can frozen orange juice concentrate
2 6-oz. cans frozen lemonade concentrate
1 6-oz. can frozen limeade concentrate
1 30-oz. can pineapple juice
2 c. cranberry juice
2 32-oz. bottles of ginger ale, chilled
1 32-oz. bottle of soda, chilled

Combine all ingredients in punch bowl; mix well. Garnish with lemon or lime slices.
Yield: 33 six-ounce servings.

Approx per serv: Cal 95; Prot 0.3 g; T Fat 0.1 g; Chl 0.0 mg; Car 24.1 g; Sod 1.0 mg; Pot 106.1 mg.

Tiffany Threadgould, Ingham

OLD ENGLISH EGGNOG

6 eggs, separated
1 c. sugar
2 qt. light cream
Flavoring to taste (opt.)
1/2 c. confectioners' sugar

Beat egg yolks in mixer bowl until thick. Add sugar gradually, beating until light. Add cream; beat well. Stir in flavoring. Chill, covered, in refrigerator. Beat egg whites until foamy. Add confectioners' sugar gradually, beating well after each addition. Beat until soft peaks form. Fold gently into chilled mixture. Chill, covered, for 1 hour. Yield: 24 four-ounce servings.

Approx per serv: Cal 301; Prot 3.6 g; T Fat 26.4 g; Chl 151.6 mg; Car 13.8 g; Sod 44.1 mg; Pot 97.8 mg.

Marjory McPherson Veliquette, Antrim

FRIENDSHIP TEA

1 1/4 c. instant tea powder
18 oz. instant orange breakfast drink mix
2 c. sugar
1 .26-oz. package unsweetened lemonade mix
1 tsp. cloves
2 tsp. cinnamon

Combine all ingredients in bowl; mix well. Store in airtight container. Add 1 tablespoon mixture to 1 cup hot water in mug for each serving.

Cathy Newkirk, Ingham

Fruits & Vegetables

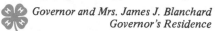

CARROTS AND APPLES

3 med. carrots, peeled, sliced
2 tbsp. butter
1 med. apple, sliced
1/2 tsp. cinnamon
1/4 c. packed brown sugar

Saute carrots in butter in skillet until tender-crisp. Add apple. Cook until heated through, stirring constantly. Stir in cinnamon and brown sugar. Spoon into serving dish.
Yield: 4 servings.

Approx per serv: Cal 156; Prot 0.7 g; T Fat 6.2 g; Chl 17.7 mg; Car 26.2 g; Sod 100.1 mg; Pot 291.5 mg.

Governor and Mrs. James J. Blanchard
Governor's Residence

BAKED PINEAPPLE

1/2 c. butter, softened
1/2 c. (or more) sugar
4 eggs
1   20-oz. can crushed pineapple
5 slices bread, cubed

Cream butter and sugar in bowl. Add eggs; beat well. Stir in pineapple and bread. Pour into greased 1 1/2-quart casserole. Bake, uncovered, at 350 degrees for 1 hour or until lightly browned. Serve hot or cold. Yield: 6 servings.

Approx per serv: Cal 397; Prot 6.8 g; T Fat 20.0 g; Chl 216.6 mg; Car 49.5 g; Sod 348.7 mg; Pot 174.8 mg.

Christy Miller, Lenawee

ASPARAGUS AND MUSHROOM CASSEROLE

2   8-oz. packages frozen cut asparagus
1 c. milk
2 tbsp. cornstarch
4 c. chopped mushrooms
1 c. chopped onion
1/4 c. butter
1 tsp. instant chicken bouillon
1/2 tsp. salt
1/2 tsp. nutmeg
1 1/2 tsp. lemon juice
1/4 c. chopped pimento (opt.)
3/4 c. soft bread crumbs
1 tbsp. butter

Cook asparagus according to package directions. Drain, reserving liquid. Add enough milk to reserved liquid to measure 1 to 1 1/2 cups. Mix in cornstarch. Saute mushrooms and onion in 1/4 cup butter and bouillon in skillet. Stir in salt, nutmeg and lemon juice. Add milk mixture. Stir in asparagus and pimento gently. Pour into 1 1/2-quart casserole. Brown bread crumbs in 1 tablespoon butter in skillet. Sprinkle over casserole. Bake at 350 degrees for 35 to 40 minutes. Yield: 6 servings.

Approx per serv: Cal 189; Prot 7.1 g; T Fat 11.7 g; Chl 35.7 mg; Car 16.6 g; Sod 444.8 mg; Pot 556.2 mg.

Marilyn McQueen, Clinton

CHEESY GREEN BEANS

3/4 c. milk
1   8-oz. package cream cheese
1/2 tsp. salt
1 tsp. garlic salt
1/2 c. Parmesan cheese
2   16-oz. cans green beans, drained

Combine milk, cream cheese, salt, garlic salt and Parmesan cheese in saucepan. Cook over low heat until cream cheese is melted, stirring constantly. Stir in green beans. Heat to serving temperature. Yield: 10 servings.

Approx per serv: Cal 136; Prot 5.5 g; T Fat 10.8 g; Chl 33.4 mg; Car 5.2 g; Sod 636.3 mg; Pot 135.4 mg.

Mary Arndt, Allegan

COMPANY VEGETABLES

2   10-oz. packages frozen broccoli spears
1 c. grated American cheese
1 can cream of mushroom soup
1 sm. can evaporated milk
1   3 1/2-oz. can French-fried onion rings

Cook broccoli according to package directions for 4 minutes; drain. Place in 2-quart baking dish. Sprinkle with cheese. Pour mixture of soup and evaporated milk over top. Bake at 350 degrees for 25 minutes. Top with onion rings. Bake for 8 to 10 minutes longer or until onion rings are crisp. Yield: 6 servings.

NOTE: May substitute asparagus spears, French-cut green beans, green peas or mixed vegetables for broccoli spears.

Marie Kondras, Cass

BROCCOLI HOT DISH

1 lg. onion, chopped
1/4 c. margarine
1   10-oz. package frozen cut broccoli
1/4 c. milk
1/2 c. Cheez Whiz
1   4-oz. can chopped mushrooms
1 can cream of mushroom soup
1 c. minute rice

Saute onion in margarine in skillet. Cook broccoli in 1/2 cup water in saucepan according to package directions. Chop broccoli. Combine with sauteed onion and remaining ingredients in bowl; mix well. Spoon into 9-inch square baking dish. Bake at 350 degrees for 45 minutes. Yield: 3 servings.

NOTE: Don't tell anyone it is broccoli. Listen to them rave about it first. I don't like broccoli but love this.

Approx per serv: Cal 495; Prot 13.3 g; T Fat 29.0 g; Chl 24.4 mg; Car 47.8 g; Sod 1314.0 mg; Pot 572.1 mg.

Jana Trembath, Luce

4-H is for kids.

ANNA'S BROCCOLI AND RICE CASSEROLE

1/2 c. brown rice
1 bunch broccoli
1 can cream of celery soup
1 soup can milk
1/2 tsp. salt
1/2 c. grated Cheddar cheese

Cook brown rice in 1 1/2 cups water in saucepan for 30 minutes or until water is absorbed. Peel broccoli stems; cut stems and flowerets into 1/2-inch pieces. Add to cooked brown rice. Stir in mixture of soup, milk and salt. Pour into 2-quart casserole. Sprinkle with cheese. Bake at 350 degrees for 45 minutes to 1 hour or until broccoli is tender. Yield: 4 servings.

Approx per serv: Cal 279; Prot 13.1 g; T Fat 11.1 g; Chl 29.1 mg; Car 34.1 g; Sod 1015.6 mg; Pot 671.1 mg.

Anna Butterfield, Lapeer

PATRICIA'S BROCCOLI AND RICE CASSEROLE

1 can cream of mushroom soup
1/4 c. butter
1   8-oz. jar Cheez Whiz
2 c. minute rice
1   10-oz. package frozen chopped broccoli, thawed

Heat soup, 1 soup can water, butter and Cheez Whiz in saucepan until Cheez Whiz melts, stirring constantly. Stir in rice and broccoli. Pour into 2-quart baking dish. Bake at 350 degrees for 45 minutes. Yield: 8 servings.

Approx per serv: Cal 283; Prot 9.3 g; T Fat 15.7 g; Chl 41.1 mg; Car 26.6 g; Sod 825.0 mg; Pot 182.7 mg.

Patricia Rumsey, Jackson

RED CABBAGE

6 slices bacon, chopped
1/4 c. vinegar
1/4 c. sugar
1 med. red cabbage, finely sliced
1 apple, chopped
Pepper to taste

Cook bacon in saucepan until crisp. Stir in vinegar and sugar. Add cabbage, apple, pepper and 1/2 cup water. Cook, covered, over low heat for about 2 hours, adding additional water if necessary. Yield: 4 servings.

Approx per serv: Cal 375; Prot 7.5 g; T Fat 24.3 g; Chl 23.8 mg; Car 36.1 g; Sod 291.0 mg; Pot 710.6 mg.

Emily Van Matre, Barry

SCALLOPED CABBAGE

1 lg. head cabbage
16 oz. Cheddar cheese, shredded
2 c. cracker crumbs
1 c. milk

Cut cabbage into bite-sized pieces. Cook in a small amount of water in saucepan until tender. Add cheese and cracker crumbs; mix well. Stir in milk and salt and pepper to taste. Pour into baking dish. Bake at 350 degrees for 45 minutes. Yield: 6 servings.

Approx per serv: Cal 501; Prot 26.4 g; T Fat 29.2 g; Chl 80.5 mg; Car 36.6 g; Sod 866.7 mg; Pot 853.1 mg.

Linda Smith, Lenawee

MARINATED CARROTS

2 lb. carrots, peeled, sliced
1 green pepper, sliced
1 med. onion, sliced
1 can tomato soup
1/2 c. oil
1/2 c. sugar
3/4 c. cider vinegar
1 tsp. prepared mustard
1 tsp. Worcestershire sauce
1 tsp. salt
1/2 tsp. pepper

Cook carrots in a small amount of water in saucepan until tender-crisp; drain and cool. Place in large bowl with green pepper and onion. Combine remaining ingredients in bowl; mix well. Pour over vegetables. Spoon into serving bowl. Serve cold as vegetable or salad. Yield: 8 servings.

Approx per serv: Cal 256; Prot 2.2 g; T Fat 14.7 g; Chl 0.0 mg; Car 31.6 g; Sod 638.8 mg; Pot 531.8 mg.

Frances Passerello, Houghton

CAULIFLOWER-BROCCOLI DELIGHT

1   10-oz. package frozen broccoli
1   10-oz. package frozen cauliflower
1 can cream of mushroom soup
2/3 c. milk
1 c. shredded Cheddar cheese
1   3-oz. can French-fried onions

Cook broccoli and cauliflower according to package directions for 3 to 5 minutes; drain. Combine soup, milk and cheese in bowl; mix well. Stir in 3/4 can onions. Combine with cooked vegetables in 2-quart casserole. Sprinkle with remaining onions. Bake at 350 degrees for 35 minutes. Yield: 5 servings.

Approx per serv: Cal 286; Prot 10.9 g; T Fat 17.0 g; Chl 31.7 mg; Car 24.1 g; Sod 925.2 mg; Pot 379.2 mg.

Jennifer S. Bieneman, Kent

CHEESY CAULIFLOWER

1 med. head cauliflower, separated
*   into flowerets*
1/4 c. chopped green pepper
1/4 c. chopped onion
1   6-oz. can sliced mushrooms, drained
1/4 c. butter

1 c. milk
1 can cream of mushroom soup
2 tbsp. flour
1 tsp. salt
6 slices pimento cheese
Paprika to taste

Cook cauliflower in a small amount of water in saucepan for 10 to 15 minutes; drain. Saute green pepper, onion and mushrooms in butter in skillet. Add milk, soup, flour and salt. Cook until thickened, stirring constantly. Spoon half the cauliflower into 1 1/2-quart casserole. Top with half the cheese and half the sauce. Repeat with remaining cauliflower, cheese and sauce. Sprinkle with paprika. Bake at 350 degrees for 30 minutes. Yield: 8 servings.

NOTE: May substitute additional 1 cup milk for soup.

Barbara J. Root, Washtenaw

TWICE-COOKED PARSNIPS

2 lg. parsnips, peeled, quartered
1/2 c. margarine
6 parsley sprigs

Cook parsnips in enough water to almost cover in saucepan until tender-crisp; drain. Brown in margarine in skillet over medium heat, turning frequently. Remove to serving dish. Garnish with parsley. Yield: 4 servings.

Approx per serv: Cal 257; Prot 1.4 g; T Fat 23.4 g; Chl 0.0 mg; Car 12.0 g; Sod 286.7 mg; Pot 309.7 mg.

Gloria Brabon, Van Buren

AUDREY ANN'S POTATO CASSEROLE

2 1-lb. packages frozen hashed brown
   potatoes, thawed
1 c. sour cream
1 can cream of chicken soup
1/2 c. butter, melted
1/2 c. chopped onion
8 oz. Cheddar cheese, shredded

Combine hashed brown potatoes, sour cream, soup and butter in bowl; mix well. Stir in onion and cheese. Spoon into 9 x 13-inch baking pan. Bake at 375 degrees for 1 hour.
Yield: 12 servings.
NOTE: May sprinkle with crushed potato chips before baking.

Approx per serv: Cal 261; Prot 7.0 g; T Fat 19.0 g; Chl 52.7 mg; Car 16.7 g; Sod 443.1 mg; Pot 201.3 mg.

Audrey Ann Keith, Mason

MASHED POTATO DISH

9 or 10 med. potatoes, peeled
1 8-oz. package cream cheese, softened
1/2 c. sour cream
2 tbsp. butter
2 tsp. garlic salt
1 tsp. salt
1/4 tsp. pepper

Cook potatoes in water to cover in saucepan until tender. Drain and mash potatoes. Add cream cheese, sour cream, butter, garlic salt, salt and pepper; mix well. Spoon into greased 9 x 13-inch baking pan. Bake at 350 degrees for 30 minutes. Yield: 8 servings.

Approx per serv: Cal 340; Prot 7.7 g; T Fat 16.8 g; Chl 46.7 mg; Car 41.3 g; Sod 919.9 mg; Pot 996.5 mg.

Ruth Salo, Houghton

SCALLOPED POTATOES

6 to 8 lg. potatoes, peeled, thinly sliced
1 can cream of mushroom soup
1 lg. can evaporated milk
1 med. onion, chopped
1 tbsp. salt
1/4 tsp. pepper
8 oz. Velveeta cheese, cut into
   1/2-in. cubes (opt.)

Place potatoes in 4-quart casserole. Mix soup, evaporated milk, onion, salt and pepper in bowl. Pour over potatoes; stir gently. Stir in cheese cubes. Bake, uncovered, at 350 degrees for 1 1/2 to 2 hours or until tender.
Yield: 10 servings.

Rachele Bogue, Cass

MASHED RUTABAGAS AND POTATOES SUPREME

2 tsp. salt
1 tbsp. sugar
4 c. chopped peeled rutabagas
3 c. chopped peeled potatoes
1 cube chicken bouillon
1/4 tsp. pepper
1 c. grated Cheddar cheese
2 tbsp. finely chopped onion

Sprinkle salt and sugar over rutabagas and potatoes in saucepan. Dissolve bouillon cube in 2 cups boiling water. Pour over vegetables. Bring to a boil; reduce heat. Simmer until vegetables are tender. Drain and mash vegetables. Add pepper, cheese and onion. Beat until fluffy. Spoon into serving dish. Yield: 6 servings.

Approx per serv: Cal 185; Prot 7.5 g; T Fat 6.3 g; Chl 19.2 mg; Car 25.8 g; Sod 1009.7 mg; Pot 550.3 mg.

Pearl McCauley, Delta

TOFU-SPINACH PIE

1 10-oz. package frozen chopped spinach
3 eggs, beaten
16 oz. tofu, at room temperature
1 tsp. salt
1/2 tsp. pepper
1/2 tsp. nutmeg
1/2 tsp. allspice
2 med. onions, minced
1/2 c. chopped green pepper
1 c. grated sharp Cheddar cheese

Cook spinach according to package directions until just thawed; drain well. Combine eggs, tofu and spices in blender container. Process until smooth. Add spinach, onions, green pepper and cheese; mix well. Pour into greased pie plate. Bake at 325 degrees for 1 hour.
Yield: 5 servings.

Approx per serv: Cal 241; Prot 19.3 g; T Fat 14.8 g; Chl 174.1 mg; Car 10.2 g; Sod 667.0 mg; Pot 408.6 mg.

Joy Jonckheere, Livingston

4-H is 30,000 Michigan volunteer leaders.

TOMATO PIE

1 1/4 c. flour
2 tsp. baking powder
1/2 tsp. salt
1/2 tsp. basil
1/2 c. shortening
1/2 c. sour cream
3/4 c. mayonnaise
1 c. shredded Cheddar cheese
1 tbsp. minced onion
1 tbsp. minced green pepper
1/2 c. sliced mushrooms
3 med. tomatoes, peeled, sliced

Mix flour, baking powder, salt and basil in bowl. Cut in shortening until crumbly. Stir in sour cream. Spread evenly in 9-inch pie plate. Combine mayonnaise, cheese, onion, green pepper and mushrooms in bowl; mix gently. Layer tomato slices and mayonnaise mixture alternately over crust. Bake at 375 degrees for 30 to 35 minutes. Yield: 6 servings.

Approx per serv: Cal 406; Prot 8.9 g; T Fat 30.6 g; Chl 28.3 mg; Car 24.7 g; Sod 443.1 mg; Pot 249.1 mg.

Cheri Booth, Gratiot

4-H is meeting the needs of today.

ZUCCHINI CASSEROLE

3 lb. zucchini, cut into 1-in. pieces
1/2 c. chopped onion
1 can cream of mushroom soup
1 c. sour cream
1 c. grated carrots
1 c. grated Cheddar cheese
1 6-oz. package chicken-flavored
   stuffing mix

Cook zucchini and onion in water to cover in saucepan for 5 minutes; drain. Mix soup, sour cream, carrots and cheese in bowl. Fold in zucchini and onion. Mix dry stuffing mix with seasoning packet. Reserve 3/4 cup stuffing mix.

Sprinkle remaining stuffing mix in greased 9 x 13-inch baking pan. Spoon zucchini mixture over top. Sprinkle with reserved stuffing mix. Bake at 350 degrees for 1 hour.
Yield: 12 servings.

Approx per serv: Cal 262; Prot 9.5 g; T Fat 10.5 g; Chl 21.1 mg; Car 34.0 g; Sod 745.5 mg; Pot 387.3 mg.

Lucille Gilchrist, Genesse

RUSSIAN VEGETABLE PIE

1 1/4 c. flour
1 tsp. sugar
1 tsp. salt
3 tbsp. butter
4 oz. cream cheese, softened
1 yellow onion, chopped
3 c. shredded cabbage
2 tbsp. butter
Basil, marjoram, dill and tarragon
   to taste
8 oz. mushrooms, sliced
1 tbsp. butter
4 oz. cream cheese, softened
4 or 5 hard-boiled eggs, sliced

Combine first 3 ingredients in bowl. Cut in 3 tablespoons butter until crumbly. Add 4 ounces cream cheese; mix well. Roll 2/3 of the dough on lightly floured surface to fit 9-inch pie plate; line pie plate. Roll remaining dough for top crust. Place in refrigerator. Saute onion and cabbage in 2 tablespoons butter in skillet until cabbage is wilted, adding herbs and salt and pepper to taste. Set cabbage mixture aside. Saute mushrooms in 1 tablespoon butter in skillet for 5 minutes. Spread 4 ounces cream cheese in pie shell. Layer hard-boiled egg slices over cream cheese; sprinkle with chopped dill. Layer cabbage mixture and mushrooms in prepared pie shell. Top with chilled pastry, sealing and fluting edge and cutting vents. Bake at 400 degrees for 15 minutes. Reduce temperature to 350 degrees. Bake for 20 to 25 minutes or until golden. Yield: 4 servings.

NOTE: Don't tell people what is in the pie until they try it. Use fresh seasonings and be generous with them. Use at least 1/8 teaspoon of each.

Approx per serv: Cal 671; Prot 21.1 g; T Fat 46.7 g; Chl 428.9 mg; Car 43.5 g; Sod 922.9 mg; Pot 821.2 mg.

Virginia Pulver, Marquette

Salads & Side Dishes

BLUEBERRY GELATIN

2 3-oz. packages black
   raspberry gelatin
1 15-oz. can blueberries with juice
1 15-oz. can crushed pineapple
   with juice
1 8-oz. package cream cheese, softened
1 c. sour cream
1/2 c. sugar
1/2 tsp. vanilla extract

Dissolve gelatin in 2 cups boiling water in bowl; cool. Stir in fruit. Pour into 9 x 13-inch dish. Chill until firm. Combine remaining ingredients in bowl; beat until smooth. Spread over gelatin. Chill until serving time. Cut into squares.
Yield: 10 servings.

Approx per serv: Cal 369; Prot 4.8 g; T Fat 13.7 g; Chl 35.3 mg; Car 60.3 g; Sod 124.5 mg; Pot 194.7 mg.

Mary Brown, Cass

FROZEN FRUIT SALAD

4 egg yolks
1/4 c. vinegar
1/4 c. sugar
1 pt. whipping cream, whipped
1 8-oz. package marshmallows, chopped
1 8-oz. bottle of maraschino cherries,
   drained, chopped
1 8-oz. can pineapple tidbits
1 c. seedless grapes
1/2 c. broken walnuts

Beat egg yolks, vinegar and sugar in saucepan. Cook over low heat until thick and smooth, stirring constantly. Cool. Fold into whipped cream. Fold in marshmallows, fruit and walnuts. Pour into 8 x 12-inch dish. Freeze until firm. Thaw for 20 minutes; cut into serving portions. Serve on lettuce-lined plates with warm hard rolls. Yield: 12 servings.

Approx per serv: Cal 251; Prot 2.9 g; T Fat 5.1 g; Chl 84.1 mg; Car 51.2 g; Sod 45.9 mg; Pot 206.2 mg.

Verna Morrison, Kalkaska

JEROMY'S GELATIN SALAD

1 8-oz. can crushed pineapple
1 6-oz. package orange gelatin
1 8-oz. package cream cheese, softened
1/2 c. grated carrots
1 8-oz. carton whipped topping

Drain pineapple, reserving juice. Add enough water to reserved juice to measure 1 cup. Bring to a boil in saucepan. Add gelatin; stir until dissolved. Cool. Combine cream cheese, carrots and pineapple in bowl; mix well. Add gelatin; mix well. Fold in whipped topping. Pour into 9 x 13-inch dish. Chill until set. Cut into serving portions. Yield: 12 servings.

Approx per serv: Cal 200; Prot 3.2 g; T Fat 11.9 g; Chl 21.0 mg; Car 21.7 g; Sod 99.3 mg; Pot 83.1 mg.

Jeromy Bogue, Cass

GOOD FRUIT SALAD

1 16-oz. can light sweet cherries
1 16-oz. can dark sweet cherries
1 16-oz. can sliced peaches
1 16-oz. can pears
1 13-oz. can pineapple tidbits
1 c. marshmallows
1/2 c. sour cream
1 c. whipped topping

Drain fruit; chop pears. Combine all ingredients in serving bowl; mix well. Chill until serving time. Yield: 12 servings.

Approx per serv: Cal 197; Prot 1.4 g; T Fat 3.7 g; Chl 4.3 mg; Car 42.5 g; Sod 10.2 mg; Pot 226.4 mg.

Beth Weidmayer, Washtenaw

STRAWBERRY-NUT SALAD

1 6-oz. package strawberry gelatin
2 10-oz. packages frozen sliced
   strawberries, thawed
1 20-oz. can crushed pineapple, drained
3 med. bananas, mashed
1 c. coarsely chopped walnuts
2 c. sour cream

Dissolve gelatin in 1 cup boiling water in large bowl. Add strawberries, pineapple, bananas and walnuts; mix well. Pour half the mixture into 9 x 13-inch dish. Chill until firm. Spread sour cream over congealed layer. Spoon remaining gelatin mixture over top. Chill until firm. Cut into serving pieces. Yield: 24 servings.

Approx per serv: Cal 158; Prot 2.4 g; T Fat 7.3 g; Chl 8.4 mg; Car 22.9 g; Sod 33.4 mg; Pot 172.0 mg.

Kathy Brouard, Allegan

STRAWBERRY-RICE SALAD

1 3-oz. package strawberry gelatin
1 c. rice, cooked
1 20-oz. can crushed pineapple, drained
2 c. miniature marshmallows
1 c. flaked coconut
1 8-oz. carton whipped topping

Prepare gelatin according to package directions. Add rice; mix well. Chill until set. Stir congealed gelatin mixture with fork until broken up. Add pineapple, marshmallows, coconut and whipped topping; mix well. Chill until serving time. Serve on crisp lettuce. Salad stays fresh in refrigerator for up to 3 days. Yield: 10 servings.

Approx per serv: Cal 319; Prot 3.1 g; T Fat 8.4 g; Chl 0.1 mg; Car 60.1 g; Sod 55.9 mg; Pot 175.1 mg.

Connie Brown, Oscoda

TEA GARDEN SALAD

1 3-oz. package orange gelatin
1 c. hot tea
1 8-oz. can mandarin oranges
1 8-oz. can crushed pineapple
1 6-oz. can water chestnuts, drained

Dissolve gelatin in hot tea in bowl. Drain fruit, reserving 1 cup juice. Stir juice into gelatin. Chill until partially set. Sliver water chestnuts. Stir into gelatin with fruit. Chill until set. Yield: 6 servings.

Approx per serv: Cal 146; Prot 2.6 g; T Fat 0.2 g; Chl 0.0 mg; Car 35.1 g; Sod 49.9 mg; Pot 213.8 mg.

Barbara MacDonald, Livingston

CORNED BEEF SALAD

1 3-oz. package lemon gelatin
2 tbsp. vinegar
1/2 c. salad dressing
1 15-oz. can corned beef, shredded
1/2 tsp. salt
1/2 c. chopped cucumber
1/2 c. chopped celery
1/2 c. chopped green pepper
4 or 5 lg. radishes, chopped
1 tbsp. chopped onion
3 hard-boiled eggs, chopped

Dissolve gelatin in 1 1/4 cups boiling water in mixer bowl. Add vinegar, salad dressing, corned beef and salt. Beat at medium speed until smooth. Stir in remaining ingredients. Pour into glass loaf pan. Chill until firm. Unmold if desired. Slice loaf. Serve each slice garnished with salad dressing and sliced pimento-stuffed olives. Yield: 8 servings.

Approx per serv: Cal 265; Prot 18.4 g; T Fat 15.4 g; Chl 156.4 mg; Car 13.0 g; Sod 831.6 mg; Pot 150.6 mg.

Dean Dernay, Oakland

SHRIMP SALAD

1 6-oz. package frozen cooked popcorn shrimp, thawed
1 10-oz. package frozen green peas, thawed
5 stalks celery
1/2 c. salad dressing
1 tsp. lemon juice
4 lettuce leaves

Drain shrimp and peas well. Slice celery 1/8 inch thick. Combine shrimp, peas and celery in bowl. Add mixture of salad dressing and lemon juice; toss to mix. Chill for 2 hours. Serve on lettuce-lined plates. Yield: 4 servings.

Approx per serv: Cal 243; Prot 15.1 g; T Fat 13.4 g; Chl 78.8 mg; Car 16.3 g; Sod 391.7 mg; Pot 368.3 mg.

Virginia Wiederhold Reeder, Van Buren

BROCCOLI-MUSHROOM SALAD

Flowerets of 1 bunch broccoli
8 oz. fresh mushrooms, sliced
1/2 c. sugar
1 tsp. salt
1 tsp. paprika
1 tsp. celery seed
1/2 tsp. garlic powder
Pinch of dillseed
3/4 c. oil
5 tbsp. wine vinegar
3 slices crisp-fried bacon, crumbled

Combine broccoli and mushrooms in serving bowl. Combine remaining ingredients except bacon in small bowl; mix well. Pour over vegetables; toss to coat. Chill for several hours. Top with bacon just before serving. Yield: 4 servings.

Approx per serv: Cal 544; Prot 7.0 g; T Fat 44.2 g; Chl 5.0 mg; Car 35.2 g; Sod 615.7 mg; Pot 683.4 mg.

Dee Little, Houghton

FRESH BROCCOLI SALAD

Flowerets of 1 bunch broccoli
1/2 c. chopped onion
1/2 c. raisins
1/2 c. sugar
1 c. salad dressing
2 tbsp. vinegar
8 slices crisp-fried bacon, crumbled

Place broccoli flowerets in serving bowl. Combine onion, raisins, sugar, salad dressing and vinegar in small bowl; mix well. Pour over broccoli; mix gently. Top with bacon. Chill for 30 minutes before serving. Yield: 6 servings.

Approx per serv: Cal 363; Prot 6.3 g; T Fat 22.4 g; Chl 28.9 mg; Car 38.0 g; Sod 352.7 mg; Pot 435.9 mg.

Shirley Herpst, Van Buren

NAVY BEAN SALAD

1 lb. dried Michigan navy beans
1 1/2 c. chopped celery
3/4 c. chopped onion
3/4 c. chopped green pepper
1/2 c. Italian salad dressing
1/2 c. white vinegar
1/2 c. sugar
1 tsp. dry mustard
1/2 tsp. garlic salt
1/4 tsp. paprika
1/2 tsp. MSG
1/2 tsp. salt
1/4 c. chili sauce

Cook beans according to package directions until tender. Drain well. Combine remaining ingredients in large serving bowl; mix well. Add beans; mix well. Chill, covered, in refrigerator overnight. Yield: 10 servings.

Approx per serv: Cal 279; Prot 11.0 g; T Fat 8.0 g; Chl 0.0 mg; Car 43.3 g; Sod 633.6 mg; Pot 687.2 mg.

Linda Bruce, Marquette

MIXED VEGETABLE SALAD

1 head cauliflower, broken into flowerets
1 bunch broccoli, cut into
*   bite-sized pieces*
8 oz. mushrooms, sliced
8 oz. green onions, chopped
1 c. oil

1/2 c. vinegar
1/2 c. sugar
1 1/2 tsp. salt
1 tsp. pepper
1 tsp. paprika
2 tsp. celery seed

Combine vegetables in serving bowl. Combine remaining ingredients in small bowl; mix well. Pour over vegetables; mix gently. Chill for 4 hours. Yield: 8 servings.

Approx per serv: Cal 326; Prot 3.7 g; T Fat 27.5 g; Chl 0.0 mg; Car 19.6 g; Sod 416.7 mg; Pot 441.3 mg.

Sarah Weidmayer, Washtenaw

CAULIFLOWER SALAD

1 head cauliflower, cut into flowerets
1   10-oz. package frozen peas, thawed
8 slices American cheese, chopped
1/4 c. salad dressing
1/4 c. mayonnaise
1/2 to 3/4 pkg. Italian salad dressing mix

Combine cauliflowerets, peas and cheese in serving bowl. Blend salad dressing and mayonnaise with salad dressing mix in small bowl. Pour over cauliflower mixture; toss lightly to coat. Chill until serving time. Yield: 4 servings.

Joyce Kies, Napoleon

TASTY COLESLAW

1 med. head cabbage, grated
1 1/2 tbsp. oil
1 sm. onion, grated
3/4 c. mayonnaise
1/2 c. sugar
2 tbsp. cider vinegar
1/2 tsp. celery seed
1 1/2 tsp. prepared mustard
1/4 tsp. salt

Toss cabbage with oil in serving bowl until well coated. Add onion; mix well. Blend remaining ingredients in small bowl. Add to cabbage mixture; mix well. Chill before serving. The oil keeps the cabbage crisp for several days. Yield: 8 servings.

Approx per serv: Cal 268; Prot 2.6 g; T Fat 19.7 g; Chl 14.7 mg; Car 23.3 g; Sod 239.0 mg; Pot 425.5 mg.

Barbara Dupras, Marquette

Marinate cucumbers in mixture of vinegar, sugar, salt, peppercorns and 3/4 cup water in large bowl for 2 to 3 hours, stirring occasionally. Drain well. Combine cucumbers, sour cream and salt to taste in serving bowl; mix gently. Yield: 6 servings.

Cecile Veeser, Menominee

MAKE-AHEAD SALAD

1 head lettuce, torn
2 stalks celery, chopped
1 sm. onion, thinly sliced into rings
1 10-oz. package frozen peas,
    cooked, drained
1 6-oz. can sliced water
    chestnuts, drained
1 1/2 c. mayonnaise
3 tbsp. Parmesan cheese
8 slices crisp-fried bacon, crumbled

Layer lettuce, celery, onion, peas and water chestnuts in salad bowl. Spread mayonnaise over top, sealing to edge. Sprinkle cheese and bacon over top. Cover tightly with plastic wrap. Chill for 3 hours to overnight. Yield: 6 servings.

Approx per serv: Cal 565; Prot 9.1 g; T Fat 51.3 g; Chl 51.7 mg; Car 19.8 g; Sod 555.0 mg; Pot 396.9 mg.

Judy Wright, Benzie

COTTAGE CHEESE SALAD

1 3-oz. package lemon gelatin
1 16-oz. carton cottage cheese
1/2 c. mayonnaise
2 green onions, chopped
2 stalks celery, chopped
1 carrot, shredded
1 c. whipped topping

Dissolve gelatin in 1/2 cup boiling water in large serving bowl. Add cottage cheese, mayonnaise and vegetables; mix well. Stir in whipped topping. Chill until firm. Yield: 10 servings.

Approx per serv: Cal 190; Prot 7.9 g; T Fat 12.7 g; Chl 17.1 mg; Car 12.0 g; Sod 221.3 mg. Pot 123.3 mg.

Bea Axford, Otsego

SEVEN-LAYER SALAD

1 lg. head lettuce, torn
1/2 c. chopped onion
1/2 c. chopped celery
2 10-oz. packages frozen peas, thawed
2 c. mayonnaise
2 tbsp. sugar
2 tbsp. Parmesan cheese
1/2 lb. sliced bacon, crisp-fried, crumbled
4 hard-boiled eggs, chopped
4 tomatoes, chopped

Layer lettuce, onion, celery and peas in 9 x 13-inch dish. Spread mayonnaise over top, sealing to edge. Sprinkle with mixture of sugar and cheese. Chill, covered, overnight. Add bacon, hard-boiled eggs, salt and pepper to taste and tomatoes just before serving. Yield: 12 servings.

Approx per serv: Cal 399; Prot 8.2 g; T Fat 35.6 g; Chl 117.2 mg; Car 13.5 g; Sod 403.8 mg; Pot 326.5 mg.

Vicky Anders, St. Joseph

4-H is the largest youth program in Michigan.

CUCUMBERS IN SOUR CREAM

4 lg. cucumbers, thinly sliced
3/4 c. vinegar
2 tbsp. sugar
1 tsp. salt
4 whole peppercorns
2 c. sour cream

SPAGHETTI SALAD

1 16-oz. package thin spaghetti
2 lg. tomatoes, chopped
1 bunch green onions, chopped
1 green pepper, chopped
1 c. chopped celery
2 or 3 cucumbers, chopped
3/4 jar Salad Supreme
1 8-oz. bottle of Italian
     salad dressing

Cook spaghetti according to package directions until just tender; drain and cool. Combine spaghetti and vegetables in salad bowl; toss to mix. Add remaining ingredients; mix well. Chill for 1 hour. Yield: 8 servings.

Katherine Beauvais, Livingston

PASTA DELIGHT

1 16-oz. package spaghetti
1 tbsp. oil
2 tomatoes, coarsely chopped
1/2 green pepper, chopped
1/2 c. chopped onion
1 sm. carrot, chopped
1 med. cucumber, coarsely chopped
1/2 c. chopped celery
1 16-oz. can kidney beans, drained
1/2 c. Parmesan cheese
2 tbsp. sugar
1 8-oz. bottle of Italian salad dressing

Cook spaghetti according to package directions adding 1 tablespoon oil. Drain, rinse and cool. Combine spaghetti and remaining ingredients in salad bowl; toss lightly. Chill for 6 to 12 hours. Garnish with hard-boiled egg wedges. Yield: 10 servings.

Approx per serv: Cal 403; Prot 11.6 g; T Fat 18.3 g; Chl 48.3 mg; Car 48.9 g; Sod 563.3 mg; Pot 358.3 mg.

Suzanne Kroetsch, Sanilac

PEA SALAD

1 16-oz. package frozen peas
1 med. onion, chopped
2 stalks celery, chopped
1/2 c. salad dressing
1/2 c. sour cream
2 tsp. sugar

2 tsp. Worcestershire sauce
1/2 tsp. garlic powder
1 c. peanuts

Cook peas according to package directions; drain and cool. Combine peas, onion and celery in bowl. Add mixture of salad dressing, sour cream, sugar, Worcestershire sauce, garlic powder and salt and pepper to taste; mix gently. Chill until serving time. Add peanuts just before serving; mix gently. Yield: 5 servings.

Approx per serv: Cal 386; Prot 12.3 g; T Fat 29.6 g; Chl 22.1 g; Car 22.2 g; Sod 389.1 mg; Pot 426.4 mg.

Peggy Baratta, St. Joseph

GREAT POTATO SALAD

1 c. salad dressing
1 tbsp. prepared mustard
1/4 c. vinegar
1/2 tsp. celery seed
1 tsp. salt
1/8 tsp. pepper
2 tbsp. sugar
4 c. chopped cooked potatoes
1/2 c. chopped onion
1/2 c. chopped celery
3 hard-boiled eggs, chopped
1/2 c. chopped sweet pickles

Combine first 7 ingredients in serving bowl; mix well. Add vegetables, eggs and pickles; mix lightly. Chill until serving time. Yield: 6 servings.

Approx per serv: Cal 384; Prot 7.3 g; T Fat 20.2 g; Chl 146.4 mg; Car 45.1 g; Sod 812.6 mg; Pot 756.2 mg.

Marion Magnus, Clare

4-H is Learning by Doing.

PENNSYLVANIA DUTCH POTATO SALAD

8 to 10 med. potatoes, cooked, chopped
1 sm. Bermuda onion, finely chopped
8 oz. Velveeta cheese, chopped
2 to 3 c. salad dressing
2 tbsp. mustard

1 tsp. salt
3 slices bacon, chopped
3 or 4 ripe olives, sliced

Combine first 6 ingredients in bowl; mix well. Spoon into greased casserole. Top with bacon and olives. Bake at 350 degrees for 30 to 45 minutes. Yield: 10 servings.

NOTE: This is a great dish for 4-H potlucks.

Caryn Brown, Cass

SAUERKRAUT SALAD

4 c. sauerkraut, well drained
1 c. finely chopped celery
1 lg. onion, finely chopped
1 green pepper, chopped
1 2-oz. can chopped pimentos
1 1/4 c. sugar
1/2 c. vinegar
1/2 c. oil

Combine first 5 ingredients in bowl; mix well. Add sugar, vinegar and oil; mix well. Let stand for 2 days, stirring occasionally. Yield: 8 servings.

Approx per serv: Cal 278; Prot 1.8 g; T Fat 13.9 g; Chl 0.0 mg; Car 40.0 g; Sod 902.2 mg; Pot 300.6 mg.

Carol Sieting, Kalkaska

SPINACH SALAD

1 8-oz. package fresh spinach
1 16-oz. can bean sprouts, drained
8 slices crisp-fried bacon, crumbled
3 hard-boiled eggs, chopped
1 tbsp. oil
1 tsp. salt
3/4 c. sugar
1/3 c. catsup
1 tbsp. Worcestershire sauce
1 med. onion, grated
1/4 c. vinegar

Combine spinach, sprouts, bacon and eggs in salad bowl. Mix remaining ingredients in small bowl. Pour over spinach mixture; toss lightly. Yield: 4 servings.

Approx per serv: Cal 396; Prot 13.6 g; T Fat 15.9 g; Chl 203.0 mg; Car 53.2 g; Sod 1171.0 mg; Pot 616.7 mg.

Cheryl Throne, Monroe

BETTY'S SALAD

1 c. oil
1/2 c. catsup
3/4 c. sugar
1 tbsp. Worcestershire sauce
1/4 c. vinegar
1 head lettuce, torn
1/2 pkg. fresh spinach, torn
1 14-oz. can bean sprouts, drained
1 lb. sliced bacon, chopped, crisp-fried
8 hard-boiled eggs, cut into quarters

Combine first 5 ingredients in tightly covered jar; shake vigorously. Chill overnight. Combine lettuce, spinach, bean sprouts and bacon in salad bowl; toss to mix. Arrange hard-boiled eggs over top. Add prepared salad dressing just before serving. Yield: 10 servings.

Approx per serv: Cal 421; Prot 10.6 g; T Fat 32.8 g; Chl 212.9 mg; Car 23.2 g; Sod 391.9 mg; Pot 378.8 mg.

Kathy Van Assche, Wayne

4-H is over 150 projects.

HOMEMADE SALAD SEASONING

2 c. Parmesan cheese
2 tsp. salt
1/2 c. sesame seed
1/2 tsp. garlic salt
1 tbsp. onion flakes
2 tbsp. parsley flakes
1/2 tsp. dillseed
2 tbsp. poppy seed
1 tsp. MSG (opt.)
3 tbsp. celery seed
2 tsp. paprika
1/2 tsp. pepper

Combine all ingredients in bowl; mix well. Store in airtight 1-quart container. Use within 3 to 4 months on salads, baked potatoes, eggs or as desired. Yield: 48 one-tablespoon servings.

Approx per serv: Cal 29; Prot 2.1 g; T Fat 2.1 g; Chl 4.7 mg; Car 0.4 g; Sod 166.0 mg; Pot 18.7 mg.

Pam Stibitz, Muskegon

Side Dishes

JEAN'S BAKED BEANS

4 c. dried navy beans
1 tsp. soda
1 lb. sliced smoked bacon
3/4 c. catsup
2 tbsp. molasses
1 1/2 tsp. nutmeg
1 1/2 tbsp. sugar
1 tbsp. salt
1 tsp. pepper
1 sm. onion, chopped

Soak beans in water to cover overnight. Add soda. Bring to a boil. Cook until skins burst. Drain. Cut bacon into squares. Combine catsup, molasses and seasonings with a small amount of hot water in bowl; mix well. Layer bacon, beans, catsup mixture and onion 1/3 at a time in beanpot. Add enough hot water to cover. Bake at 350 degrees for 4 to 6 hours or until of desired consistency, adding a small amount of additional water if necessary.
Yield: 15 servings.

Approx per serv: Cal 401; Prot 14.9 g; T Fat 21.8 g; Chl 21.2 mg; Car 37.4 g; Sod 660.9 mg; Pot 729.6 mg.

Jean Anthony, Schoolcraft

BACHELOR BEANS

1 20-oz. jar baked beans
1 onion, chopped
1 green pepper, chopped
6 tbsp. brown sugar
Barbecue sauce to taste

Combine beans, onion, green pepper and brown sugar in casserole. Mix until brown sugar dissolves. Add a small amount of barbecue sauce; mix well. Bake at 300 degrees for 20 minutes. Yield: 4 servings.

Quincy Stewart, Oakland

MEXICAN BEANS

1 16-oz. can pork and beans
1 16-oz. can kidney beans, drained
1 16-oz. can butter beans

6 slices crisp-fried bacon, crumbled
1 sm. onion, finely chopped
1/2 c. sugar
1/3 c. packed brown sugar
1 to 2 tbsp. chili powder
2 tsp. (or more) Worcestershire sauce

Combine all ingredients in casserole; mix well. Bake at 300 degrees for 2 hours or longer.
Yield: 6 servings.
NOTE: May be cooked in electric skillet or Crock·Pot.

Approx per serv: Cal 395; Prot 15.3 g; T Fat 6.6 g; Chl 10.1 mg; Car 70.5 g; Sod 628.0 mg; Pot 624.1 mg.

Sally Richardson, Kalkaska

OLD SETTLER'S BEANS

1/2 lb. ground beef
1/4 lb. bacon, chopped
1 sm. onion, chopped
1 16-oz. can kidney beans
1 16-oz. can pork and beans
1 16-oz. can butter beans
1/2 c. packed brown sugar
1/2 c. sugar
1/4 c. catsup
1/2 tsp. prepared mustard
2 tbsp. molasses

Brown ground beef and bacon with onion in skillet; drain. Combine with remaining ingredients in casserole. Bake at 350 degrees for 1 hour. Yield: 6 servings.
NOTE: May be baked in Crock·Pot for 8 hours.

Approx per serv: Cal 604; Prot 21.7 g; T Fat 21.4 g; Chl 42.2 mg; Car 83.1 g; Sod 792.0 mg; Pot 812.2 mg.

Barbara Miller, Macomb

BAKED MACARONI AND CHEESE

2 tbsp. butter, melted
2 tbsp. flour
1 tsp. salt
1/2 tsp. pepper
2 1/2 c. milk
1 1/2 c. shredded Cheddar cheese
2 c. macaroni, cooked
1/2 c. shredded Cheddar cheese

Blend butter, flour, salt and pepper in saucepan. Stir in milk. Cook until thickened, stirring constantly. Add 1 1/2 cups cheese. Stir until cheese melts. Combine with macaroni in casserole; mix well. Sprinkle with 1/2 cup cheese. Bake at 375 degrees for 20 to 25 minutes or until bubbly and golden brown. Yield: 6 servings.

Approx per serv: Cal 353; Prot 16.5 g; T Fat 19.9 g; Chl 63.4 mg; Car 26.9 g; Sod 717.1 mg; Pot 230.9 mg.

Pat Eickhoff, Ionia

DIANE'S NOODLE DOUGH

    4 c. flour
    3/4 tsp. salt
    2 eggs, lightly beaten
    2 tbsp. oil

Sift flour and salt into large bowl. Make well in center. Add eggs and oil; mix well. Stir in about 1 cup boiling water to make stiff dough. Knead on floured surface for about 5 minutes or until smooth and shiny. Cover with bowl. Let rest for 10 minutes. Roll on floured surface. Cut into noodles. Cook as desired. Yield: 6 servings.

Approx per serv: Cal 371; Prot 10.9 g; T Fat 7.3 g; Chl 84.3 mg; Car 63.6 g; Sod 288.5 mg; Pot 100.8 mg.

Patricia Barra, Menominee

4-H is for everyone.

FRIED RICE

    1/2 lb. bacon, chopped
    1 med. onion, chopped
    6 eggs, beaten
    4 c. cooked rice
    1/4 c. (or less) soy sauce

Brown bacon and onion in skillet; push to one side. Add eggs. Cook until set, stirring frequently; drain. Add cooled rice and soy sauce. Cook until heated through, stirring frequently. Serve with additional soy sauce. Yield: 4 servings.

Approx per serv: Cal 748; Prot 20.1 g; T Fat 48.4 g; Chl 418.9 mg; Car 55.3 g; Sod 2565.7 mg; Pot 344.1 mg.

Angel Frost, Barry

LONG GRAIN AND WILD RICE

    1/2 c. wild rice
    2 stalks celery, chopped
    1 lg. onion, chopped
    3 tbsp. butter
    3 c. chicken broth
    3 tbsp. chopped fresh parsley
    1/2 tsp. Kitchen Bouquet
    1/4 tsp. each salt and pepper
    1/4 tsp. sage
    1/2 tsp. basil
    1 c. long grain rice
    2 tbsp. slivered almonds

Saute wild rice, celery and onion in butter in skillet until onion is tender. Add broth, parsley and seasonings. Bring to a boil; reduce heat. Simmer, covered, for 40 minutes. Add long grain rice. Bring to a boil. Simmer, covered, for 14 minutes. Stir in almonds. Serve immediately with sour cream if desired. Yield: 4 servings.

Approx per serv: Cal 361; Prot 8.2 g; T Fat 11.1 g; Chl 28.9 mg; Car 57.9 g; Sod 992.8 mg; Pot 274.9 mg.

Rene Givens, Oakland

ZESTY BROWN RICE

    2 beef bouillon cubes
    1 tsp. parsley flakes
    1/2 tsp. celery salt
    3/8 tsp. pepper
    2/3 c. brown rice
    1/2 c. chopped celery
    1 sm. onion, chopped
    1 tbsp. butter
    1 tbsp. soy sauce
    1   4-oz. can sliced mushrooms (opt.)
    1 can sliced water chestnuts (opt.)

Combine bouillon cubes, seasonings and 1 1/4 cups boiling water in saucepan. Bring to a boil. Stir in rice. Bring to a boil; reduce heat. Simmer, covered, for 20 minutes or until rice is tender. Saute celery and onion in butter in skillet until tender. Add soy sauce, mushrooms and water chestnuts. Stir into rice. Heat to serving temperature. Yield: 4 servings.

NOTE: Cooked chicken or beef may be added if desired.

Approx per serv: Cal 208; Prot 5.1 g; T Fat 3.8 g; Chl 10.4 mg; Car 39.0 g; Sod 1143.0 mg; Pot 320.8 mg.

Dorothy Wisniewski, Cass

RICE AND MUSHROOM CASSEROLE

1 c. rice
1 8-oz. can mushrooms, drained
1 env. dry onion soup mix
1 stick butter, melted

Combine all ingredients and 2 1/2 cups water in 1 1/2-quart casserole. Bake at 350 degrees for 45 minutes to 1 hour or until rice is tender. Yield: 4 servings.

NOTE: May bake browned pork chops or chicken on top of rice.

Approx per serv: Cal 419; Prot 5.7 g; T Fat 24.4 g; Chl 86.9 mg; Car 44.6 g; Sod 1005.5 mg; Pot 253.4 mg.

Vera R. DeMille, Menominee

MOM'S EASY PICKLED BEETS

1/2 c. beet juice
1/2 c. cider vinegar
2 whole cloves
3 peppercorns
1/4 bay leaf
1 tsp. salt
2 tbsp. sugar
1 20-oz. can sliced beets, drained
1 med. onion, thinly sliced

Combine first 7 ingredients in saucepan. Bring to a boil; remove from heat. Pour hot liquid over mixture of beets and onion in bowl. Chill, covered, for 1 to 24 hours. Yield: 6 servings.

NOTE: May add shelled hard-boiled eggs to marinade with beets if desired.

Approx per serv: Cal 64; Prot 1.0 g; T Fat 0.1 g; Chl 0.0 mg; Car 13.6 g; Sod 524.8 mg; Pot 171.8 mg.

Linda Mayes, Baraga

SLIPPERY JACKS

Cucumbers, peeled
2 c. white vinegar
1 c. packed brown sugar
1/2 tsp. mustard seed
1 tsp. turmeric
1 tsp. mixed pickling spice
Salt

Cut cucumbers in half lengthwise; scoop out seed. Cut each half into fourths. Soak in cold water overnight. Drain well. Combine vinegar, brown sugar and remaining ingredients except salt in saucepan. Cook until sugar dissolves. Add cucumbers. Boil for 3 minutes or until cucumbers are transparent. Pack into hot sterilized 1-quart jars. Add 1 teaspoon salt per jar. Seal with 2-piece lids. Process in boiling water bath for 5 minutes.

NOTE: This recipe comes from my mother-in-law who was Finnish.

Madalynn Sundell, Missaukee

SOLAR PICKLES

48 sm. cucumbers
Dillweed
1 clove of garlic
1 qt. vinegar
3/4 c. salt
1 tbsp. pickling spice
2 slices dark rye bread

Layer cucumbers and dillweed alternately in 1-gallon glass jar until jar is filled. Add garlic. Combine vinegar, salt, pickling spice and 3 1/2 quarts water in saucepan. Bring to a boil. Pour over cucumbers. Place bread on top. Seal with lid. Let stand in full sun for 3 days. Remove and discard bread. Store in refrigerator. Yield: 48 servings.

Ruth Wilson, Menominee

4-H is in the city, suburb and farm.

SWEET PICKLES

24 sm. cucumbers
1/2 c. salt
1 qt. vinegar
2 c. sugar
2 tsp. mustard seed
2 tsp. turmeric
1 tsp. celery seed

Soak cucumbers with salt in water to cover for 1 hour. Rinse and drain. Combine remaining ingredients in saucepan. Bring to a boil. Add cucumbers. Bring to a boil. Pack into hot sterilized jars. Seal with 2-piece lids. Process in boiling water bath for 5 minutes. Yield: 24 servings.

Jake Curtiss, Isabella

Meats, Poultry & Fish

BAJA CALIFORNIA CHICKEN

8 boned chicken breasts
Seasoned salt and pepper
1/4 c. tarragon vinegar
1/4 c. olive oil
2 cloves of garlic, crushed
2/3 c. dry Sherry

Sprinkle chicken breasts with seasoned salt and pepper to taste. Combine vinegar, olive oil and garlic in skillet. Saute chicken in mixture until golden brown, turning frequently. Place chicken in baking dish. Add Sherry. Bake at 350 degrees for 10 minutes. Yield: 8 servings.

Approx per serv: Cal 268; Prot 33.9 g; T Fat 11.7 g; Chl 82.9 mg; Car 1.7 g; Sod 51.1 mg; Pot 342.4 mg.

 President and Mrs. Ronald Reagan
The White House

HAM CURRY CASSEROLE

1 10-oz. package frozen chopped broccoli
1 8-oz. package long grain and wild
  rice, cooked
12 oz. ham, cubed
1 c. cubed Cheddar cheese
1 can cream of celery soup
1 sm. can evaporated milk
1 c. mayonnaise
2 tsp. dry mustard
3/4 tsp. curry powder

Cook broccoli using package directions until tender-crisp; drain. Layer rice, ham, broccoli and cheese in 9 x 13-inch casserole. Combine remaining ingredients in bowl; mix well. Pour over layers. Bake at 350 degrees for 45 minutes. Yield: 6 servings.

Dr. and Mrs. Russell G. Mawby
Chairman, W. K. Kellogg Foundation
Former State 4-H Director, 4-H Alumni, Kent County

ONE-POUND PORK CHOPS

6 1-lb. loin pork chops
2 c. soy sauce
1/2 c. packed brown sugar
1 tsp. salt
1 tbsp. dark molasses
1/2 c. packed brown sugar
1 tbsp. dry mustard

1 14-oz. bottle of catsup
1 12-oz. bottle of chili sauce

Place pork chops bone side up in dish. Combine soy sauce, 1/2 cup brown sugar, salt, molasses and 1 cup water in saucepan. Bring to a boil. Pour over pork chops. Marinate in refrigerator overnight. Drain. Place pork chops in baking dish; seal with foil. Bake at 375 degrees for 2 hours or until tender. Blend 1/2 cup brown sugar, dry mustard and 1/3 cup water in saucepan. Stir in remaining ingredients. Simmer until thickened. Dip pork chops in sauce; place in baking pan. Bake at 350 degrees or until slightly glazed. Let stand at room temperature until ready to grill. Grill over low heat for 15 minutes or less or until heated through. Yield: 6 servings.

NOTE: Marinating mixture and sauce may be brought to a boil, poured into storage containers and stored in refrigerator or freezer for future use. Nutritional information includes total amount of marinating mixture.

Approx per serv: Cal 1378; Prot 68.9 g; T Fat 90.8 g; Chl 222.2 mg; Car 70.4 g; Sod 8780.6 mg; Pot 1837.1 mg.

Mr. and Mrs. Michael Pridgeon
President, Michigan 4-H Foundation, 4-H Alumni

FILE GUMBO

2 chickens, cut up
2 tsp. salt
1/2 c. flour
1 lb. hot sausage, thickly sliced
1/2 c. oil
1/2 c. flour
1 c. finely chopped onion
1/2 c. finely chopped scallions
1 c. finely chopped celery
1 c. finely chopped green pepper
2 tsp. salt
1 1/2 tbsp. cayenne pepper
1/2 tsp. Tabasco sauce
1 lb. cooked medium shrimp
1 lb. cooked crab meat
1/4 c. chopped parsley
2 tsp. file powder
8 c. cooked long grain rice

Rinse chicken; pat dry. Season with 2 teaspoons salt and pepper to taste. Coat with 1/2 cup flour. Cook sausage in heavy skillet until dark brown. Remove sausage; drain on paper towel. Brown chicken in sausage drippings; add a small amount of oil if necessary. Drain on paper towel. Combine 1/2 cup oil and 1/2 cup flour in heavy skillet. Cook over very low heat for 45 minutes or until dark brown, stirring constantly. Do not burn. Combine with onion, scallions and celery in 12-quart stockpot. Cook over medium heat for 3 minutes. Stir in green pepper and 4 quarts water. Bring to a boil, stirring constantly. Add sausage, chicken, salt, cayenne pepper and Tabasco sauce. Simmer for 1 3/4 hours. Add shrimp and crab. Simmer for 15 to 20 minutes longer. Skim surface. Stir in parsley and file. Mound 1 cup rice in each soup bowl. Ladle gumbo over rice.

Yield: 8 servings.

NOTE: Roux may be stored, covered, in refrigerator for up to 2 weeks. Stir and warm before using.

Approx per serv: Cal 954; Prot 76.1 g; T Fat 40.2 g; Chl 282.8 mg; Car 66.5 g; Sod 2254.9 mg; Pot 802.9 mg.

Mr. and Mrs. Michael J. Tate
Director, Michigan 4-H Youth Programs

4-H is learning skills for life.

ENCHILADA CASSEROLE

1 1/2 lb. ground beef
1 tsp. salt
1 10-oz. can tomato sauce
1 10-oz. can enchilada sauce
10 tortillas
1 lg. onion, chopped
2 c. shredded sharp Cheddar cheese
1/2 c. chopped ripe olives

Saute ground beef in skillet until no longer pink. Do not brown. Add salt; set aside. Combine tomato and enchilada sauces in saucepan. Bring to a boil. Dip tortillas 1 at a time into sauce. Layer tortillas, ground beef, onion, cheese and olives in casserole. Pour remaining tomato sauce mixture over layers. Bake at 350 degrees for 30 minutes or until bubbly.

Dr. and Mrs. Wally J. Moline
Director of Extension and Associate Dean of the
College of Agriculture and Natural Resources
4-H Alumni

VEGETABLE AND HAM PIE

1 stick butter, softened
5 eggs, separated
1/2 c. sour cream
1/4 c. flour
3/4 c. Parmesan cheese
4 oz. ham, coarsely chopped
1/2 c. cooked green peas
2 c. cooked cauliflowerets
1 c. sauteed sliced mushrooms

Cream butter in bowl until light and fluffy. Add egg yolks, sour cream and 2 tablespoons flour; beat well. Beat egg whites until stiff peaks form. Fold in remaining 2 tablespoons flour and 2 tablespoons cheese gently. Fold egg whites gently into egg yolk mixture. Spoon half the mixture into buttered casserole. Layer ham and 2 tablespoons cheese over egg mixture. Add layers of peas and cauliflowerets, sprinkling each layer with 2 tablespoons cheese. Top with mushrooms and remaining cheese. Spoon remaining egg mixture over top. Place in cold oven. Bake at 350 degrees for 45 minutes or until set and browned. Do not overbake. Serve immediately.

President and Mrs. John A. DiBiaggio
Michigan State University

BEEF BARBECUE

1 6-lb. beef roast
1 stalk celery, chopped
1 lg. onion, chopped
1 green pepper, chopped
1 12-oz. bottle of catsup
3 tbsp. barbecue sauce
3 tbsp. vinegar
1 tsp. Tabasco sauce
2 tbsp. chili sauce
2 tbsp. salt
1 tsp. pepper

Cut roast into 6 pieces; place in roasting pan. Combine remaining ingredients in bowl; mix well. Pour over beef. Bake at 300 degrees for 6 hours or until very tender. Trim and shred beef. Combine with pan juices; mix well.

Yield: 30 servings.

Approx per serv: Cal 211; Prot 16.1 g; T Fat 14.7 g; Chl 57.2 mg; Car 2.7 g; Sod 332.7 mg; Pot 175.0 mg.

Jean Minner, Jackson

BEEF AND PORK BARBECUE

1 5-lb. beef roast
1 3-lb. pork roast
1 onion, chopped
1 green pepper, chopped
1/3 c. pickle relish
1/3 c. vinegar
1/2 c. catsup
2 tsp. mustard
2 tsp. horseradish
2 tbsp. brown sugar

Season beef and pork with salt and pepper to taste. Place in roasting pan. Roast, covered, at 350 degrees for several hours or until very tender. Bone, trim and shred roasts. Combine with pan drippings and remaining ingredients in saucepan; mix well. Simmer for 30 minutes or longer. Serve on buns. Yield: 12 servings.

Approx per serv: Cal 441; Prot 41.1 g; T Fat 25.7 g; Chl 134.3 mg; Car 9.2 g; Sod 265.7 mg; Pot 557.4 mg.

Darlene S. Fitzgerald, Shiawassee

LEMON-MARINATED CHUCK ROAST

1 4-lb. beef chuck roast, 1 1/2 in. thick
1/2 c. lemon juice
1 tsp. grated lemon rind
1/3 c. oil
1 tsp. Worcestershire sauce
2 tbsp. sliced green onions with tops
4 tsp. sugar
1 tsp. prepared mustard
1 1/2 tsp. salt
1/8 tsp. pepper

Score fatty edges of roast; place in shallow baking dish. Combine remaining ingredients in bowl. Pour over roast. Marinate, covered, at room temperature for 3 hours or in refrigerator overnight. Turn roast several times. Drain, reserving marinade. Grill over medium-hot coals for 17 to 20 minutes on each side or to desired degree of doneness. Carve cross grain into thin slices. Arrange on serving platter. Spoon heated reserved marinade over top. Yield: 6 servings.

Joan Hoggard, Emmet

REUBEN CASSEROLE

1 pkg. scalloped potatoes mix
1 8-oz. can sauerkraut
2 2-oz. packages sliced corned beef, chopped
2/3 c. milk
1 1/2 c. shredded Swiss cheese

Layer dried potatoes, sauerkraut and corned beef in deep 8 x 8-inch baking dish. Sprinkle with scalloped potato sauce mix. Pour 2 1/2 cups boiling water and milk over top. Sprinkle with cheese. Bake at 350 degrees for 35 to 45 minutes or until potatoes are tender.

Jo Hannah Steiner, Barry

OVEN SWISS STEAK

1/4 c. flour
1 tsp. salt
1 1/2 lb. boneless round steak, cut into 4 pieces
3 tbsp. shortening
1 16-oz. can stewed tomatoes
1/2 c. chopped celery
1/2 c. chopped carrot
2 tbsp. chopped onion
1/2 tsp. Worcestershire sauce
1/4 c. shredded process American cheese

Pound mixture of flour and salt into steak with meat mallet. Shake off and reserve excess flour. Brown steak on both sides in shortening in skillet. Place in shallow 2-quart baking dish. Blend reserved flour into pan drippings in skillet. Add next 5 ingredients; mix well. Cook until mixture is thickened and bubbly, stirring constantly. Pour over steak. Bake at 350 degrees for 2 hours or until very tender. Sprinkle cheese over top. Bake until cheese melts.
Yield: 4 servings.

Approx per serv: Cal 514; Prot 38.1 g; T Fat 33.5 g; Chl 120.8 mg; Car 13.8 g; Sod 945.9 mg; Pot 931.3 mg.

Peggy Hamminga, Antrim

SUPER STEAK AND BLACK-EYED PEAS

4 c. cooked wild rice
1 lg. onion, chopped
3/4 c. chopped celery
3/4 c. chopped green pepper
1 c. sliced mushrooms
1 c. chopped tomatoes

2 tbsp. olive oil
1 8-oz. can French-style green
  beans, drained
1 8-oz. can black-eyed peas, drained
2 lb. round steak, cut into 1-in. strips
3/4 tsp. seasoned salt
1/4 tsp. garlic salt
1/4 tsp. pepper
2 tbsp. olive oil
6 tbsp. Worcestershire sauce

Place rice in large buttered baking dish. Saute onion, celery, green pepper, mushrooms and tomatoes in 2 tablespoons olive oil in skillet for 3 minutes. Add green beans and peas; mix well. Cook for 3 minutes longer; set aside. Sprinkle steak with seasoned salt, garlic salt and pepper. Brown in 2 tablespoons olive oil in skillet for 3 minutes. Stir in sauteed vegetables; mix well. Pour over rice in baking dish. Sprinkle Worcestershire sauce over top. Bake at 350 degrees until heated through. Yield: 12 servings.

Approx per serv: Cal 313; Prot 21.6 g; T Fat 14.3 g; Chl 51.4 mg; Car 25.1 g; Sod 433.7 mg; Pot 737.1 mg.

Nancy Hampton, Oakland

FIVE-HOUR OVEN BEEF STEW

1 1/2 lb. stew beef
1 16-oz. can tomatoes
1 c. chopped celery
3 to 5 potatoes, peeled, chopped
3 carrots, chopped
2 sm. onions, sliced
1 clove of garlic, minced
1 tbsp. tapioca
1 tsp. sugar
1 tbsp. salt
Pepper to taste

Combine all ingredients in large casserole; mix well. Bake, covered, at 250 degrees for 5 hours. Yield: 5 servings.

Approx per serv: Cal 652; Prot 41.5 g; T Fat 33.0 g; Chl 127.9 mg; Car 46.5 g; Sod 1518.6 mg; Pot 1529.4 mg.

David Risner, Calhoun

LAZY STEW

1 16-oz. can potatoes
1 16-oz. can whole kernel corn, drained
1 4-oz. can sliced mushrooms, drained

4 to 5 cubed beef steaks, cut into
  bite-sized pieces
1 can cream of mushroom soup

Combine potatoes with liquid, corn, mushrooms and steak in slow cooker. Season to taste. Mix soup with 1/2 soup can water in bowl. Stir into stew. Cook on Medium for several hours or until tender. Yield: 4 servings.

NOTE: May thicken sauce with cornstarch if desired and serve over noodles.

Approx per serv: Cal 467; Prot 29.3 g; T Fat 20.7 g; Chl 83.1 mg; Car 42.8 g; Sod 873.2 mg; Pot 1041.6 mg.

Patt Lambert, Clare

PIZZA CASSEROLE

1 lb. ground beef
1 lb. ground pork
1/2 c. chopped onion (opt.)
1 12-oz. package egg noodles, cooked
1 12-oz. jar spaghetti sauce
1 15-oz. can tomato sauce
1 tsp. oregano
2 c. grated mozzarella cheese

Brown ground beef and pork with onion and salt and pepper to taste in skillet, stirring frequently. Add noodles, sauces and oregano. Layer half the noodle mixture and 1 cup cheese in 9 x 13-inch baking dish. Repeat layers. Bake at 325 degrees for 30 minutes. Yield: 8 servings.

Sandy Saari, Marquette

SADIE'S SPECIAL CASSEROLE

1 c. rice
1 lb. ground beef
1 lg. onion, chopped
1 c. chopped celery
1 can chicken with rice soup
1 can cream of celery soup

Cook rice using package directions for 10 minutes. Partially brown ground beef with onion and celery in skillet; drain. Add soups, 1 soup can water and rice with cooking liquid. Pour into casserole. Bake at 350 degrees for 1 1/4 hours. Yield: 6 servings.

Approx per serv: Cal 337; Prot 17.8 g; T Fat 13.8 g; Chl 60.0 mg; Car 34.0 g; Sod 836.6 mg; Pot 373.7 mg.

Connie Hoy, Luce

COMPANY CASSEROLE

2 lb. ground beef
1/2 c. chopped onion
1/4 c. chopped green pepper
1 4-oz. can sliced mushrooms
1 8-oz. can tomato sauce
1 1/2 tsp. salt
1/4 tsp. pepper
1/2 c. milk
1 8-oz. package cream cheese, softened
1 tbsp. lemon juice
1 1/2 tsp. Worcestershire sauce
1/4 tsp. garlic salt
1 8-oz. package wide egg noodles, cooked

Brown ground beef in skillet, stirring until crumbly. Add vegetables, tomato sauce, salt and pepper; mix well. Simmer for several minutes. Cream milk, cream cheese, lemon juice, Worcestershire sauce and garlic salt in bowl. Add noodles. Layer noodle mixture and ground beef mixture alternately in 4-quart casserole until all ingredients are used. Bake at 350 degrees for 20 minutes or until bubbly. Yield: 8 servings.

Approx per serv: Cal 479; Prot 27.1 g; T Fat 29.2 g; Chl 136.9 mg; Car 26.1 g; Sod 770.7 mg; Pot 491.3 mg.

Patricia Roach, Antrim

ALICE'S LASAGNA

2 lb. ground beef
1 onion, chopped
1/2 tsp. salt
1/2 tsp. pepper
1 tsp. garlic powder
1/2 tsp. basil
1/2 tsp. oregano
1 8-oz. can tomato sauce
2 6-oz. cans tomato paste
1 8-oz. carton cottage cheese
2 eggs
8 oz. lasagna noodles, cooked
1 8-oz. package shredded
   mozzarella cheese
1 tbsp. chopped parsley

Brown ground beef with onion in skillet, stirring frequently; drain. Add seasonings, tomato sauce and paste and 1 3/4 cups water; mix well. Mix cottage cheese and eggs in bowl. Layer ground beef mixture, noodles, cottage cheese and mozzarella alternately in greased 9 x 13-inch baking dish, ending with ground beef and mozzarella. Bake at 350 degrees for 35 minutes. Sprinkle with parsley. Yield: 12 servings.

Approx per serv: Cal 359; Prot 25.0 g; T Fat 18.5 g; Chl 131.5 mg; Car 22.9 g; Sod 378.1 mg; Pot 568.2 mg.

Alice R. Gauthier, Houghton

LAZY CABBAGE ROLL CASSEROLE

1 lb. ground beef
1 med. onion, chopped
3 tbsp. rice
1 can tomato soup
3 c. chopped cabbage

Brown ground beef with onion and salt and pepper to taste in skillet, stirring frequently; drain. Add rice, soup and 1 soup can water. Simmer for 10 minutes. Place cabbage in greased 2-quart casserole. Pour ground beef mixture over cabbage. Bake, covered, at 325 degrees for 1 1/2 hours. Yield: 5 servings.

Approx per serv: Cal 279; Prot 18.3 g; T Fat 14.7 g; Chl 61.3 mg; Car 18.5 g; Sod 535.5 mg; Pot 463.7 mg.

Kristyn Kurka, Shiawassee

GOULASH

1 lb. ground beef
1/4 tsp. garlic salt
1/2 tsp. salt
1/2 tsp. pepper
1/2 med. onion, chopped
1 8-oz. package noodles, cooked
4 c. canned tomatoes
1 6-oz. can tomato paste
1 16-oz. can kidney beans
1 4-oz. can sliced mushrooms
1/4 c. (or more) sugar

Brown ground beef in skillet, stirring until crumbly; drain. Add seasonings and onion; mix well. Add noodles, tomatoes, tomato paste, beans and mushrooms. Simmer until thick. Add sugar; mix well. Spoon into serving dish. Yield: 6 servings.

Approx per serv: Cal 474; Prot 25.8 g; T Fat 13.6 g; Chl 86.6 mg; Car 63.0 g; Sod 513.7 mg; Pot 1073.6 mg.

Debra Daggett, Oceana

PERFECT MEAT LOAF

4 slices bread, cubed
1/2 c. milk
2 eggs
1 tbsp. Worcestershire sauce
1 1/2 lb. ground beef
1/2 lb. ground pork
1/4 c. finely chopped onion
2 tbsp. finely chopped celery
2 tsp. salt
1/2 tsp. poultry seasoning
1/4 tsp. pepper
1/4 tsp. dry mustard

Soak bread in milk in bowl until soft. Add eggs and Worcestershire sauce. Beat with rotary beater until smooth. Combine ground beef and pork in bowl; mix well. Add onion, celery, seasonings and bread mixture; mix well. Shape into loaf in loaf pan. Bake at 350 degrees for 1 hour. Yield: 8 servings.

Approx per serv: Cal 367; Prot 22.6 g; T Fat 26.0 g; Chl 137.5 mg; Car 8.9 g; Sod 715.7 mg; Pot 387.9 mg.

Theresa Thome, Kent

MEATBALLS SUPREME

1 1/4 lb. lean ground beef
1/4 lb. lean ground pork
1 egg, beaten
1 sm. can evaporated milk
2 tbsp. milk
1 tbsp. grated onion
1/4 tsp. pepper
1/4 tsp. nutmeg
1 tsp. salt
1/3 c. instant cream of rice
1/4 c. margarine
1 can cream of mushroom soup

Combine first 10 ingredients in bowl; mix well. Chill in refrigerator. Shape into walnut-sized balls. Brown in margarine in skillet. Place in casserole. Spoon soup over meatballs. Bake at 325 degrees for 1 1/2 hours. Yield: 8 servings.
NOTE: May substitute 1/4 pound additional ground beef for pork or ground veal for part of ground beef. Meats should be finely ground.

Approx per serv: Cal 331; Prot 20.7 g; T Fat 21.9 g; Chl 98.7 mg; Car 11.6 g; Sod 727.5 mg; Pot 391.9 mg.

Louisa Lange, Jackson

PORCUPINES

1 lb. ground beef
1/2 c. brown rice
1 egg
1 tbsp. oil
1 sm. onion, chopped
1 tsp. thyme
3/4 tsp. salt
3/4 tsp. pepper
1 tbsp. minced parsley
2 c. tomato juice

Combine all ingredients except tomato juice in bowl; mix well. Shape into balls. Place in casserole. Add tomato juice. Bake, covered, at 350 degrees for 1 hour. Yield: 4 servings.

Approx per serv: Cal 590; Prot 27.6 g; T Fat 30.1 g; Chl 140.3 mg; Car 51.1 g; Sod 736.6 mg; Pot 777.9 mg.

Donna Cook, Isabella

JASON'S HAMBURGER PIE

1 c. buttermilk baking mix
1 lb. ground beef
1/2 tsp. oregano
1/2 tsp. salt
1/4 tsp. pepper
1/2 c. fine dry bread crumbs
1 8-oz. can tomato sauce
1/4 c. chopped onion
1/4 c. chopped green pepper
1 egg
1/4 c. milk
2 c. shredded Cheddar cheese
1/2 tsp. dry mustard
1/2 tsp. salt

Combine baking mix and 1/4 cup cold water in bowl; mix well. Beat for 20 strokes. Knead 5 times on floured surface. Roll out. Fit into 9-inch pie plate; flute edge. Brown ground beef in skillet, stirring until crumbly; drain. Add oregano, 1/2 teaspoon salt, pepper, crumbs, tomato sauce, onion and green pepper; mix well. Spoon into prepared pie plate. Beat egg and milk. Add cheese, mustard and 1/2 teaspoon salt. Spoon over ground beef mixture. Bake at 375 degrees for 30 minutes. Yield: 6 servings.

Approx per serv: Cal 508; Prot 29.1 g; T Fat 27.9 g; Chl 132.8 mg; Car 34.8 g; Sod 1488.0 mg; Pot 578.0 mg.

Jason W. Schumacher, Huron

SLOPPY JOE TURNOVERS

1 lb. ground beef
1/4 c. chopped onion
1/2 tsp. salt
1/4 tsp. garlic powder
1/2 c. catsup
1/4 c. sour cream
1 10-count can refrigerator
  flaky biscuits

Brown ground beef with onion in skillet, stirring frequently; drain. Add seasonings, catsup and sour cream; mix well. Separate biscuits. Roll each into 4-inch square. Spoon 1/4 cup ground beef mixture onto each square. Fold over to form triangle; seal edges with fork. Cut three 1/2-inch slits in top of each. Place on baking sheet. Bake at 375 degrees for 15 minutes or until golden brown. Brush with melted margarine if desired. Yield: 10 servings.

Approx per serv: Cal 219; Prot 11.0 g; T Fat 10.1 g; Chl 48.6 mg; Car 20.3 g; Sod 575.6 mg; Pot 175.9 mg.

Melinda Bloodworth, Van Buren

PIZZABURGERS

1 lb. ground beef
1 8-oz. can tomato sauce
1/4 c. sliced olives
1/4 tsp. garlic salt
Oregano to taste
12 hamburger buns
2 c. chopped mozzarella cheese

Brown ground beef in skillet, stirring until crumbly; drain. Add next 4 ingredients and salt to taste; mix well. Spoon onto hamburger buns. Sprinkle filling with cheese; cover with bun tops. Wrap each filled bun in foil. Bake at 350 degrees for 15 minutes. Yield: 12 servings.
NOTE: Foil-wrapped Pizzaburgers may be frozen.

Approx per serv: Cal 299; Prot 16.0 g; T Fat 12.7 g; Chl 43.9 mg; Car 31.0 g; Sod 666.1 mg; Pot 224.9 mg.

Amy Larson, Marquette

SAUCY BURRITOS

2 lb. ground beef
1 env. taco seasoning mix
1 pkg. flour tortillas
2 15-oz. cans tomato sauce
1/2 tsp. oregano
1/2 tsp. onion salt
1/2 tsp. garlic powder
2 tbsp. chili powder
1 lb. Colby cheese, grated

Brown ground beef in skillet, stirring frequently. Add taco seasoning mix according to package directions. Soften tortillas, using package directions. Fill with ground beef mixture; roll to enclose filling. Place in 9 x 13-inch casserole. Combine remaining ingredients except cheese with 1 tomato sauce can water in bowl. Pour over casserole. Top with cheese. Bake at 350 degrees for 20 minutes or until bubbly. Yield: 8 servings.

Khoi Huynh, Ionia

ITALIAN SPAGHETTI

1 lb. ground beef
2 med. onions, chopped
2 cloves of garlic, minced
2 tbsp. chopped parsley
1 tbsp. each basil, oregano, Italian
  seasoning and sweet pepper flakes
1 tsp. salt
Red and green pepper flakes to taste
1 tbsp. Worcestershire sauce
2 8-oz. cans tomato sauce
2 6-oz. cans tomato paste

Brown ground beef in skillet, stirring until crumbly; drain. Add onions, garlic and parsley. Cook until onions are golden. Add seasonings, tomato sauce and paste. Simmer for 2 hours. Serve over spaghetti with Parmesan cheese. Yield: 6 servings.
NOTE: May substitute ground fresh turkey for ground beef.

Approx per serv: Cal 483; Prot 26.8 g; T Fat 12.6 g; Chl 51.1 mg; Car 74.3 g; Sod 983.5 mg; Pot 3575.6 mg.

Dorothy Quirk, Marquette

FOIL LAMB CHOPS

4 lamb chops
2 med. tomatoes, sliced
1 4-oz. can mushrooms
1 env. dry onion soup mix

Place 4 squares heavy foil on baking sheet. Place 1 lamb chop on each. Layer remaining ingredients over chops. Fold foil to enclose filling; seal tightly. Bake at 325 degrees for 1 1/2 to 2 hours. Serve with baked potatoes, green vegetable and salad. Yield: 4 servings.

Violet Civis, Muskegon

ROAST LEG OF LAMB

1   5 to 6-lb. leg of lamb
2 cloves of garlic, chopped
2 tbsp. Worcestershire sauce
3 tbsp. chopped parsley
1 tsp. thyme
4 bay leaves
2 med. onions, sliced

Cut 1-inch slits in roast; insert garlic. Sprinkle with Worcestershire sauce and seasonings. Place fat side up on rack in roasting pan. Add onions and 2 cups water to pan. Bake at 325 degrees until tender. Serve with mint jelly. Yield: 10 servings.

Approx per serv: Cal 460; Prot 41.0 g; T Fat 30.3 g; Chl 157.0 mg; Car 2.8 g; Sod 131.7 mg; Pot 525.7 mg.

Ken Wahl, Bay

LAMB SAUSAGE

3 lb. lean lamb
1 lb. smoked ham, cubed
1/2 lb. bacon
1 1/2 tsp. sage
1 tsp. thyme
1 tsp. each salt and pepper

Put lamb, ham and bacon through food chopper twice. Add seasonings; mix well. Shape into patties. Grill or fry as desired. Yield: 16 servings.

Linda L. Davis, Benzie

STIR-FRIED SWEET AND SOUR LAMB

1 1/2 to 2 lb. lean lamb, cut into
    3/4-in. cubes
1 egg, beaten
1/3 c. cornstarch
3 tbsp. oil

1 c. 1/4-in. thick diagonally
    sliced carrots
1 lg. clove of garlic, minced
1 1/2 tbsp. cornstarch
1/2 c. pineapple juice
3 tbsp. apple cider vinegar
1/4 tsp. ginger
1 tsp. Worcestershire sauce
2 tbsp. soy sauce
3 tbsp. sugar or honey
1   15-oz. can pineapple chunks, drained
1/2 c. diagonally sliced green onions
1 tomato, cut into 1-in. wedges
1 c. sliced mushrooms
1   6-oz. package frozen Chinese pea
    pods with water
Hot cooked rice
1/4 c. sliced almonds

Dip lamb cubes in beaten egg; coat with 1/3 cup cornstarch. Stir-fry lamb 1/2 at a time in 2 tablespoons hot oil in wok for 5 minutes or until brown on all sides; drain on paper towels. Add remaining tablespoon oil. Stir-fry carrots and garlic in wok for 2 minutes. Add 2 tablespoons water. Cook, covered, until tender-crisp. Combine 1 1/2 tablespoons cornstarch, next 6 ingredients and 1/4 cup water in small bowl; mix well. Add to wok with lamb, pineapple chunks and vegetables. Cook until thickened, stirring constantly. Serve over rice. Top with almonds. Yield: 4 servings.

Mary E. Wahl, Bay

RIBS AND SAUERKRAUT

4 c. sauerkraut
2 med. apples, chopped
1/2 to 1 c. chopped celery
1 med. onion, chopped
2 tsp. brown sugar
3 lb. pork ribs
1/2 c. raisins (opt.)

Combine first 5 ingredients in bowl; mix well. Place 1 rack ribs in baking pan. Spread sauerkraut over ribs. Top with remaining ribs. Season with salt and pepper. Bake at 350 degrees for 1 1/2 hours. Serve sprinkled with raisins if desired. Yield: 5 servings.

Approx per serv: Cal 744.5; Prot 26.7 g; T Fat 55.2 g; Chl 101.2 mg; Car 38.4 g; Sod 1526.2 mg; Pot 982.8 mg.

Carol Majors, Monroe

PORK CHOPS AND STUFFING

4 pork chops
2 tbsp. chopped onion
2 tbsp. chopped celery
1/4 c. melted butter
1/2 tsp. poultry seasoning
3 c. soft bread cubes
1 can mushroom soup

Brown pork chops in skillet. Arrange in casserole. Saute onion and celery in butter in skillet. Add seasoning, 1/4 cup water and bread cubes; mix well. Spoon onto pork chops. Pour mixture of soup and 1/3 cup water over pork chops. Bake at 300 degrees for 1 hour.
Yield: 4 servings.

Approx per serv: Cal 569; Prot 20.6 g; T Fat 41.1 g; Chl 98.3 mg; Car 28.4 g; Sod 1007.1 mg; Pot 376.1 mg.

Sue Maschke, Otsego

APPLE-GLAZED PORK CHOPS

2 lb. pork chops
1/4 c. flour
1/2 tsp. salt
1/8 tsp. pepper
1/2 tsp. dry mustard
2 tbsp. margarine
2 tbsp. flour
2 tbsp. brown sugar
1 1/2 c. apple juice
2 apples, peeled, sliced
1/3 c. raisins
1/2 tsp. cinnamon

Coat pork chops with mixture of 1/4 cup flour, salt, pepper and mustard. Brown on both sides in margarine in skillet. Remove pork chops. Stir in 2 tablespoons flour and brown sugar. Add apple juice gradually. Cook until thickened, stirring constantly. Place pork chops in 2-quart casserole. Arrange apples and raisins over pork chops. Pour apple juice mixture over top. Sprinkle with cinnamon. Bake, covered, at 350 degrees for 1 hour. Yield: 4 servings.

Approx per serv: Cal 794.6; Prot 32.5 g; T Fat 51.1 g; Chl 111.1 mg; Car 51.6 g; Sod 451.3 mg; Pot 829.3 mg.

Rosalind A. Lehman, Midland

CHOP SUEY

1 lb. pork, cut into bite-sized pieces
1 lb. veal, cut into bite-sized pieces
2 c. chopped onions
1/4 c. oil
2 c. chopped celery
1 16-oz. can bean sprouts, drained
3 tbsp. cornstarch
1 tbsp. brown sugar
3 tbsp. soy sauce
1 8-oz. can mushrooms, drained
1 6-oz. can water chestnuts, drained

Brown pork, veal and onions in oil in skillet; drain. Stir in enough water to cover. Simmer until almost tender. Add celery. Simmer for 20 minutes longer. Stir in bean sprouts. Blend next 3 ingredients and 1/4 cup water in bowl. Add to skillet. Cook until mixture thickens, stirring constantly. Season with salt and pepper to taste. Stir in mushrooms and sliced water chestnuts. Cook just until heated through.
Yield: 6 servings.

Approx per serv: Cal 546; Prot 32.1 g; T Fat 35.9 g; Chl 100.5 mg; Car 23.9 g; Sod 821.4 mg; Pot 921.8 mg.

Maudie Ritt, Antrim

HAM AND CHICKEN CASSEROLE

1/2 c. chopped green pepper
1 c. chopped celery

2 c. fine noodles, cooked
1/4 c. chopped pimento
1 c. chopped cooked ham
1 c. chopped cooked chicken
2 cans cream of mushroom soup
Chicken broth
1   3-oz. can French-fried onions
1   8-oz. package shredded Cheddar cheese

Cook green pepper and celery in a small amount of water in saucepan until tender; drain. Combine with noodles, pimento, ham and chicken in 9 x 13-inch casserole. Blend soup with enough chicken broth to make smooth gravy. Pour over noodle mixture; mix lightly. Top with onions and cheese. Bake at 350 degrees for 30 minutes. Yield: 6 servings.

Approx per serv: Cal 569; Prot 27.6 g; T Fat 31.8 g; Chl 114.9 mg; Car 42.5 g; Sod 1489.9 mg; Pot 387.9 mg.

Tracy Roehm, Washtenaw

STOVE TOP HAM CASSEROLE

2 c. chopped ham
1/4 c. chopped onion
1/4 c. chopped green pepper
2 tbsp. butter
2 cans cream of chicken soup
3/4 c. milk

Saute ham, onion and green pepper with salt and pepper to taste in butter in skillet until vegetables are tender. Add soup and milk. Simmer for 1 hour. Serve over cooked rice. Yield: 4 servings.

Approx per serv: Cal 204; Prot 5.5 g; T Fat 14.5 g; Chl 36.1 mg; Car 13.6 g; Sod 1300.6 mg; Pot 202.5 mg.

Sharon Andrews, Kalkaska

HAM-NOODLE CASSEROLE

2 c. noodles, cooked
1 c. chopped cooked ham
1 c. peas
1 c. chopped American cheese
2 tbsp. chopped onion
1/2 tsp. salt
1/4 tsp. pepper
1/4 tsp. paprika
1 tbsp. butter
1 c. milk
1/3 c. bread crumbs

Layer noodles, ham, peas, cheese and onion alternately in greased 2-quart casserole until all ingredients are used. Season with salt, pepper and paprika. Dot with butter. Add milk. Sprinkle crumbs over top. Bake at 350 degrees for 45 minutes. Yield: 4 servings.

NOTE: May make the following substitutions: luncheon meat or chicken for ham; tomato juice or soup for milk; mushrooms, green pepper or olives for peas; dry mustard or Worcestershire sauce for paprika.

Approx per serv: Cal 493; Prot 23.6 g; T Fat 22.0 g; Chl 111.9 mg; Car 48.9 g; Sod 1185.4 mg; Pot 353.9 mg.

Cleo Williams, Shiawassee

MICKIE'S LASAGNA

1 lb. hot Italian sausage
1 clove of garlic, minced
1 tbsp. basil
1 1/2 tsp. salt
1   16-oz. can stewed tomatoes
2   6-oz. cans tomato paste
3 c. cottage cheese
1/2 c. Parmesan cheese
2 tbsp. parsley flakes
2 eggs, beaten
2 tsp. salt
1/2 tsp. pepper
10 oz. lasagna noodles, cooked
1   16-oz. can spinach, drained
1 c. chopped ripe olives
1/2 c. chopped green olives
1   16-oz. can sliced mushrooms
1/2 c. finely chopped onion
16 oz. mozzarella cheese, thinly sliced

Brown sausage in skillet, stirring until crumbly; drain. Add garlic, basil, salt, tomatoes and tomato paste. Simmer for 30 minutes, stirring occasionally. Combine cottage cheese, Parmesan cheese, parsley, eggs, salt and pepper in bowl; mix well. Layer noodles, sausage mixture, cottage cheese mixture, spinach, olives, mushrooms, onion and cheese 1/2 at a time in 9 x 13-inch baking dish. Bake at 375 degrees for 30 minutes or until bubbly and cheese melts. Let stand for 10 minutes before serving. Yield: 12 servings.

Mickie L. Hackworth, Clare

PIZZA CASSEROLE

1 lb. sausage
1 16-oz. package noodles, cooked
2 8-oz. cans pizza sauce
1 8-oz. package sliced pepperoni
2 tsp. oregano
1 8-oz. can mushrooms, drained
2 8-oz. packages shredded
   mozzarella cheese

Brown sausage in skillet, stirring until crumbly; drain. Layer noodles, sauce, pepperoni, oregano, mushrooms, sausage and cheese in 9 x 13-inch casserole 1/2 at a time. Bake at 350 degrees for 30 minutes. Yield: 8 servings.

Sara Persons, Mecosta

HOT DOG BAKE

3 tbsp. butter, melted
2 tbsp. flour
1 tsp. salt
1/4 tsp. pepper
3/4 tsp. dry mustard
1 1/2 c. milk
3/4 c. salad dressing
1 16-oz. can wax beans, drained
1 med. onion, chopped
6 med. potatoes, cooked, chopped
8 to 10 hot dogs, sliced 1 in. thick
1/2 c. cracker crumbs

Blend butter, flour and seasonings in saucepan. Stir in milk gradually. Cook until thickened, stirring constantly. Cool slightly. Add salad dressing; mix well. Add beans, onion, potatoes and hot dogs; mix well. Sprinkle with cracker crumbs. Bake at 350 degrees for 45 minutes. Yield: 4 servings.

Approx per serv: Cal 1066; Prot 29.4 g; T Fat 70.5 g; Chl 148.7 mg; Car 81.2 g; Sod 2755.9 mg; Pot 1735.0 mg.

Jeanine Clemens, Ogemaw

RABBIT BARBECUE

4 cloves of garlic, chopped
1/2 c. margarine
1 c. packed brown sugar
2 tbsp. celery seed
2/3 c. lemon juice
3 tbsp. vinegar
1/3 c. mustard with horseradish
1/2 c. Worcestershire sauce
1 14-oz. bottle of catsup
2 to 4 tsp. Tabasco sauce
1 rabbit, cooked, chopped

Saute garlic in margarine in large saucepan until lightly browned. Add remaining ingredients except rabbit; mix well. Simmer for 40 minutes. Remove and discard garlic. Stir in rabbit. Simmer for 30 minutes. Serve on buns.
Yield: 15 servings.

NOTE: May cook rabbit in pressure cooker according to manufacturer's instructions for 30 minutes for mature rabbit or 10 minutes for young tender rabbit.

Approx per serv: Cal 294; Prot 20.3 g; T Fat 13.2 g; Chl 59.5 mg; Car 23.9 g; Sod 538.2 mg. Pot 483.1 mg.

Arlene Parker, Muskegon

FRENCH HERBED RABBIT

2 young rabbits, cut up
2 tbsp. oil
1 med. onion, chopped
2 stalks celery, chopped
2 c. chopped carrots
2 cloves of garlic, chopped
1 c. sliced mushrooms
1 c. Sauterne
1 bay leaf
2 tbsp. chopped parsley
1/2 tsp. thyme

Brown rabbit in hot oil in skillet; drain. Arrange in roaster. Saute onion, celery, carrots, garlic and mushrooms in pan drippings for 5 minutes. Add wine. Cook for several minutes. Pour over rabbit. Add bay leaf, parsley, thyme and salt and pepper to taste. Bake at 400 degrees for 45 minutes or until tender. Remove and discard bay leaf. Arrange rabbit pieces in center of serving plate. Spoon vegetable mixture around edge. Yield: 8 servings.

Approx per serv: Cal 394; Prot 42.0 g; T Fat 17.7 g; Chl 127.4 mg; Car 7.3 g; Sod 87.5 mg; Pot 735.9 mg.

Annette L. Dedic, Delta

VENISON PATTIES

1 lb. ground venison
1/2 lb. bacon, chopped

1 sm. onion, minced
1/2 tsp. grated lemon rind
1/8 tsp. thyme
1/8 tsp. marjoram
1 egg
1/4 to 1/3 c. bread crumbs

Combine all ingredients in bowl; mix well. Shape into 3-inch patties. Broil or fry as desired. Yield: 4 servings.

Approx per serv: Cal 447; Prot 11.6 g; T Fat 41.8 g; Chl 116.9 mg; Car 5.2 g; Sod 449.1 mg; Pot 196.8 mg.

Gordon Worth, Barry

VENISON ROAST

1 4-lb. venison rump roast
2 cloves of garlic, sliced
4 slices bacon
1 onion, quartered

Trim roast well. Cut slits in roast; insert garlic. Place in baking pan. Sprinkle with salt and pepper to taste. Arrange bacon over top. Add onion and 1/2 inch water. Cook, covered, at 350 degrees for 1 1/2 to 2 hours or until venison is tender. Yield: 8 servings.

Jon Rund, Gogebic

VENISON SUPREME

1 lb. venison, cut into 1/2-in. cubes
1/4 c. flour
1 tsp. salt
1/2 tsp. pepper
1/4 c. shortening
1/2 c. sliced mushrooms
1/4 c. chopped onion
1 c. tomato juice
Oregano to taste
1/2 bay leaf
3/4 c. sour cream
1 c. chopped celery (opt.)
1 8-oz. package egg noodles, cooked

Coat venison with mixture of flour, salt and pepper. Brown in shortening in skillet. Add mushrooms and onion. Saute until onion is tender. Add tomato juice, 1/2 cup water and seasonings. Bring to a boil; reduce heat. Simmer, uncovered, for 25 minutes or until venison is tender. Stir in sour cream and celery. Simmer, covered, for 15 minutes. Spoon hot cooked noodles into ring on serving platter. Spoon venison mixture into ring. Serve with broccoli. Yield: 6 servings.

Shirley Charlier, Menominee

CHICKEN AND RICE

1 c. rice
2 tsp. instant bouillon
1 env. dry onion soup mix
1 4-oz. can mushrooms
1 3-lb. chicken, cut up
1/4 c. butter
2 tbsp. chopped parsley (opt.)

Place rice in 9 x 13-inch baking dish. Add mixture of 2 cups water and bouillon. Add soup mix and mushrooms. Arrange chicken over rice. Dot with butter. Sprinkle with salt and pepper to taste and parsley. Bake at 350 degrees for 1 hour. Yield: 6 servings.

Approx per serv: Cal 563; Prot 33.3 g; T Fat 33.8 g; Chl 188.0 mg; Car 29.3 g; Sod 798.1 mg; Pot 436.3 mg.

Patricia Perry, Kent

PARMESAN CHICKEN

1/2 c. fine dry bread crumbs
1/4 c. Parmesan cheese
1/2 tsp. oregano
Garlic powder to taste
Pepper to taste
4 lb. chicken pieces
2 cans cream of chicken soup
1 c. milk
Paprika to taste
1/4 c. Parmesan cheese

Combine first 5 ingredients in shallow dish. Coat chicken with crumb mixture. Arrange skin side down in 10 x 15-inch baking dish. Bake at 400 degrees for 20 minutes on each side. Blend soup and milk. Pour over chicken. Sprinkle with paprika and 1/4 cup Parmesan cheese. Bake at 400 degrees for 20 minutes longer or until chicken is tender. Yield: 8 servings.

Approx per serv: Cal 487; Prot 36.0 g; T Fat 32.1 g; Chl 170.8 mg; Car 11.3 g; Sod 780.8 mg; Pot 422.4 mg.

Leora Anderson, Muskegon

CHICKEN TETRAZZINI

1 med. onion, chopped
1/4 c. butter
1/4 c. flour
1 1/2 c. chicken broth
1 c. cream
1 tsp. salt
1/8 tsp. pepper
1/2 c. dry vermouth
1/4 c. Parmesan cheese
1/2 lb. mushrooms, sliced
2 tbsp. butter
12 oz. spaghetti, cooked
3 c. chopped cooked chicken
1/2 c. Parmesan cheese

Saute onion in 1/4 cup butter in saucepan until almost tender. Stir in flour. Stir in broth and cream gradually. Bring to a boil over low heat, stirring constantly. Add salt, pepper, vermouth and 1/4 cup cheese. Saute mushrooms in 2 tablespoons butter in skillet until brown. Add spaghetti and chicken. Turn into shallow 2 1/2-quart casserole. Pour cream sauce over top. Sprinkle with 1/2 cup cheese. Bake at 350 degrees for 30 to 45 minutes or until heated through. Yield: 4 servings.

Approx per serv: Cal 879; Prot 53.9 g; T Fat 33.7 g; Chl 166.4 mg; Car 82.9 g; Sod 1209.6 mg; Pot 967.9 mg.

Maurene Schumann, Ogemaw

CHINESE CASSEROLE

1 c. chopped celery
1 c. chopped onion
4 c. chopped cooked chicken
1 can cream of mushroom soup
1 can cream of chicken soup
1 c. minute rice
1/4 c. soy sauce
1 16-oz. can Chinese vegetables, drained
1 3-oz. can Chinese noodles

Saute celery and onion in skillet until tender. Add remaining ingredients except noodles. Turn into greased 2-quart casserole. Bake at 350 degrees for 45 minutes. Sprinkle noodles over top. Bake for 5 minutes longer. Yield: 8 servings.

Kathleen Bragiel, Bay

TURKEY AMANDINE

3 c. chopped cooked turkey
1 can cream of chicken soup
1 8-oz. can sliced water chestnuts, drained
1 4-oz. can mushroom pieces, drained
2/3 c. mayonnaise
1/2 c. chopped celery
1/2 c. chopped onion
1/2 c. sour cream
1 8-oz. can refrigerator crescent dinner rolls
2/3 c. shredded Swiss cheese
1/2 c. slivered almonds
2 to 4 tbsp. butter, melted

Combine first 8 ingredients in large saucepan. Cook over medium heat until bubbly. Pour into 9 x 13-inch casserole. Separate rolls into 2 rectangles. Place over hot turkey mixture. Combine cheese, almonds and butter in bowl. Sprinkle over top. Bake at 375 degrees for 20 to 25 minutes or until brown. Yield: 6 servings.

Pat Bancroft, Lenawee

MARINATED SALMON STEAKS

4 1-in. thick salmon steaks
1/3 c. orange juice
1/3 c. soy sauce
2 tbsp. chopped parsley
2 tbsp. oil
1 clove of garlic, crushed
1/2 tsp. basil

Arrange salmon steaks in shallow dish. Combine remaining ingredients in bowl; mix well. Pour over salmon. Marinate at room temperature for 2 hours or in refrigerator for 4 to 6 hours, turning occasionally. Drain, reserving marinade. Grill salmon steaks over medium-hot coals for 8 minutes or until lightly browned. Baste with reserved marinade; turn steaks over. Grill for 8 to 10 minutes or until fish flakes easily. Bring reserved marinade to a boil in saucepan. Place salmon steaks on serving plate. Drizzle hot marinade over top. Yield: 4 servings.

Approx per serv: Cal 320; Prot 36.0 g; T Fat 16.6 g; Chl 60.0 mg; Car 4.8 g; Sod 1906.0 mg; Pot 710.7 mg.

Debra Richer, Dickinson

Breads

OLD-FASHIONED BISCUITS

2 1/2 c. flour
1 1/2 tsp. baking powder
1/2 tsp. soda
1 tsp. salt
1/2 c. shortening
1 c. buttermilk

Sift dry ingredients into bowl. Cut in shortening until crumbly. Stir in buttermilk with fork. Pat 1/4 to 1/2 inch thick on floured surface. Cut with biscuit cutter. Place on baking sheet. Bake at 400 degrees for 10 to 12 minutes or until golden brown. Yield: 12 servings.

Approx per serv: Cal 185; Prot 3.5 g; T Fat 9.6 g; Chl 0.4 mg; Car 21.0 g; Sod 280.0 mg; Pot 53.9 mg.

Kathryn Robotham, Osceola

HERB-BUTTERED BREAD

1 long loaf French bread
1 c. butter, softened
2 tsp. finely chopped green onion
2 tsp. finely chopped ripe olives
2 tsp. finely chopped parsley
1 tsp. basil
1/2 tsp. thyme
1/2 tsp. marjoram
1/2 tsp. tarragon
1 tsp. garlic powder

Slice bread diagonally. Combine butter and remaining ingredients in bowl; mix well. Spread bread slices with mixture; place on baking sheet. Bake at 350 degrees for 15 minutes. Serve warm. Yield: 10 servings.

Approx per serv: Cal 368; Prot 6.5 g; T Fat 20.8 g; Chl 58.9 mg; Car 39.0 g; Sod 640.5 mg; Pot 71.2 mg.

Julee Nordin, Menominee

APPLE BREAD

1 c. sugar
1/2 c. margarine, softened
2 eggs
2 tbsp. sour milk
2 c. flour
1 tsp. soda
1/2 tsp. baking powder
1 tsp. salt
1 tsp. vanilla extract

2 c. chopped apples
1/4 c. sugar
1/4 c. flour
1/4 c. butter
1 tbsp. cinnamon

Combine first 4 ingredients in bowl; mix well. Add flour, soda, baking powder, salt and vanilla; mix well. Stir in apples. Pour into greased loaf pan. Combine remaining ingredients in small bowl; mix well. Mixture will be crumbly. Sprinkle over batter. Bake at 325 degrees for 1 hour or until loaf tests done. Remove to wire rack to cool. Yield: 8 servings.

Approx per serv: Cal 482; Prot 5.8 g; T Fat 19.4 g; Chl 81.0 mg; Car 73.6 g; Sod 622.2 mg; Pot 182.0 mg.

Bridget Pinkston, Ionia

EASY BANANA BREAD

1/4 c. shortening
3/4 c. sugar
2 eggs
1 c. mashed bananas
2 c. buttermilk baking mix
1/3 c. chopped pecans (opt.)

Cream shortening, sugar and eggs in mixer bowl for 2 minutes. Add bananas and baking mix; mix until blended. Stir in pecans. Pour into 2 greased 3 1/2 x 7-inch loaf pans. Bake at 350 degrees for 25 to 30 minutes or until loaves test done. Remove to wire rack to cool completely. Yield: 12 servings.

Approx per serv: Cal 568; Prot 7.7 g; T Fat 45.5 g; Chl 42.1 mg; Car 39.2 g; Sod 270.6 mg; Pot 431.3 mg.

Melissa Stanfield, Shiawassee

BOSTON BROWN BREAD

1 1/2 c. raisins
1 c. sugar
1 egg
1/4 c. melted shortening
1 tsp. vanilla extract
2 c. flour
1 tsp. soda
1 tsp. salt
1/2 c. chopped walnuts

Combine raisins and 1 1/2 cups water in saucepan. Boil for 5 minutes. Cool. Combine with sugar, egg, shortening and vanilla in bowl; mix well. Add mixture of flour, soda and salt; mix well. Stir in walnuts. Pour into 3 greased 16-ounce cans. Bake at 350 degrees for 1 hour. Cool in cans for 10 minutes. Remove to wire rack to cool completely. Yield: 20 servings.

Approx per serv: Cal 164; Prot 2.4 g; T Fat 5.2 g; Chl 12.6 mg; Car 28.4 g; Sod 154.0 mg; Pot 111.9 mg.

Lillian Bartholomew, Antrim

BLUEBERRY BREAD

3 tbsp. oil
2 eggs
1 c. sugar
1 c. milk
2 c. flour
1 tbsp. baking powder
1/2 tsp. salt
1 c. fresh blueberries

Cream oil, eggs and sugar in bowl until light. Add milk; mix well. Sift in dry ingredients; mix well. Fold in blueberries. Pour into greased loaf pan. Bake at 350 degrees for 1 hour. Cool in pan for 30 minutes. Remove to wire rack to cool completely. Yield: 8 servings.

Approx per serv: Cal 308; Prot 6.1 g; T Fat 8.0 g; Chl 67.5 mg; Car 53.4 g; Sod 288.1 mg; Pot 106.9 mg.

Audra Dohm, Cass

BUTTERMILK RAISIN BREAD

5 c. flour
3/4 c. sugar
1 tbsp. baking powder
1 tsp. salt
1 tsp. soda
1/2 c. margarine
2 1/2 c. golden raisins
3 tbsp. caraway seed (opt.)
2 1/2 c. buttermilk
1 egg, slightly beaten

Combine first 5 ingredients in bowl. Cut in margarine until crumbly. Stir in raisins and caraway seed. Add buttermilk and egg; stir until just mixed. Mixture will be lumpy. Pour into generously buttered 11-inch cast-iron skillet. Bake at 350 degrees for 1 hour or until brown. Cool completely. Garnish with dusting of confectioners' sugar. Cut into wedges. Yield: 20 servings.

Approx per serv: Cal 252; Prot 5.2 g; T Fat 5.3 g; Chl 13.3 mg; Car 47.0 g; Sod 301.4 mg; Pot 216.3 mg.

Katie Moon, Livingston

CRANBERRY-NUT BREAD

2 c. flour
1 1/2 tsp. baking powder
1/2 tsp. soda
1 c. sugar
1/2 tsp. salt
1 tbsp. grated orange rind
2 tbsp. butter, melted
1/2 c. plus 2 tbsp. orange juice
1 egg, beaten
1/2 c. chopped walnuts
1 c. finely chopped cranberries

Combine first 6 ingredients in bowl. Add butter, orange juice and egg; stir until just moistened. Fold in walnuts and cranberries. Spoon into greased loaf pan. Bake at 350 degrees for 1 hour and 10 minutes or until loaf tests done. Remove from pan. Cool on wire rack. Yield: 12 servings.

Approx per serv: Cal 207; Prot 3.6 g; T Fat 5.9 g; Chl 27.0 mg; Car 35.8 g; Sod 193.6 mg; Pot 83.7 mg.

Leigh Ann Hammons, Monroe

4-H is securing the future.

DATE-NUT BREAD

1 1/2 c. chopped dates
2 tsp. soda
2 tbsp. shortening
2 c. sugar
2 eggs
1 tsp. vanilla extract
4 c. flour
1 tsp. salt
1 c. chopped pecans

Combine dates, soda and 2 cups hot water in bowl. Let stand for several minutes. Cream shortening and sugar in bowl. Add eggs and vanilla; mix well. Add mixture of flour and salt alternately with date mixture, mixing well after each addition. Stir in pecans. Fill 6 well-greased soup cans 1/2 full. Bake at 350 degrees for 45 minutes or until bread tests done. Cool for 10 minutes. Remove from cans to cool completely. Yield: 24 servings.

Approx per serv: Cal 221; Prot 3.4 g; T Fat 5.4 g; Chl 21.1 mg; Car 41.3 g; Sod 163.0 mg; Pot 127.4 mg.

Wanda J. Hoffman, Sanilac

GRAHAM BREAD

2 tbsp. shortening
1/2 c. sugar
1 egg
3/4 c. graham flour
1 c. all-purpose flour
1 tsp. soda
1/2 tsp. salt
1 c. sour milk
1/2 c. chopped pecans
1/2 c. raisins

Cream shortening and sugar in bowl. Add egg; mix well. Combine flours, soda and salt. Add to creamed mixture alternately with sour milk, mixing well after each addition. Stir in pecans and raisins. Pour into greased loaf pan. Bake at 350 degrees for 30 to 40 minutes or until loaf tests done. Remove to wire rack to cool. Yield: 8 servings.

Approx per serv: Cal 273; Prot 6.0 g; T Fat 9.9 g; Chl 32.2 mg; Car 42.3 g; Sod 286.6 mg; Pot 223.1 mg.

Alma Barr, Ionia

HEALTH BREAD

1 c. bran cereal
1 c. quick-cooking oats
1 c. flour
1 c. sugar
1 tsp. soda
1/2 tsp. baking powder
1 egg
1 c. buttermilk
1 c. chopped walnuts (opt.)
1/2 c. raisins (opt.)

Combine first 6 ingredients in bowl. Stir in egg and buttermilk. Fold in walnuts and raisins. Pour into 2 greased 8-inch round cake pans. Bake at 450 degrees for 10 minutes. Remove to wire rack to cool. Yield: 16 servings.

Approx per serv: Cal 180; Prot 4.2 g; T Fat 5.7 g; Chl 16.1 mg; Car 31.0 g; Sod 110.0 mg; Pot 141.5 mg.

Nancy Beukema, Marquette/Delta

HOBO BREAD

2 1/2 c. raisins
4 tsp. soda
2 c. sugar

4 c. flour
1/4 c. oil
1 tsp. salt

Combine raisins and soda in bowl. Add enough boiling water to cover by 2 inches. Let stand, covered, overnight. Combine remaining ingredients in bowl. Add raisins; mix well. Spoon into 3 greased 1-pound coffee cans. Bake at 350 degrees for 1 1/4 hours. Cool in cans for 10 minutes. Remove to wire rack to cool completely. Yield: 30 servings.

Approx per serv: Cal 163; Prot 2.1 g; T Fat 2.0 g; Chl 0.0 mg; Car 35.3 g; Sod 184.3 mg; Pot 108.4 mg.

Mrs. Donald H. Todd, Ingham

PEANUT BUTTER BREAD

2 c. flour
2 tsp. baking powder
1/2 tsp. salt
1/2 c. sugar
3 tbsp. shortening
1/2 c. peanut butter
2 eggs, lightly beaten
1 c. milk

Sift dry ingredients into bowl. Cut in mixture of shortening and peanut butter until crumbly. Beat eggs with milk. Add to peanut butter mixture; mix well. Pour into greased loaf pan. Bake at 350 degrees for 1 1/2 hours. Remove to wire rack to cool. Yield: 12 servings.

Approx per serv: Cal 229; Prot 6.7 g; T Fat 10.8 g; Chl 45.0 mg; Car 27.4 g; Sod 229.0 mg; Pot 127.7 mg.

Val Cox, Cass

PRUNE BREAD

1 1/2 c. sifted flour
1 tsp. soda
1 tsp. salt
1 tsp. margarine
1 c. sugar
1 egg, beaten
1 jar baby food strained prunes
1 tsp. vanilla extract

Combine first 3 ingredients in bowl. Cut in margarine until crumbly. Add sugar, egg, prunes and vanilla; mix well. Pour into greased loaf pan. Bake at 350 degrees for 1 hour. Remove to wire rack to cool. Yield: 12 servings.

Approx per serv: Cal 133; Prot 2.1 g; T Fat 0.7 g; Chl 21.1 mg; Car 30.1 g; Sod 255.6 mg; Pot 33.1 mg.

Sylvia Vander Mevlen, Missaukee

POPPY SEED BREAD

1   2-layer pkg. yellow cake mix
1 sm. package coconut cream instant
    pudding mix
4 eggs, beaten
1/2 c. oil
2 tbsp. poppy seed

Combine all ingredients in bowl; mix well. Spoon into 2 small greased loaf pans. Bake at 350 degrees for 40 to 50 minutes or until bread tests done. Cool in pans for 10 minutes. Remove to wire rack to cool completely. Yield: 24 servings.

Approx per serv: Cal 163; Prot 2.2 g; T Fat 7.1 g; Chl 42.1 mg; Car 22.4 g; Sod 233.7 mg; Pot 15.3 mg.

Todd Langshaw, Barry

SPICED PUMPKIN BREAD

1 c. sugar
1/2 c. oil
2 eggs, beaten
1 c. canned pumpkin
1 1/4 c. all-purpose flour
3/4 c. whole wheat flour
1 tsp. soda
1/2 tsp. salt
1/4 tsp. baking powder
1/2 tsp. each allspice, cinnamon,
    cloves and nutmeg
1/2 c. raisins

Mix sugar and oil in bowl. Add eggs, pumpkin and 1/3 cup water; mix well. Add mixture of dry ingredients; stir until just mixed. Stir in raisins. Pour into greased loaf pan. Bake at 350 degrees for 1 hour or until loaf tests done. Remove from pan. Cool completely on wire rack before slicing. Yield: 12 servings.

Approx per serv: Cal 181; Prot 3.6 g; T Fat 1.8 g; Chl 42.1 mg; Car 38.3 g; Sod 176.9 mg; Pot 125.7 mg.

Lara Norman, Benzie

RHUBARB BREAD

1 1/2 c. packed brown sugar
2/3 c. oil
1 egg
1 tsp. vanilla extract
1 c. buttermilk
2 3/4 c. flour
1 tsp. soda
1 tsp. salt
1 1/2 c. chopped rhubarb
1/2 c. chopped pecans
3 tbsp. melted margarine
1/4 c. sugar

Combine first 4 ingredients in bowl; blend well. Stir in buttermilk gradually. Add mixture of flour, soda and salt; mix well. Stir in rhubarb and pecans. Pour into 2 well-greased loaf pans. Drizzle mixture of margarine and sugar over top. Bake at 325 degrees for 1 hour or until loaves test done. Remove from pans. Cool completely before slicing. Store in refrigerator or freezer. Yield: 24 servings.

Approx per serv: Cal 153; Prot 2.4 g; T Fat 4.0 g; Chl 10.7 mg; Car 27.4 g; Sod 161.0 mg; Pot 112.3 mg.

Penny Arnold, Gratiot

STRAWBERRY BREAD

3 c. flour
1 tsp. soda
1 tsp. cinnamon
2 c. sugar
1 tsp. salt
4 eggs
1 1/4 c. oil
1 3/4 c. chopped strawberries
1 c. chopped pecans
1   8-oz. package cream cheese, softened
1/2 c. strawberry juice

Combine first 5 ingredients in bowl. Make well in center. Pour eggs, oil and strawberries into well; stir until mixed. Stir in pecans. Pour into 2 greased and floured loaf pans. Bake at 350 degrees for 40 to 60 minutes or until loaves test done. Remove to wire rack to cool. Blend cream cheese with strawberry juice in small bowl. Serve cream cheese mixture as spread. Yield: 24 servings.

Approx per serv: Cal 327; Prot 4.2 g; T Fat 19.7 g; Chl 58.9 mg; Car 34.7 g; Sod 159.0 mg; Pot 85.5 mg.

Carlie Parmalee, Isabella

WHEAT GERM-ZUCCHINI BREAD

3 eggs, beaten
1 c. sugar
1 c. packed brown sugar
1 c. oil
1 tbsp. maple flavoring
2 c. coarsely shredded peeled zucchini
2 tsp. soda
1/2 tsp. baking powder
1 tsp. salt
1/2 c. wheat germ
2 1/2 c. flour
1 c. chopped pecans
1/3 c. sesame seed

Combine first 5 ingredients in bowl. Beat until thick and foamy. Stir in zucchini. Add next 5 dry ingredients; mix well. Fold in pecans. Pour into greased and floured 5 x 9-inch loaf pans. Sprinkle with sesame seed. Bake at 350 degrees for 1 hour or until bread tests done. Cool in pans for 10 minutes. Remove to wire rack to cool completely. Yield: 12 servings.

Approx per serv: Cal 521; Prot 7.6 g; T Fat 29.5 g; Chl 63.2 mg; Car 59.5 g; Sod 352.5 mg; Pot 297.4 mg.

Matthew Marinelli, Monroe

4-H is traveling to Michigan State University, Washington, D.C., and even international adventures.

ALL-BRAN MUFFINS

3 c. All-Bran
2 1/2 c. milk
1 1/2 c. whole wheat flour
1 c. all-purpose flour
2 tbsp. baking powder
1/2 tsp. salt
1 c. sugar
2 eggs
2/3 c. oil

Combine All-Bran and milk in bowl. Let stand for 1 minute. Mix dry ingredients in bowl. Add eggs, oil and All-Bran mixture. Stir just until moistened. Spoon into greased muffin cups. Bake at 400 degrees for 20 to 25 minutes or until muffins test done. Remove from pans. Yield: 48 servings.

Approx per serv: Cal 88; Prot 2.0 g; T Fat 3.9 g; Chl 12.3 mg; Car 13.2 g; Sod 95.4 mg; Pot 60.2 mg.

Douglas Sweeney, Huron

BLUEBERRY MUFFINS

1 1/2 c. flour
1/2 c. sugar
2 tsp. baking powder
1/2 tsp. salt
1/4 c. margarine
1 egg
1/2 c. milk
1 c. blueberries

Combine dry ingredients in bowl. Add margarine, egg and milk. Beat with rotary beater until blended. Fold in blueberries. Spoon into paper-lined muffin cups. Bake at 400 degrees for 20 to 25 minutes or until muffins test done. Remove from pan. Yield: 12 servings.

Approx per serv: Cal 145; Prot 2.6 g; T Fat 4.9 g; Chl 22.5 mg; Car 22.7 g; Sod 201.0 mg; Pot 46.8 mg.

Kent Rintala, Houghton

OATMEAL MUFFINS

1 c. flour
1/4 c. sugar
1 tbsp. baking powder
1/2 tsp. salt
1/4 c. shortening
1 c. oats
1 egg, beaten
1 c. milk

Sift first 4 ingredients into bowl. Cut in shortening until crumbly. Add oats. Stir in egg and milk just until moistened. Fill greased muffin cups 2/3 full. Bake at 425 degrees for 20 minutes. Remove from pan. Yield: 12 servings.

Approx per serv: Cal 142; Prot 3.3 g; T Fat 6.5 g; Chl 23.9 mg; Car 17.9 g; Sod 186.6 mg; Pot 69.3 mg.

Iris Hambleton, Muskegon

MANDARIN ORANGE MUFFINS

1 1/2 c. flour
1/2 c. sugar
1 3/4 tsp. baking powder

1/2 tsp. salt
1/4 tsp. allspice
1/2 tsp. nutmeg
1/3 c. shortening
1 egg, slightly beaten
1/4 c. milk
1 8-oz. can mandarin oranges, drained
1/4 c. melted butter
1/4 c. sugar
1/2 tsp. cinnamon

Sift first 6 ingredients into bowl. Cut in short-ening until crumbly. Add mixture of egg and milk; mix just until moistened. Batter will be thick. Fold in oranges. Fill greased muffin cups 3/4 full. Bake at 350 degrees for 20 to 25 min-utes or until muffins test done. Dip hot muffins in butter. Coat with mixture of 1/4 cup sugar and cinnamon. Yield: 12 servings.

Approx per serv: Cal 211; Prot 2.5 g; T Fat 10.9 g; Chl 33.6 mg; Car 26.5 g; Sod 191.8 mg; Pot 47.7 mg.

Lisa Dobbins, Jackson

PEACH UPSIDE-DOWN MUFFINS

2 c. flour
1 1/2 c. sugar
1 tbsp. baking powder
1/2 tsp. salt
1/4 c. melted shortening
2 eggs
1 c. milk
6 tbsp. butter
1 c. plus 2 tbsp. packed brown sugar
6 peaches, sliced

Sift first 4 ingredients together 3 times. Com-bine with shortening, eggs and milk in bowl. Beat until smooth and light. Place 1 teaspoon butter and 1 tablespoon brown sugar in each muffin cup. Heat in 375-degree oven until melted. Arrange peaches in each cup. Fill 1/2 full with batter. Bake for 25 minutes. Invert on serving plate. Serve plain or with ice cream. Yield: 18 servings.

Approx per serv: Cal 223; Prot 3.0 g; T Fat 8.3 g; Chl 41.8 mg; Car 35.2 g; Sod 179.2 mg; Pot 191.7 mg.

Frank Bogedain, Monroe

PINEAPPLE MUFFINS

2 c. flour
2 tsp. baking powder
1/2 tsp. soda

1/2 tsp. salt
1/2 c. packed brown sugar
1 egg, well beaten
1 c. sour cream
1 8-oz. can crushed pineapple
1/3 c. melted shortening
1/2 c. chopped pecans

Combine first 5 ingredients in bowl; mix well. Make well in center. Mix egg, sour cream, pine-apple and shortening. Pour into well. Stir just until moistened. Fold in pecans. Fill greased muffin cups 2/3 full. Bake at 400 degrees for 20 to 25 minutes or until brown. Remove from pans. Yield: 18 servings.

Approx per serv: Cal 175; Prot 2.6 g; T Fat 9.6 g; Chl 19.7 mg; Car 20.4 g; Sod 131.0 mg; Pot 90.1 mg.

Julie Blaser, Monroe

PUMPKIN-PECAN MUFFINS

1 1/4 c. oats
1 c. flour
1/3 c. chopped pecans
1 tsp. baking powder
1 tsp. cinnamon
1/2 tsp. soda
1/2 tsp. salt
1/2 tsp. nutmeg
1 c. canned pumpkin
3/4 c. packed brown sugar
1 c. oil
1/4 c. milk
1 egg
1 tsp. vanilla extract
1/4 c. oats
1/4 c. flour
1/4 c. packed brown sugar
3 tbsp. chopped pecans
1 tsp. cinnamon
1/4 c. margarine, softened

Combine first 8 ingredients in bowl. Add pump-kin, 3/4 cup brown sugar, oil, milk, egg and vanilla. Mix just until moistened. Fill paper-lined muffin cups 3/4 full. Combine remaining ingredients in bowl; mix until crumbly. Sprin-kle over batter. Bake at 400 degrees for 15 to 20 minutes or until muffins test done. Remove from pans. Yield: 18 servings.

Approx per serv: Cal 175; Prot 2.9 g; T Fat 7.5 g; Chl 14.5 mg; Car 24.8 g; Sod 140.8 mg; Pot 143.0 mg.

Kathy LaMarche, Delta

PRUNE MUFFINS

1 egg, beaten
1 c. milk
1/4 c. oil
2 c. flour
1/4 c. packed brown sugar
1 tbsp. baking powder
1 tsp. salt
1/4 tsp. nutmeg
3/4 c. chopped cooked prunes

Combine egg, milk and oil in bowl; mix well. Mix dry ingredients in bowl. Stir in liquid ingredients just until moistened. Do not overmix. Fold in prunes. Grease muffin cup bottoms. Fill 2/3 full. Bake at 400 degrees for 20 to 25 minutes or until golden brown. Remove from pans immediately. Serve warm. Yield: 12 servings.

Approx per serv: Cal 133; Prot 3.7 g; T Fat 1.8 g; Chl 27.0 mg; Car 25.7 g; Sod 278.1 mg; Pot 115.6 mg.

Marsha Alt, Monroe

CHRISTY'S CINNAMON LOAF

1 pkg. dry yeast
1/2 c. sugar
1 tsp. salt
6 tbsp. butter
2/3 c. milk, scalded
2 eggs
3 c. flour
2 tbsp. melted butter
1/4 c. sugar
1 1/2 tsp. cinnamon
2 tbsp. butter

Dissolve yeast in 2 tablespoons warm water. Combine 1/2 cup sugar, salt, 6 tablespoons butter and milk in mixer bowl. Cool to lukewarm. Add eggs, yeast and half the flour. Beat until smooth. Stir in remaining flour. Let rise, covered, until doubled in bulk. Knead lightly on floured surface. Roll into 9 x 18-inch rectangle. Brush with 2 tablespoons butter; sprinkle with mixture of 1/4 cup sugar and cinnamon. Roll up from narrow end as for jelly roll. Place in greased 5 x 9-inch loaf pan. Brush with 2 tablespoons butter. Let rise for 45 minutes or until doubled in bulk. Bake at 350 degrees for 30 minutes. Yield: 12 servings.

Approx per serv: Cal 271; Prot 5.1 g; T Fat 11.3 g; Chl 72.9 mg; Car 37.2 g; Sod 312.4 mg; Pot 74.3 mg.

Christy Derby, Oceana

SPOON BREAD

2 c. cornmeal
2 tbsp. melted shortening
1 1/2 tsp. salt
2 eggs, separated
1 1/2 c. sour milk
1 tsp. soda

Stir cornmeal gradually into 2 1/2 cups boiling water in saucepan. Cool. Add shortening, salt, egg yolks, sour milk and soda. Beat for 2 minutes. Fold in stiffly beaten egg whites gently. Pour into well-oiled baking dish. Bake at 435 degrees for 40 minutes. Yield: 6 servings.

Approx per serv: Cal 276; Prot 7.9 g; T Fat 9.3 g; Chl 92.8 mg; Car 39.2 g; Sod 769.0 mg; Pot 164.8 mg.

Sally Kopella, Calhoun

EGG CUSTARD BREAD

1 pkg. dry yeast
1 c. milk, scalded, cooled
1 1/2 tbsp. shortening
1 tsp. salt
2 c. flour
1/2 3-oz. package egg custard mix
1 1/2 to 2 c. flour
2 to 4 tbsp. melted margarine

Dissolve yeast in 1/2 cup warm water in mixer bowl. Add milk, shortening, salt and 2 cups flour. Beat until smooth. Add custard mix and enough flour to make medium dough. Knead on lightly floured surface for 10 minutes. Place in greased bowl, turning to grease surface. Let rise, covered, in warm place for 1 hour. Roll into 9 x 18-inch rectangle. Fold into thirds, overlapping ends. Roll up tightly, folding ends under. Place seam side down in greased loaf pan; brush with margarine. Let rise until doubled in bulk. Place on lowest oven rack in preheated 425-degree oven. Bake for 25 to 30 minutes or until loaf tests done. Remove from pan; brush with margarine. Cool on wire rack. Yield: 12 servings.

Approx per serv: Cal 216; Prot 5.4 g; T Fat 4.9 g; Chl 2.8 mg; Car 37.2 g; Sod 233.3 mg; Pot 85.0 mg.

Keith Kellersohn, Monroe

DILLY CASSEROLE BREAD

1 pkg. dry yeast
1 c. cream-style cottage cheese

2 tbsp. sugar
1 tbsp. dried onion flakes
1 tbsp. butter
2 tsp. dillseed
1 tsp. salt
1 egg
1/4 tsp. soda
2 1/4 to 2 1/2 c. flour
1 tbsp. butter, softened
1 tsp. salt (opt.)

Dissolve yeast in 1/4 cup warm water. Heat cottage cheese to lukewarm. Combine cottage cheese, next 7 ingredients and yeast in large bowl; mix well. Add enough flour to make stiff dough. Let rise, covered, in warm place for 1 hour or until doubled in bulk. Stir dough down. Pour into well-greased 1 1/2-quart casserole. Let rise in warm place for 30 minutes or until light. Bake at 350 degrees for 40 to 50 minutes or until golden brown. Brush with softened butter; sprinkle with salt. Yield: 12 servings.

NOTE: Delicious served with ham or toasted.

Approx per serv: Cal 151; Prot 6.3 g; T Fat 3.6 g; Chl 33.4 mg; Car 22.8 g; Sod 448.5 mg; Pot 59.5 mg.

Elaine Poole, Van Buren
Tanya Saunders, Gratiot

LISA'S SWEDISH RYE BREAD

1 pkg. yeast
1/2 tsp. sugar
1 c. packed brown sugar
1/2 c. dark corn syrup
1 tbsp. salt
1 1/2 tbsp. shortening
4 c. rye flour
4 c. (about) all-purpose flour

Dissolve yeast and sugar in 1/4 cup warm water. Combine brown sugar, corn syrup, salt, shortening and 3 cups water in bowl; mix well. Add rye flour and yeast mixture; mix well. Add enough all-purpose flour to make stiff dough. Knead on floured surface until smooth and elastic. Place in greased bowl, turning to grease surface. Let rise until doubled in bulk. Shape into 4 loaves; place in greased loaf pans. Let rise until doubled in bulk. Bake at 350 degrees for 45 minutes. Cool on wire rack.
Yield: 48 servings.

Approx per serv: Cal 90.4; Prot 1.9 g; T Fat 0.6 g; Chl 0.0 mg; Car 19.2 g; Sod 135.1 mg; Pot 41.9 mg.

Lisa Nelson, Monroe

FRENCH BREAD

1 pkg. dry yeast
1 tbsp. sugar
2 tsp. salt
5 3/4 c. sifted flour
1 egg white

Dissolve yeast in 2 cups warm water in bowl. Add sugar, salt and 3 cups flour; beat until smooth and shiny. Stir in 2 1/2 cups flour. Sprinkle 1/4 cup flour on bread board or pastry cloth. Turn dough onto surface. Knead for 5 to 7 minutes or until smooth and elastic. Place in greased bowl turning to grease surface. Cover with waxed paper and towel. Let rise for 1 hour or until doubled in bulk. Divide into 2 portions; shape each into ball. Let rest, covered, for 5 minutes. Shape each ball into 3-inch diameter loaf rolling from center toward ends between greased hands. Place 4 inches apart on lightly greased baking sheet. Cut 3/4-inch deep diagonal slashes 1 1/2 inches apart in each loaf. Let rise, covered, until doubled in bulk. Bake at 425 degrees for 30 to 35 minutes. Brush with egg white. Bake for 2 minutes longer. Remove loaves to wire rack to cool. Yield: 24 servings.

Approx per serv: Cal 104; Prot 3.2 g; T Fat 0.3 g; Chl 0.0 mg; Car 21.6 g; Sod 180.4 mg; Pot 33.9 mg.

Margaret Stryker, Kalamazoo

JEAN'S MINI LOAVES

1 c. milk
1/4 c. butter
2 tbsp. sugar
1 tsp. salt
2 pkg. dry yeast
4 to 4 1/2 c. flour

Heat milk, butter and 1/2 cup water in saucepan until very warm. Combine sugar, salt, yeast and 2 cups flour in mixer bowl. Add warm liquid; mix well. Add remaining 2 to 2 1/2 cups flour; mix well. Knead on floured surface for 5 minutes. Place in greased bowl. Cover with greased waxed paper. Let rise in very warm place for 15 minutes. Shape into miniature loaves on baking sheet. Let rise for 15 minutes. Bake at 425 degrees for 12 minutes or until brown. Yield: 20 servings.

Approx per serv: Cal 138; Prot 3.7 g; T Fat 3.0 g; Chl 8.8 mg; Car 23.6 g; Sod 141.7 mg; Pot 59.0 mg.

Jean A. Cousineau, Mecosta

WHOLE-GRAIN BREAD

1/4 c. honey
1/4 c. molasses
2 pkg. dry yeast
2/3 c. nonfat dry milk powder
2 eggs
2 tbsp. oil
2 tsp. salt
1/2 c. quick-cooking oats
1/2 c. wheat germ
1/2 c. bran cereal
2 c. whole wheat flour
2 1/2 to 3 1/4 c. all-purpose flour

Combine first 3 ingredients and 1 3/4 cups warm water in large bowl. Let stand, covered, for 10 minutes or until frothy. Add dry milk powder, eggs, oil and salt; mix well. Add oats, wheat germ, cereal and whole wheat flour; mix well. Add enough all-purpose flour to make moderately stiff dough. Knead on floured surface for 5 to 8 minutes. Place in greased bowl, turning to grease surface. Let rise, covered, until doubled in bulk. Divide into 2 portions. Let rest for 10 minutes. Shape into loaves; place in greased loaf pans. Let rise until doubled in bulk. Bake at 350 degrees for 40 minutes. Remove to wire rack to cool. Yield: 24 servings.

Approx per serv: Cal 278; Prot 4.9 g; T Fat 2.2 g; Chl 21.5 mg; Car 61.4 g; Sod 206.4 mg; Pot 615.9 mg

Jeanette Katt, Antrim

GOLDEN HONEY ROLLS

1 c. milk
1/2 c. oil
2 tbsp. honey
1 1/2 c. flour
1 pkg. dry yeast
1 tsp. salt
2 eggs
1 3/4 c. flour
1/3 c. sugar
2 tbsp. butter
1 tbsp. honey

Heat first 3 ingredients in saucepan until warm. Combine with 1 1/2 cups flour, yeast, salt and eggs in mixer bowl. Beat at medium speed for 3 minutes. Stir in remaining flour. Let rise, covered, for 45 minutes or until doubled in bulk. Beat for 30 seconds. Drop by tablespoonfuls

into 2 well-greased 9-inch round baking pans. Combine sugar and remaining ingredients in bowl; mix well. Drizzle half the mixture over rolls. Let rise, covered, for 20 minutes or until doubled in bulk. Drizzle with remaining honey mixture. Bake at 350 degrees for 25 to 30 minutes or until golden brown. Remove from pans immediately. Yield: 20 servings.

Approx per serv: Cal 177; Prot 3.5 g; T Fat 7.8 g; Chl 30.5 mg; Car 23.3 g; Sod 133.6 mg; Pot 53.9 mg.

Lisa Jagielski, Monroe

CRESCENT ROLLS

2 pkg. dry yeast
1/4 c. margarine, softened
1/2 tsp. salt
1   4 1/2-oz. package egg custard mix
3 1/2 c. flour

Dissolve yeast in 1 1/4 cups warm water in bowl. Add margarine, salt and custard mix; stir until dissolved. Add flour gradually, mixing well after each addition. Knead on floured surface until smooth and elastic. Roll into circles; cut into wedges. Roll from wide end. Place on greased baking sheet; shape into crescents. Let rise for 45 minutes. Bake at 400 degrees for 10 to 15 minutes or until brown. Serve hot. Yield: 24 servings.

Approx per serv: Cal 102; Prot 2.3 g; T Fat 2.2 g; Chl 0.0 mg; Car 18.4 g; Sod 89.5 mg; Pot 34.0 mg.

Kevin Diuble, Washtenaw

OLD-FASHIONED DINNER ROLLS

1/2 c. butter, softened
2 pkg. dry yeast
1/2 c. sugar
3 eggs
1 1/2 tsp. salt
9 to 10 c. flour

Combine butter and 2 cups boiling water in bowl. Stir until butter melts. Cool to lukewarm. Dissolve yeast in 1/2 cup warm water in bowl. Add butter mixture, sugar, eggs, salt and 3 cups flour. Beat at medium speed until smooth. Stir in enough remaining flour to make stiff dough. Knead on floured surface for about 10 minutes. Place in greased bowl, turning to grease surface.

Let rise, covered, for 1 hour or until doubled in bulk. Shape into 24 rolls. Place in 2 greased 9 x 13-inch baking pans. Let rise, covered, until doubled in bulk. Bake at 400 degrees for 20 to 25 minutes or until browned. Remove from pans. Yield: 48 servings.

Approx per serv: Cal 126; Prot 3.3 g; T Fat 2.5 g; Chl 21.7 mg; Car 22.0 g; Sod 94.5 mg; Pot 35.2 mg.

Julie Savery, Washtenaw

PARSLEY PAN ROLLS

2 pkg. dry yeast
1/2 c. sugar
1/4 c. margarine, softened
1 egg
2 tsp. salt
6 1/2 to 7 c. sifted flour
1/4 c. melted margarine
1 tsp. garlic salt
1/4 c. chopped parsley

Dissolve yeast in 2 cups warm water in bowl. Add sugar, softened margarine, egg, salt and half the flour. Beat until smooth. Stir in remaining flour. Place in greased bowl, turning to grease surface. Chill, loosely covered, for 2 hours or longer. Punch dough down occasionally. Shape into 1-inch balls. Place in greased 8-inch round baking pan. Let rise, covered, until doubled in bulk. Brush with mixture of melted margarine and garlic salt. Sprinkle with parsley. Bake at 400 degrees for 15 minutes. Remove from pan. Yield: 72 servings.

Approx per serv: Cal 59; Prot 1.4 g; T Fat 1.5 g; Chl 3.5 mg; Car 10.0 g; Sod 105.7 mg; Pot 17.3 mg.

Teresa Zelling, Monroe

4-H is Making the Best Better.

PULL-APART ONION ROLLS

3/4 c. milk
2 tbsp. butter
1 tbsp. sugar
1/2 tsp. salt
1 c. flour
1 pkg. dry yeast
1 egg
1 1/2 c. flour
2 tsp. onion flakes
3 tbsp. melted butter
1 tbsp. Parmesan cheese
1 tbsp. sesame seed
1/2 tsp. paprika
1 tsp. garlic powder

Heat first 4 ingredients in saucepan until butter is almost melted, stirring constantly. Add to mixture of 1 cup flour and yeast in mixer bowl. Add egg. Beat at low speed for 30 seconds. Beat at high speed for 3 minutes. Stir in 1 1/2 cups flour. Knead on floured surface for 5 minutes. Place in greased bowl, turning to grease surface. Let rise, covered, until doubled in bulk. Punch dough down. Let rest, covered, for 10 minutes. Roll into 8-inch square. Soak onion in 2 teaspoons water. Combine with remaining ingredients in bowl; mix well. Brush over dough. Cut into 2-inch squares. Layer buttered side up in greased 1 1/2-quart casserole. Let rise, covered, for 45 minutes. Bake, covered with foil, for 15 minutes. Remove foil. Bake for 10 to 20 minutes longer or until brown. Cool in casserole for 5 minutes. Turn onto serving plate. Serve warm. Yield: 16 servings.

Joan Secord, Clinton

ROLLS A LA BURELEAN

1 pkg. yeast
3 tbsp. shortening
1/4 c. sugar
1 tsp. salt
1 egg
3 c. flour
6 tbsp. butter

Dissolve yeast in 1 cup lukewarm water. Cream shortening, sugar and salt in bowl until light and fluffy. Add egg; mix well. Add yeast and 1 1/2 cups flour; mix well. Add remaining 1 1/2 cups flour; mix well. Knead on floured surface until smooth and elastic. Place in greased bowl, turning to grease surface. Let rise until doubled in bulk. Knead on floured surface. Roll out; cut out with glass. Place a small amount of butter in center of each; fold over. Place in 9-inch round baking pan. Bake at 350 degrees for 30 minutes. Remove from pan. Yield: 18 servings.

Approx per serv: Cal 147; Prot 2.7 g; T Fat 6.7 g; Chl 25.9 mg; Car 18.8 g; Sod 169.2 mg; Pot 32.3 mg.

Burelean Densmore, Calhoun

WHOLE WHEAT ROLLS

2 pkg. yeast
1 c. nonfat dry milk powder
1/2 c. oil
2 eggs
1/3 c. sugar
2 tsp. salt
6 c. all-purpose flour
4 c. whole wheat flour

Combine first 6 ingredients and 3 cups warm water in bowl; mix well. Add 5 cups all-purpose flour; beat well. Add 1 cup all-purpose flour and 2 cups whole wheat flour; mix well. Knead in remaining whole wheat flour until smooth and elastic. Place in greased bowl, turning to grease surface. Let rise until doubled in bulk. Shape into dinner rolls. Place in glass baking pan. Let rise until doubled in bulk. Bake at 375 degrees for 20 to 25 minutes or until golden. Remove from pan. Yield: 48 servings.

Approx per serv: Cal 125; Prot 3.9 g; T Fat 2.9 g; Chl 10.8 mg; Car 21.2 g; Sod 99.6 mg; Pot 84.9 mg.

Valerie Zieske, Monroe

MAPLE NUT CINNAMON ROLLS

1 c. milk
1/2 c. shortening
1 c. oats
1/3 c. packed brown sugar
1 1/2 tsp. salt
1 pkg. yeast
1 1/2 c. flour
2 eggs
1 1/2 to 2 c. flour
2 tbsp. melted butter
2/3 c. packed brown sugar
1 tsp. cinnamon
1/4 c. maple syrup
1 1/4 c. packed brown sugar
1/4 c. butter, softened
1/4 tsp. maple flavoring
2/3 c. chopped walnuts

Heat milk and shortening in saucepan until shortening melts. Combine oats, 1/3 cup brown sugar, salt, yeast and 1 1/2 cups flour in mixer bowl. Add milk mixture and eggs. Beat at low speed until moistened. Beat at medium speed for 3 minutes. Stir in 1 1/2 to 2 cups flour to make stiff dough. Let rise, covered, in warm place for 1 1/2 hours or until doubled in bulk. Roll into 12 x 24-inch rectangle. Brush with melted butter. Sprinkle with mixture of 2/3 cup brown sugar and cinnamon. Roll from long side as for jelly roll. Combine maple syrup and remaining ingredients in bowl; mix well. Spread in 9 x 13-inch baking pan. Cut dough into 1-inch slices; place in prepared pan. Let rise for 1 hour or until doubled in bulk. Bake at 350 degrees for 30 minutes or until browned. Invert onto serving plate.

Chris Leicht, Monroe

PECAN ROLLS

1 c. milk, scalded
1 cake yeast, crumbled
1 1/2 c. flour
1/4 c. sugar
1 1/2 tsp. salt
2 eggs
1/3 c. butter
2 1/4 c. (about) flour
2 tbsp. melted butter
1/2 c. packed brown sugar
1 tsp. cinnamon
1 c. chopped pecans
1/4 c. brown sugar
1/4 c. butter

Cool milk to lukewarm. Dissolve yeast in milk in bowl. Add 1 1/2 cups flour; beat well. Let stand, covered, until light and bubbly. Add sugar, salt, eggs, 1/3 cup butter and 2 1/4 cups flour. Knead on floured surface until smooth and elastic. Let rise until doubled in bulk. Roll 1/4 inch thick on floured surface. Brush with melted butter. Sprinkle with 1/2 cup brown sugar and cinnamon. Roll as for jelly roll. Cut into 1-inch slices. Butter sides of muffin cups. Sprinkle pecans in bottom. Combine 1/4 cup brown sugar, 1/4 cup butter and 1 tablespoon water in saucepan. Boil for 2 minutes. Spoon over pecans. Place dough slices cut side down in prepared muffin cups. Let rise, covered, until doubled in bulk. Bake at 375 degrees for 25 minutes. Invert onto serving plate.
Yield: 36 servings.

Approx per serv: Cal 137; Prot 2.5 g; T Fat 6.7 g; Chl 26.2 mg; Car 17.3 g; Sod 141.5 mg; Pot 67.0 mg.

Pam Durocher, Monroe

Desserts

FRESH PEACH COBBLER

3 c. sliced fresh peaches
1 c. sugar
1 tsp. grated lemon rind
1 tbsp. lemon juice
1/4 tsp. almond extract
1 1/2 c. flour
1 tbsp. baking powder
1 tbsp. sugar
1/2 tsp. salt
1/3 c. shortening
1 /2 c. milk
1 egg, well beaten
2 tbsp. sugar

Arrange peaches in greased 8-inch square baking dish. Sprinkle with mixture of 1 cup sugar, lemon rind, lemon juice and almond extract. Bake at 400 degrees for about 5 minutes. Sift next 4 dry ingredients into bowl. Cut in shortening until crumbly. Stir in milk and egg just until moistened. Spread over peaches. Sprinkle with 2 tablespoons sugar. Bake for 35 to 40 minutes or until brown and bubbly.
Yield: 8 servings.

Approx per serv: Cal 329; Prot 4.1 g; T Fat 11.1 g; Chl 33.7 mg; Car 45.0 g; Sod 272.5 mg; Pot 187.0 mg.

 Theresa Thome, Kent

PUMPKIN SQUARES

1 c. sifted flour
1/2 c. quick-cooking oats
1/2 c. packed brown sugar
1/2 c. melted butter
1 20-oz. can pumpkin
1 13-oz. can evaporated milk
2 eggs
3/4 c. sugar
1/2 tsp. salt
1 tsp. cinnamon
1/2 tsp. ginger
1/4 tsp. cloves
2 tbsp. butter, melted
3/4 c. chopped pecans
1/2 c. packed brown sugar

Combine first 4 ingredients in bowl; mix until crumbly. Press into 9 x 13-inch baking pan. Bake at 350 degrees for 15 minutes. Mix pumpkin, evaporated milk, eggs, sugar, salt and spices in bowl. Pour over baked layer. Bake for 20 minutes. Sprinkle mixture of remaining ingredi-

ents over top. Bake for 20 minutes longer. Cool. Cut into squares. Serve with whipped topping. Yield: 12 servings.

Approx per serv: Cal 480; Prot 7.0 g; T Fat 26.2 g; Chl 86.7 mg; Car 58.3 g; Sod 409.5 mg; Pot 446.6 mg.

Dr. and Mrs. James A. Anderson
Vice Provost, Michigan State University
Dean, College of Agriculture and Natural Resources
4-H Alumni

ENGLISH ALMOND PUFF

1/2 c. butter
1 c. flour
1/2 c. butter
1 c. flour
1 tbsp. almond extract
3 eggs, beaten
1 1/2 c. confectioners' sugar
2 tbsp. butter
1 to 1 1/2 tsp. almond extract
1/2 c. chopped almonds

Cut 1/2 cup butter into 1 cup flour in bowl until crumbly. Sprinkle 2 tablespoons water over mixture; mix with fork. Shape into 2 balls. Pat each ball into 3 x 12-inch strip 3 inches apart on ungreased baking sheet. Bring 1/2 cup butter and 1 cup water to a boil in saucepan; blend well. Stir in 1 cup flour and almond flavoring all at once. Cook over low heat for 1 minute or until mixture forms ball, stirring constantly. Remove from heat. Add eggs; beat until smooth. Spread evenly over dough strips. Bake at 350 degrees for 1 hour or until crisp and brown; cool. Combine next 3 ingredients and 1 to 2 tablespoons warm water in bowl; mix well. Spread on puffs; sprinkle with almonds.

Robin Evans, Monroe

SUPREME APPLE DUMPLINGS

2 c. flour
1/2 tsp. salt
1 tbsp. baking powder
2 tbsp. shortening
6 tbsp. milk
4 med. apples, peeled, cored
1/4 c. sugar
4 tsp. butter
Cinnamon to taste
1 c. sugar

Combine first 3 ingredients in bowl. Cut in shortening until crumbly. Stir in milk and 6 tablespoons cold water. Pat out into 1/2-inch thick square on floured surface. Cut into 4 squares. Place 1 apple on each square. Place 1 tablespoon sugar, 1 teaspoon butter and cinnamon in cavity of each apple. Bring corners of dough up to enclose apple; seal. Place in baking pan. Combine 1 cup sugar and 1 cup water in saucepan. Boil for 5 minutes, stirring occasionally. Pour over dumplings. Bake at 450 degrees for 20 minutes. Reduce temperature to 350 degrees. Bake for 30 minutes longer. Baste several times during baking. Yield: 4 servings.

Approx per serv: Cal 702; Prot 7.8 g; T Fat 13.3 g; Chl 14.3 mg; Car 142.3 g; Sod 572.0 mg; Pot 330.9 mg.

Tricia Alexander, Monroe

APPLE CRUNCH

8 to 10 med. apples, peeled, sliced
3/4 c. quick-cooking oats
1/2 c. flour
3/4 c. packed brown sugar
1 tsp. cinnamon
1/2 c. melted butter

Arrange apples in buttered baking dish. Combine remaining ingredients in bowl; mix well. Sprinkle over apples. Bake at 350 degrees for 30 to 35 minutes or until top is brown and apples are tender. Yield: 8 servings.

Approx per serv: Cal 390; Prot 2.5 g; T Fat 13.7 g; Chl 35.5 mg; Car 69.4 g; Sod 149.3 mg; Pot 399.0 mg.

Cliff Curtiss, Isabella

MARGARET'S CHEESECAKE

30 graham crackers, crushed
1 stick margarine, melted
1 3-oz. package lemon gelatin
1 lg. can evaporated milk, chilled
1 c. sugar
1 8-oz. package cream cheese, softened
1 tsp. vanilla extract

Mix cracker crumbs and margarine in bowl. Reserve 1/2 cup for topping. Press remaining crumbs into 9 x 13-inch dish. Chill in refrigerator. Dissolve gelatin in 1 cup boiling water in bowl. Chill for 30 minutes or until partially set. Beat evaporated milk in bowl until stiff peaks form. Add sugar gradually. Beat in gelatin, cream cheese and vanilla. Pour into prepared dish. Sprinkle reserved crumbs over top. Chill until set. Yield: 16 servings.

Approx per serv: Cal 259; Prot 4.6 g; T Fat 14.4 g; Chl 23.9 mg; Car 29.7 g; Sod 242.8 mg; Pot 154.5 mg.

Margaret Shinew, Newaygo

EASY LEMONY
RICOTTA CHEESECAKE

3 3-oz. packages lemon gelatin
1 1/2 c. graham cracker crumbs
1/3 c. packed light brown sugar
1/3 c. melted butter
1/4 tsp. cinnamon
1 16-oz. carton ricotta cheese
2 8-oz. packages cream cheese, softened
1/2 tsp. salt

Dissolve gelatin in 3 cups boiling water in bowl. Chill for 1 hour or until partially set. Combine cracker crumbs, brown sugar, butter and cinnamon in bowl; mix until crumbly. Press over bottom of 9-inch springform pan. Press ricotta cheese through sieve. Combine with cream cheese, salt and gelatin in bowl. Beat just until smooth, scraping bowl. Pour into prepared pan. Chill, covered, until set. Yield: 10 servings.

NOTE: May substitute raspberry gelatin for lemon and garnish with raspberries.

Joyce E. McLain, Hillsdale

CHERRY SURPRISE

2 c. flour
1/2 c. packed brown sugar
1 c. chopped pecans
1 c. butter
2 pkg. whipped topping mix, prepared
1 c. confectioners' sugar
1 8-oz. package cream cheese, softened
2 cans cherry pie filling

Combine first 4 ingredients in bowl; mix well. Spoon into 9 x 13-inch baking pan. Bake at 375 degrees for 15 minutes. Combine whipped topping, confectioners' sugar and cream cheese in bowl; mix until smooth. Spread over baked layer. Top with pie filling. Chill in refrigerator. Yield: 18 servings.

Approx per serv: Cal 383; Prot 3.7 g; T Fat 21.5 g; Chl 47.0 mg; Car 44.8 g; Sod 167.6 mg; Pot 107.6 mg.

Marylee Parker, Shiawassee

CHERRY CRUNCH

4 c. fresh sour cherries, pitted
3 tbsp. cornstarch
1 c. sugar
1/4 tsp. almond extract
1 c. flour
1 c. quick-cooking oats
1 c. packed brown sugar
3/4 tsp. cinnamon
1 stick margarine, melted

Place cherries in 9 x 9-inch baking pan. Combine cornstarch, sugar and 1 cup water in saucepan. Cook until thick and clear, stirring constantly. Stir in almond flavoring. Pour over cherries. Combine remaining ingredients in bowl; mix until crumbly. Sprinkle over cherries. Bake at 350 degrees for 30 to 40 minutes or until topping is brown and crisp.
Yield: 8 servings.
NOTE: If cherries have been frozen, reduce water by half and use juice from cherries.

Approx per serv: Cal 453; Prot 4.1 g; T Fat 12.6 g; Chl 0.0 mg; Car 83.9 g; Sod 150.7 mg; Pot 296.7 mg.

Frances Furney, Branch

CREAM PUFF SHELLS

1/2 c. butter
1 c. flour
4 eggs

Bring butter and 1 cup water to a rolling boil. Remove from heat; cool slightly. Add flour gradually, mixing with fork until ball forms. Chill in refrigerator. Add eggs 1 at a time, mixing well after each addition. Drop by teaspoonfuls onto ungreased baking sheet. Bake at 400 degrees for 25 minutes. Cut tops off and fill as desired. Yield: 36 servings.
NOTE: May make larger shells, allowing more time to bake.

Approx per serv: Cal 44; Prot 1.1 g; T Fat 3.2 g; Chl 36.0 mg; Car 2.7 g; Sod 38.0 mg; Pot 11.2 mg.

Mitzi Zanotti Brown, Bay

PA GEESEMAN'S ICE CREAM

12 eggs
1 c. sugar
4 c. half and half
10 c. milk
Vanilla extract to taste

Beat eggs in large bowl until thick and lemon colored. Add remaining ingredients and salt to taste; mix well. Pour into ice cream freezer container. Freeze, using manufacturer's directions. Yield: 16 servings.

Approx per serv: Cal 289; Prot 12.1 g; T Fat 16.7 g; Chl 236.8 mg; Car 23.0 g; Sod 149.9 mg; Pot 345.9 mg.

Lisa Anger, Midland

ECLAIR DESSERT

1 12-oz. package graham crackers
1 lg. package French vanilla instant
pudding mix
3 c. milk
1 9-oz. container whipped
topping, thawed
2 1-oz. squares unsweetened chocolate
3 tbsp. margarine
2 tbsp. light corn syrup
3 tbsp. milk
1 tsp. vanilla extract
1 1/2 c. sifted confectioners' sugar

Line 9 x 13-inch dish with graham crackers. Combine pudding mix with milk in mixer bowl. Beat at low speed for 2 minutes. Fold in whipped topping. Spread half the pudding, another layer of crackers and remaining pudding over crackers. Top with third layer of crackers. Melt chocolate and margarine in saucepan. Add remaining ingredients and several drops of hot water if necessary to make of spreading consistency. Pour over cracker layer. Chill for 6 hours or longer. Cut into squares to serve.
Yield: 6 servings.

Approx per serv: Cal 784; Prot 11.7 g; T Fat 33.3 g; Chl 18.2 mg; Car 120.7 g; Sod 661.4 mg; Pot 521.7 mg.

Laura Ingalls, Clinton

OREO COOKIE DESSERT

1 16-oz. package Oreo cookies
1 stick margarine, melted
1 8-oz. package cream cheese, softened
1/2 c. confectioners' sugar
1 16-oz. container whipped topping
1 lg. package chocolate instant pudding
mix, prepared

Reserve 6 cookies for topping. Crush remaining cookies. Mix with margarine in 9 x 13-inch pan. Pat evenly over bottom of pan. Combine cream cheese, confectioners' sugar and half the whipped topping in bowl; mix until smooth. Spread over crumbs. Pour chocolate pudding over cream cheese layer. Top with remaining whipped topping. Cut reserved cookies in half. Arrange on top of dessert. Chill for 3 hours. Yield: 12 servings.

Approx per serv: Cal 521; Prot 4.4 g; T Fat 33.0 g; Chl 35.7 mg. Car 54.7 g; Sod 396.9 mg; Pot 50.9 mg.

Lori Haas, Arenac

BROWNIE PUDDING

1 c. flour
3/4 c. sugar
2 tbsp. (heaping) cocoa
2 tsp. baking powder
1/2 tsp. salt
1/2 c. milk
2 tbsp. oil
1 tsp. vanilla extract
3/4 to 1 c. chopped walnuts
3/4 c. packed brown sugar
1/4 c. cocoa

Sift first 5 ingredients together into bowl. Add milk, oil and vanilla; mix well. Stir in walnuts. Pour into greased 8 x 8-inch baking pan. Mix brown sugar and 1/4 cup cocoa in bowl. Sprinkle over batter. Pour 1 3/4 cups hot water over top. Do not mix. Bake at 350 degrees for 40 to 45 minutes or until set. Serve warm with ice cream. Yield: 9 servings.

Approx per serv: Cal 313; Prot 4.3 g; T Fat 12.6 g; Chl 1.9 mg; Car 49.1 g; Sod 204.6 mg; Pot 195.0 mg.

Dian Schlack, Allegan

STEAMED CARROT PUDDING

1 c. mashed cooked carrots
1 c. grated potato
1 c. sugar
1 c. flour
1/2 c. melted shortening
3/4 tsp. salt
1 tsp. soda
1 tsp. cinnamon
1 tsp. (or less) nutmeg
2 c. raisins

Combine all ingredients in bowl; mix well. Spoon into greased pudding mold; cover tightly. Place in deep 8-quart saucepan. Add enough boiling water to cover half the mold. Steam, covered, for 2 1/2 hours. Place, uncovered, in hot oven for 1 minute to dry top if desired. Invert onto serving dish. Serve with hard sauce. Store in refrigerator; reheat to serve again. Yield: 10 servings.

NOTE: Steamed pudding molds with lids are available at many hardware stores.

Approx per serv: Cal 325; Prot 2.6 g; T Fat 11.4 g; Chl 0.0 mg; Car 56.2 g; Sod 255.9 mg; Pot 344.5 mg.

Kris Sorgenfrei, Presque Isle

VARIETY FRUIT TORTE

1 1/2 c. flour
1/2 c. chopped pecans
1 1/2 sticks margarine
4 c. raspberries
1/4 c. cornstarch
1 c. sugar
2 c. miniature marshmallows
3 c. whipped topping
1 sm. package vanilla instant pudding mix
2 c. milk

Mix flour and pecans in bowl. Cut in margarine until crumbly. Press over bottom of 9 x 13-inch baking pan. Bake at 350 degrees for 15 to 20 minutes or until lightly browned. Stir with fork. Press down again; cool. Combine raspberries, cornstarch and sugar in saucepan. Cook until thick and bubbly; cool. Pour over crust. Spread mixture of marshmallows and whipped topping over raspberries. Combine pudding mix and milk in bowl; mix using package directions. Spread over marshmallow layer. Chill in refrigerator. Garnish with additional chopped pecans. Yield: 12 servings.

NOTE: For rhubarb torte, use 4 cups chopped rhubarb, 1 1/2 cups sugar, 3 tablespoons cornstarch and 1/2 cup water; prepare as for raspberries. For pineapple torte, use two 20-ounce cans drained unsweetened crushed pineapple, 1 cup sugar, 3 tablespoons cornstarch and 1/2 cup pineapple juice; prepare as for raspberries.

Approx per serv: Cal 422; Prot 4.8 g; T Fat 20.3 g; Chl 5.8 mg; Car 58.1 g; Sod 210.8 mg; Pot 187.6 mg.

Holly Jablonski, Mason

EMILY'S STRAWBERRY DESSERT

3/4 angel food cake, cut into pieces
1 6-oz. package strawberry gelatin
2 16-oz. packages frozen
*   strawberries, thawed*
1 lg. package vanilla instant pudding mix
2 1/2 c. milk
1 sm. package whipped topping
*   mix, prepared*

Place cake pieces in 9 x 13-inch pan. Dissolve gelatin in 2 cups hot water in bowl. Stir in strawberries. Pour over cake. Chill until set. Combine pudding mix and milk in bowl. Mix using package directions. Fold in whipped topping. Spread over congealed layer. Store in refrigerator. Yield: 15 servings.

Approx per serv: Cal 422; Prot 13.5 g; T Fat 15.8 g; Chl 49.1 mg; Car 58.3 g; Sod 1190.0 mg; Pot 366.4 mg.

Emily Barton, Muskegon

STRAWBERRY FLUFF

1 c. flour
1/2 c. packed brown sugar
1/2 c. chopped pecans
1 stick margarine
2 egg whites
2/3 c. sugar
1 10-oz. package frozen
*   strawberries, thawed*
2 tbsp. lemon juice
1 8-oz. carton whipped topping

Mix first 4 ingredients in bowl until crumbly. Spread in 9 x 13-inch baking pan. Bake at 325 degrees for 15 minutes, stirring several times. Reserve 1/2 cup crumbs for topping. Press remaining crumbs into pan. Beat egg whites in mixer bowl until stiff. Add sugar gradually, beating constantly. Add strawberries and lemon juice. Beat at medium speed for 15 minutes. Fold in whipped topping. Spoon into prepared pan. Top with reserved crumbs. Freeze overnight. May store in freezer for up to 1 week. Yield: 15 servings.

Approx per serv: Cal 245; Prot 2.1 g; T Fat 12.8 g; Chl 0.0 mg; Car 31.8 g; Sod 87.6 mg; Pot 91.7 mg.

Diann Axford, Otsego

LISA'S APPLE CAKE

3 eggs
1 3/4 c. sugar
2 1/2 c. flour
1/2 tsp. soda
1 tsp. cinnamon
1 tsp. salt
1 c. oil
2 c. chopped apples
1 c. chopped pecans

Beat eggs in mixer bowl until light. Add sugar; mix well. Sift remaining dry ingredients. Add to batter alternately with oil, mixing well after each addition. Fold in apples and pecans. Pour into greased and floured 9 x 13-inch pan. Bake at 350 degrees for 40 minutes. Increase temperature to 375 degrees. Bake for 10 minutes longer. Cool. Cut into squares.
Yield: 12 servings.

Approx per serv: Cal 465; Prot 5.3 g; T Fat 26.9 g; Chl 63.2 mg; Car 53.0 g; Sod 228.1 mg; Pot 121.3 mg.

Lisa Passerella, Houghton

APPLESAUCE CAKE

2/3 c. shortening
1 1/4 c. sugar
1 1/4 c. packed brown sugar
3 eggs
1 3/4 c. applesauce
2 3/4 c. flour
1 3/4 tsp. soda
1/2 tsp. baking powder
1 3/4 tsp. salt
1 1/2 tsp. cinnamon
3/4 tsp. allspice
1/2 tsp. cloves
1/4 tsp. nutmeg
1 c. raisins
1 1/2 c. chopped walnuts

Cream shortening and sugars in mixer bowl until light and fluffy. Add eggs and applesauce; mix well. Stir in dry ingredients and spices alternately with 1/2 cup water. Mix in raisins and walnuts. Pour into greased and lightly floured 9 x 13-inch cake pan. Bake at 350 degrees for about 1 hour or until cake tests done. Cool on wire rack. Cut into squares. Yield: 16 servings.

Approx per serv: Cal 425; Prot 5.4 g; T Fat 17.9 g; Chl 47.4 mg; Car 64.0 g; Sod 353.7 mg; Pot 230.2 mg.

Vicki Mallay, Isabella

DAFFODIL ANGEL CAKE

6 egg yolks
1 1/4 c. egg whites
1/2 tsp. salt
1 tsp. cream of tartar
1 1/3 c. sifted sugar
1/2 tsp. each vanilla, almond extract
2/3 c. sifted cake flour, sifted 3 times
1/2 c. sifted cake flour, sifted 3 times

Beat egg yolks in mixer bowl until thick and lemon colored. Beat egg whites and salt in mixer bowl until foamy. Add cream of tartar. Beat until stiff peaks form. Fold in sugar gently 1 tablespoon at a time. Fold half the egg whites, half the flavorings and 2/3 cup flour into egg yolks. Fold remaining flavorings and 1/2 cup flour into remaining egg whites. Drop batters by alternating spoonfuls into ungreased tube pan. Bake at 300 degrees for 1 hour. Invert on funnel to cool. Loosen side of cake with spatula. Remove to serving plate.
Yield: 12 servings.

Approx per serv: Cal 162; Prot 4.8 g; T Fat 2.7 g; Chl 125.8 mg; Car 29.8 g; Sod 147.6 mg; Pot 61.9 mg.

Ila Mae Methner, Midland

FANNIE'S BANANA CAKE

1 c. shortening
1 c. sugar
1 c. packed brown sugar
4 eggs
1/2 c. milk
2 1/2 c. flour
2 tsp. soda
1/8 tsp. salt
2 bananas, mashed
2 tsp. vanilla extract

Cream shortening and sugars in mixer bowl until light and fluffy. Add eggs and milk; mix well. Combine dry ingredients. Add to batter alternately with bananas and vanilla. Pour into greased and floured 9 x 13-inch cake pan. Bake at 350 degrees for 40 to 45 minutes or until cake tests done. Yield: 12 servings.
NOTE: This recipe was received from the previous owners of our farm and has been in the family — and — house for more than 50 years.

Approx per serv: Cal 440; Prot 5.4 g; T Fat 21.2 g; Chl 85.7 mg; Car 58.2 g; Sod 191.8 mg; Pot 183.2 mg.

Eric J. Sweeney, Huron

BELGIUM ZUTAKUKA

2 1/2 c. sugar
2 eggs, well beaten
1 c. honey
3 c. milk
1 tsp. cinnamon
4 tsp. soda
5 c. flour

Combine all ingredients in large mixer bowl. Beat at medium-high speed for 10 minutes. Pour into 3 greased and floured loaf pans. Bake at 350 degrees for 45 minutes or until loaves test done. Remove to wire rack to cool.
Yield: 30 servings.

Approx per serv: Cal 195; Prot 3.5 g; T Fat 1.4 g; Chl 20.3 mg; Car 42.9 g; Sod 126.9 mg; Pot 65.5 mg.

Sandi Salenbien, Monroe

BEST-OF-SHOW BLUEBERRY CAKE

1/2 c. butter, softened
1 c. sugar
3 eggs
1 c. sour cream
1 tsp. vanilla extract
2 c. fresh blueberries
2 c. sifted flour
1 tsp. soda
1/2 tsp. salt
1/2 c. packed brown sugar
1/2 c. chopped pecans
1/2 tsp. cinnamon

Cream butter and sugar in mixer bowl until light and fluffy. Add eggs 1 at a time, mixing well after each addition. Stir in sour cream and vanilla. Toss blueberries with a small amount of flour. Add remaining flour, soda and salt to batter; mix well. Fold in blueberries. Pour half the batter into greased and floured 9 x 13-inch pan. Combine remaining ingredients in small bowl. Sprinkle over batter. Spread remaining batter carefully over top. Bake at 350 degrees for about 40 minutes or until cake tests done.
Yield: 8 servings.

Approx per serv: Cal 519; Prot 7.4 g; T Fat 25.4 g; Chl 143.0 mg; Car 68.1 g; Sod 419.5 mg; Pot 218.1 mg.

Audra Dohm, Cass

CHERRY DELIGHT CAKE

6 egg whites
3/4 tsp. cream of tartar
2 c. sugar
3/4 tsp. vanilla extract
2 c. crushed soda crackers
3/4 c. chopped walnuts
1   16-oz. carton whipped topping
1 can cherry pie filling

Beat egg whites in mixer bowl until peaks form. Add cream of tartar and sugar gradually, beating until stiff. Stir in vanilla, cracker crumbs and walnuts. Pour into greased 9 x 13-inch cake pan. Bake at 350 degrees for 25 minutes. Cool completely. Spread whipped topping over cake. Top with pie filling. Store in refrigerator. Yield: 12 servings.

Approx per serv: Cal 411; Prot 4.5 g; T Fat 15.6 g; Chl 0.0 mg; Car 65.1 g; Sod 175.0 mg; Pot 85.1 mg.

Cheryl VanAssche, Osceola

QUICK AND EASY COCOA CAKES

2 c. buttermilk biscuit mix
1/3 c. sugar
3 tbsp. cocoa
1/2 c. milk
3 tbsp. margarine, melted

Combine all ingredients in bowl; mix well. Knead 8 to 10 times on work surface dusted with additional baking mix. Roll out and cut into 3-inch circles. Place on ungreased baking sheet. Bake at 425 degrees for 8 to 10 minutes or until cakes test done. Place in individual serving dishes. Top with ice cream and fruit or chocolate sauce. Yield: 6 servings.

NOTE: Nutritional information does not include toppings.

Approx per serv: Cal 283; Prot 4.3 g; T Fat 12.0 g; Chl 2.8 mg; Car 40.8 g; Sod 600.5 mg; Pot 104.3 mg.

Tracey Morrison, Livingston

TEXAS SHEET CAKE

2 sticks margarine
1/4 c. cocoa
2 c. sugar
2 c. flour
3/4 tsp. salt

2 eggs
1/2 c. buttermilk
1 tsp. soda
1 tsp. vanilla extract
1 stick margarine
1/4 c. cocoa
6 tbsp. milk
1   16-oz. package confectioners' sugar
1 tsp. vanilla extract

Combine 2 sticks margarine, 1/4 cup cocoa and 1 cup water in saucepan. Bring to a boil; remove from heat. Add sugar, flour and salt; mix well. Combine eggs, buttermilk, soda and 1 teaspoon vanilla in bowl. Add to cocoa mixture; mix well. Pour into greased and floured 10 x 15-inch baking pan. Bake at 350 degrees for 20 minutes. Bring 1 stick margarine, 1/4 cup cocoa and milk to a boil in saucepan. Beat in confectioners' sugar and 1 teaspoon vanilla until smooth. Pour over hot cake. Yield: 25 servings.

Approx per serv: Cal 290; Prot 2.3 g; T Fat 12.1 g; Chl 20.8 mg; Car 45.2 g; Sod 245.1 mg; Pot 57.4 mg.

Jennifer Lefcheck, Monroe

EDITH'S CHOCOLATE TORTE

1 c. flour
1 tsp. baking powder
1/2 tsp. salt (opt.)
6 eggs, separated
1 c. sugar
2 tbsp. lemon juice
Grated rind of 1/2 lemon
2 c. whipping cream
1 sm. package chocolate instant
   pudding mix
1 tbsp. instant coffee granules
3 tbsp. coffee liqueur (opt.)

Sift flour, baking powder and salt together. Beat egg whites in bowl until stiff peaks form. Beat egg yolks in bowl until thick and lemon colored. Add sugar, lemon juice and lemon rind; mix well. Fold in half the egg whites gently. Fold in sifted ingredients and remaining egg whites gently. Pour into ungreased tube pan. Bake at 325 degree for 10 minutes. Increase temperature to 350 degrees. Bake for 20 minutes. Increase temperature to 375 degrees. Bake for 20 minutes longer or until golden brown. Invert cake pan to cool. Loosen side with spatula. Remove to serving plate. Whip cream in bowl until mixture begins to thicken.

Add remaining ingredients. Beat until soft peaks form. Split cake into 2 layers. Spread whipped cream mixture between layers and over top and side of cake. Yield: 16 servings.

Approx per serv: Cal 159; Prot 4.1 g; T Fat 2.4 g; Chl 94.8 mg; Car 31.7 g; Sod 169.2 mg; Pot 179.4 mg.

Edith Nickel, Berrien

PAUL'S MOLASSES CAKE

    1/2 c. shortening
    1 c. sugar
    1/2 c. blackstrap molasses
    1 egg, beaten
    3/4 c. sour milk
    2 c. flour
    1 tsp. soda
    1/2 tsp. salt

Cream shortening, sugar and molasses in bowl with wooden spoon. Beat egg with sour milk until foamy. Add to creamed mixture alternately with mixture of dry ingredients 1/3 at a time, mixing well after each addition. Do not beat. Pour into greased loaf pan. Bake at 350 degrees for 35 to 45 minutes or until toothpick inserted in center comes out clean. Remove to wire rack to cool. Yield: 6 servings.

NOTE: This traditional Thanksgiving family dessert is 100 years old. It was dated November 12, 1885, in my great great-grandmother June Chapman's handwritten "Receipt Journal."

Approx per serv: Cal 537; Prot 6.5 g; T Fat 21.1 g; Chl 46.4 mg; Car 81.5 g; Sod 367.3 mg; Pot 895.4 mg.

Paul Carey, Montmorency

PEACH UPSIDE-DOWN CAKE

    1 8-oz. can sliced peaches
    1/2 c. packed brown sugar
    3 tbsp. butter, melted
    10 (about) maraschino cherries
    1/3 c. shortening
    1/2 c. sugar
    1 egg
    1 tsp. vanilla extract
    1 c. flour
    1 1/4 tsp. baking powder
    1/4 tsp. salt

Drain peaches, reserving syrup. Mix 1 tablespoon reserved syrup and brown sugar with butter in 8-inch cake pan. Arrange peaches and cherries in prepared pan. Cream shortening and sugar in mixer bowl until light and fluffy. Mix in egg and vanilla. Add enough water to remaining reserved peach syrup to measure 1/2 cup. Add to creamed mixture alternately with sifted dry ingredients, mixing well after each addition. Pour over peaches. Bake at 350 degrees for 40 to 45 minutes or until cake tests done. Invert on serving plate to cool. Yield: 6 servings.

Approx per serv: Cal 437; Prot 3.5 g; T Fat 19.4 g; Chl 59.9 mg; Car 63.9 g; Sod 244.4 mg; Pot 152.2 mg.

Todd Iott, Monroe

PUMPKIN CAKE ROLL

    3 eggs, beaten
    1 c. sugar
    2/3 c. pumpkin
    1 tsp. lemon juice
    3/4 c. flour
    1 tsp. baking powder
    1/2 tsp. salt
    2 tsp. cinnamon
    1 tsp. ginger
    1/2 tsp. nutmeg
    1 c. finely chopped pecans
    1 1/2 c. confectioners' sugar
    2 3-oz. packages cream cheese, softened
    1/4 c. butter, softened
    1/2 tsp. vanilla extract

Beat eggs in mixer bowl at high speed for 5 minutes. Add sugar gradually, beating until smooth. Stir in pumpkin and lemon juice. Fold in next 6 dry ingredients. Pour in 10 x 15-inch baking pan lined with greased and floured waxed paper. Sprinkle with pecans. Bake at 375 degrees for 15 minutes. Invert on towel sprinkled with 1/2 cup confectioners' sugar. Peel off waxed paper and trim brown edges if necessary. Roll up in towel as for jelly roll from narrow side; cool. Combine 1 cup confectioners' sugar and remaining ingredients in bowl; mix well. Unroll cooled cake. Spread with cream cheese mixture; reroll. Chill in refrigerator. Slice to serve. Yield: 8 servings.

Approx per serv: Cal 495; Prot 7.0 g; T Fat 26.6 g; Chl 136.2 mg; Car 60.8 g; Sod 321.6 mg; Pot 193.8 mg.

Brenda Beutler, Isabella
Kimberly Whybrew, Delta

FANCY JIFFY CAKE

    1 1-layer pkg. Jiffy cake mix
    1 sm. package vanilla instant pudding mix
    2 c. milk
    1 8-oz. package cream cheese, softened
    1 8-oz. can crushed pineapple, drained
    2 c. whipped topping
    1/4 c. chopped walnuts

Prepare cake mix using package directions. Pour into greased and floured 9 x 13-inch cake pan. Bake at 350 degrees for 20 minutes or until cake tests done. Combine pudding mix, milk and cream cheese in bowl. Beat until thick and smooth. Spread on cooled cake. Layer pineapple, whipped topping and walnuts over pudding mixture. Store in refrigerator.
Yield: 10 servings.
NOTE: Nutritional information does not include ingredients used in preparing cake mix.

Approx per serv: Cal 329; Prot 5.7 g; T Fat 15.8 g; Chl 32.0 mg; Car 42.4 g; Sod 377.1 mg; Pot 137.1 mg.

Maredda Magnus, Clare

MELT-IN-YOUR-MOUTH RASPBERRY CAKE

    3/4 c. butter, softened
    1 1/4 c. sugar
    1/2 tsp. salt
    1 1/2 tsp. vanilla extract
    3 eggs, separated
    2 3/4 c. flour
    2 tsp. baking powder
    1/2 c. milk
    2 c. fresh raspberries
    1 tbsp. flour
    1/4 c. sugar
    1 1/2 c. confectioners' sugar
    3 tbsp. raspberry juice

Cream butter and 1 1/4 cups sugar in mixer bowl until light and fluffy. Add salt, vanilla and egg yolks; beat until smooth. Add mixture of 2 3/4 cups flour and baking powder alternately with milk, mixing well after each addition. Toss raspberries with 1 tablespoon flour in bowl, coating well. Stir into batter. Beat egg whites in bowl until soft peaks form. Add 1/4 cup sugar 1 tablespoon at a time, beating until stiff. Fold gently into batter. Pour into greased and floured bundt pan. Bake at 350 degrees for 50 to 60 minutes or until cake tests done. Remove to wire rack to cool. Invert on cake plate. Mix confectioners' sugar and raspberry juice in bowl. Drizzle over cake. Yield: 16 servings.

Approx per serv: Cal 303; Prot 4.1 g; T Fat 10.4 g; Chl 75.1 mg; Car 49.4 g; Sod 228.8 mg; Pot 80.8 mg.

Kirsten Bancroft, Lenawee

RHUBARB TORTE

    1/2 c. margarine, softened
    1 c. sugar
    1 egg
    2 c. flour
    1 tsp. soda
    1/2 tsp. salt
    3/4 c. milk
    2 c. chopped rhubarb
    1/2 c. packed brown sugar
    1/2 c. sugar
    1/2 c. chopped pecans

Cream margarine, 1 cup sugar and egg in mixer bowl until light and fluffy. Add sifted flour, soda and salt alternately with milk, mixing well after each addition. Stir in rhubarb. Pour into greased and floured 9 x 13-inch cake pan. Sprinkle with mixture of remaining ingredients. Bake at 375 degrees for 30 minutes.
Yield: 12 servings.

Approx per serv: Cal 328; Prot 3.9 g; T Fat 12.4 g; Chl 23.2 mg; Car 51.9 g; Sod 267.2 mg; Pot 162.3 mg.

Berniece Peterson, Menominee

FRESH RHUBARB CAKE

    1/2 c. margarine, softened
    1 1/2 c. packed brown sugar
    1 egg
    2 c. flour
    1 tsp. soda
    1/2 tsp. salt
    1 c. milk
    2 1/2 c. chopped rhubarb
    1 tsp. vanilla extract
    1/2 c. sugar
    1 tbsp. cinnamon

Cream margarine and brown sugar in mixer bowl until light and fluffy. Mix in egg. Add flour, soda and salt alternately with milk, mixing well after each addition. Fold in rhubarb and vanilla. Pour into greased and floured 9 x 13-inch cake pan. Sprinkle with mixture of sugar and cinnamon. Bake at 350 degrees for 40 minutes. Yield: 12 servings.

Approx per serv: Cal 303; Prot 3.6 g; T Fat 9.1 g; Chl 23.9 mg; Car 52.7 g; Sod 275.2 mg; Pot 215.3 m g.

Amy Long, Shiawassee

LOUISIANA YAM CROWN CAKE

1 1/4 c. oil
2 c. sugar
4 eggs
2 tsp. vanilla extract
2 c. sifted flour
1 1/2 tsp. soda
1 tsp. salt
1 1/2 tsp. cinnamon
1 tsp. nutmeg
1/2 tsp. cloves
2 c. mashed cooked yams
1/2 c. chopped pecans
1/4 c. butter, softened
1   3-oz. package cream cheese, softened
1/2 tsp. vanilla extract
2 c. (about) confectioners' sugar
1/2 c. chopped pecans

Combine oil and sugar in mixer bowl. Add eggs 1 at a time, mixing well after each addition. Mix in 2 teaspoons vanilla. Add sifted flour, soda, salt and spices; mix well. Stir in yams and 1/2 cup pecans. Pour into greased and floured bundt pan. Bake at 350 degrees for 1 1/4 hours. Invert on serving plate. Cool completely. Split cake into 2 layers. Cream butter and cream cheese in mixer bowl. Add vanilla and enough confectioners' sugar to make of spreading consistency. Stir in 1/2 cup pecans. Spread between cake layers. Sprinkle with additional confectioners' sugar. Yield: 15 servings.

Approx per serv: Cal 523; Prot 4.7 g; T Fat 28.9 g; Chl 66.6 mg; Car 64.0 g; Sod 296.7 mg; Pot 137.0 mg.

Pam Snyder, Grand Traverse

BASIC YELLOW CAKE

2 c. sifted cake flour
1 1/2 c. sugar
2 1/2 tsp. baking powder
3/4 tsp. salt
1/2 c. shortening
1/2 c. milk
1 1/4 tsp. vanilla extract
2 eggs
1/4 c. milk

Sift flour, sugar, baking powder and salt in mixer bowl. Cut in shortening until crumbly. Add 1/2 cup milk and vanilla. Beat at low speed for 1 1/2 minutes or until moistened. Add eggs and remaining milk. Beat at high speed for 1 1/2 minutes. Pour into greased and floured 9 x 9-inch cake pan. Bake at 350 degrees for 25 to 30 minutes or until cake tests done. Yield: 6 servings.

Approx per serv: Cal 523; Prot 5.6 g; T Fat 21.9 g; Chl 88.5 mg; Car 77.2 g; Sod 440.2 mg; Pot 99.3 mg.

Stacey Barkenquast, Monroe

WHITE LEMON CAKE YUMMY

1   2-layer pkg. white cake mix
3/4 c. sugar
1/4 tsp. salt
2 tbsp. cornstarch
3 tbsp. lemon juice
1 egg, separated
1 tbsp. butter
1/2 c. shortening
1/2 c. margarine, softened
1 c. sugar
1/2 c. milk, scalded
1/2 tsp. lemon extract
1/2 tsp. vanilla extract

Prepare cake mix using package directions. Pour into 3 greased and floured 8-inch cake pans. Bake at 350 degrees for 10 to 12 minutes or until cake tests done. Turn onto wire racks to cool. Combine 3/4 cup sugar, salt and cornstarch in saucepan. Blend in 3/4 cup cold water, lemon juice and beaten egg yolk. Cook until thick, stirring constantly. Stir in butter; cool. Reserve 2 tablespoons filling for topping. Spread remaining filling between layers of cake. Cream shortening, margarine and 1 cup sugar in bowl until light and fluffy. Add egg white and cooled milk. Beat until smooth and very creamy. Add flavorings. Spread over top and side of cake. Garnish with reserved lemon filling. Store in refrigerator for up to 1 week. Yield: 15 servings.

Approx per serv: Cal 377; Prot 2.4 g; T Fat 17.5 g; Chl 20.4 mg; Car 52.9 g; Sod 451.2 mg; Pot 23.0 mg.

Mary Ellen Leppek, Bay

WHITE BUTTERMILK CAKE

1 c. shortening
3 c. sugar
1/2 c. buttermilk
4 c. sifted cake flour
1 tbsp. baking powder
1/2 tsp. soda
1 tsp. salt
1 1/2 c. buttermilk
1 tsp. vanilla extract
4 egg whites, stiffly beaten
Fluffy Bakershop Icing

Cream shortening and sugar in mixer bowl until light and fluffy. Add 1/2 cup buttermilk, beating until fluffy. Add sifted dry ingredients alternately with remaining buttermilk, mixing well after each addition. Stir in vanilla. Fold in egg whites gently. Pour into 3 greased and floured 9-inch cake pans. Bake at 350 degrees for 35 to 40 minutes or until cake tests done. Cool on wire racks. Spread Fluffy Bakershop Icing between layers and over top and side of cake.

FLUFFY BAKERSHOP ICING

1 1/2 c. milk
2 tbsp. cornstarch
1/2 c. shortening
1/2 c. margarine
1 c. sugar
1 tsp. vanilla extract
1 tsp. almond extract

Combine milk and cornstarch in saucepan. Cook until thick, stirring constantly; cool. Cream shortening, margarine and sugar in mixer bowl until light and fluffy. Beat for 10 minutes. Add cooled mixture and vanilla. Beat until creamy. Blend in almond flavoring. Yield: 20 servings.

Approx per serv: Cal 441; Prot 3.7 g; T Fat 22.2 g; Chl 3.1 mg; Car 58.1 g; Sod 283.9 mg; Pot 91.3 mg.

Mary Jo Barr, Ionia

PEANUT BUTTER CUPCAKES

1 1/2 c. flour
2 tsp. baking powder
1/2 tsp. salt
1/2 c. peanut butter
1/4 c. shortening
1 c. packed brown sugar
2 eggs

1/2 c. milk
1 tsp. vanilla extract

Combine flour, baking powder and salt in bowl. Add peanut butter and shortening; mix until creamy. Add brown sugar gradually, mixing well after each addition. Blend in eggs alternately with milk and vanilla, mixing just until smooth. Spoon into paper-lined muffin cups. Bake at 350 degrees for 20 minutes. Remove to wire racks to cool. Yield: 8 servings.

Approx per serv: Cal 376; Prot 8.6 g; T Fat 17.3 g; Chl 65.3 mg; Car 48.4 g; Sod 343.8 mg; Pot 256.5 mg.

Lisa Dental, Monroe

SELF-FILLED CUPCAKES

1 2-layer pkg. chocolate cake mix
1/3 c. sugar
1 8-oz. package cream cheese, softened
1 egg
1/8 tsp. salt
1 6-oz. package chocolate chips

Prepare cake mix using package directions. Fill greased and floured muffin cups 2/3 full. Cream sugar and cream cheese in bowl until fluffy. Mix in egg and salt. Stir in chocolate chips. Drop 1 rounded teaspoonful on batter in each muffin cup. Bake at 350 degrees for 20 to 25 minutes or until cupcakes test done. Cool. Frost with favorite chocolate frosting if desired. Yield: 30 servings.

NOTE: Nutritional information does not include ingredients used in preparing cake mix.

Approx per serv: Cal 140; Prot 1.9 g; T Fat 6.3 g; Chl 10.8 mg; Car 19.0 g; Sod 191.9 mg; Pot 20.2 mg.

Jean L. Rought, Muskegon

WONDERFUL CUPCAKES

1 c. chopped dates
1 tsp. soda
3/4 c. shortening
1 c. sugar
2 eggs, beaten
1 tsp. milk
1 c. plus 10 tbsp. flour
1/4 tsp. salt
3/4 tsp. soda
1 c. chocolate chips

1/2 c. chopped pecans
1/4 c. sugar

Combine dates, 1 teaspoon soda and 1 1/2 cups boiling water in bowl; cool. Cream shortening and 1 cup sugar in mixer bowl until light and fluffy. Add eggs, milk, flour, salt and 3/4 teaspoon soda; mix well. Stir in date mixture. Spoon into 12 greased and floured muffin cups. Sprinkle remaining ingredients over top. Bake at 375 degrees for 35 minutes. Cool on wire rack. Yield: 12 servings.

Approx per serv: Cal 426; Prot 4.2 g; T Fat 23.8 g; Chl 42.2 mg; Car 53.4 g; Sod 175.5 mg; Pot 200.0 mg.

Joshua Zimmerman, Monroe

APPLE BARS

1 c. shortening
2 1/2 c. flour
1 tbsp. sugar
1 tsp. salt
1 egg, separated
2/3 c. milk
2 c. crushed cornflakes
10 apples, peeled, sliced
1/4 c. sugar
1 tsp. cinnamon
3/4 c. confectioners' sugar

Cut shortening into flour, 1 tablespoon sugar and salt in bowl until crumbly. Add mixture of egg yolk and milk; mix well. Roll out half the dough into a 12 x 17-inch rectangle on floured surface. Place on baking sheet. Sprinkle with cornflake crumbs. Arrange apples over surface. Sprinkle with 1/4 cup sugar and cinnamon. Roll out remaining dough; place over top. Brush with beaten egg white. Bake at 400 degrees for 50 to 55 minutes or until golden brown. Sprinkle with confectioners' sugar. Cut into bars when cool. Yield: 48 servings.

Approx per serv: Cal 121; Prot 1.3 g; T Fat 5.2 g; Chl 5.7 mg; Car 17.9 g; Sod 83.6 mg; Pot 65.3 mg.

Marsha Salo, Houghton

KITTY'S BROWNIES

1/2 c. butter, softened
1 c. sugar
4 eggs
1 tsp. vanilla extract

1   16-oz. can chocolate syrup
1 c. sifted flour
1/2 tsp. salt
1 c. chopped pecans
1   6-oz. package semisweet
    chocolate chips

Cream butter and sugar in mixer bowl until light and fluffy. Add eggs, vanilla and chocolate syrup; beat until well mixed. Blend in flour and salt. Stir in pecans and chocolate chips. Spread in greased and floured 9 x 13-inch baking pan. Bake at 350 degrees for 30 to 35 minutes or until brownies test done. Cut into squares when cool. Yield: 24 servings.

Approx per serv: Cal 228; Prot 2.9 g; T Fat 11.4 g; Chl 54.0 mg; Car 32.5 g; Sod 114.6 mg; Pot 139.9 mg.

Kitty Nebel, Macomb

4-H is sponsored by your county, state, and federal government, and private contributions through Michigan State University Extension Service.

STACIE TAYLOR'S CHOCOLATE BROWNIES

4 eggs
2 c. sugar
1 tsp. vanilla extract
1 c. butter, melted
1 c. flour
2/3 c. cocoa
1/2 tsp. baking powder
1/2 tsp. salt
1 c. chopped pecans

Beat eggs in mixer bowl until frothy. Add sugar and vanilla gradually; mix well. Blend in butter. Add mixture of dry ingredients gradually, mixing well after each addition. Stir in pecans. Pour into greased and floured 9 x 9-inch cake pan. Bake at 350 degrees for 30 to 35 minutes or until brownies test done. Cool. Frost with favorite frosting if desired. Cut into squares. Yield: 16 servings.

Approx per serv: Cal 307; Prot 3.8 g; T Fat 19.0 g; Chl 98.7 mg; Car 33.9 g; Sod 233.0 mg; Pot 127.0 mg.

Stacie Taylor, Calhoun

CARAMEL CHIP BARS

1 1/2 c. flour
1 c. packed brown sugar
3/4 tsp. soda
1/2 tsp. salt
1 c. margarine, melted
32 caramels
5 tbsp. cream
1 6-oz. package chocolate chips

Combine dry ingredients in bowl. Add margarine; mix well. Press half the mixture into 9 x 13-inch baking pan. Bake at 350 degrees for 10 minutes. Melt caramels with cream in double boiler, blending well. Sprinkle chocolate chips on baked layer. Pour caramel mixture over chocolate chips. Sprinkle crumb mixture over top. Bake for 15 minutes longer. Cut into squares when cool. Yield: 24 servings.

Approx per serv: Cal 234; Prot 1.9 g; T Fat 12.0 g; Chl 0.3 mg; Car 31.9 g; Sod 206.6 mg; Pot 105.7 mg.

Matt Severin, Monroe

ENGLISH TOFFEE BARS

1 c. margarine, softened
1 c. sugar
1 egg, separated
2 c. flour
1 tsp. cinnamon
1 c. chopped pecans
*2 1-oz. squares semisweet
    chocolate, melted*

Cream margarine in mixer bowl. Add sugar gradually, beating until light and fluffy. Mix in egg yolk. Blend in flour and cinnamon. Spread evenly in greased baking sheet. Brush with lightly beaten egg white. Press pecans lightly into top. Bake at 275 degrees for 1 hour. Cut into squares while hot. Drizzle with melted chocolate. Remove to wire rack to cool. Yield: 36 servings.

Approx per serv: Cal 125; Prot 1.3 g; T Fat 8.2 g; Chl 7.0 mg; Car 12.2 g; Sod 64.1 mg; Pot 34.8 mg.

Julie Racz, Macomb

MAGIC COOKIE BARS

1/2 c. margarine, melted
1 1/2 c. graham cracker crumbs
1 can sweetened condensed milk
*1 6-oz. package semisweet
    chocolate chips*
1 1/3 c. flaked coconut
1 c. chopped pecans

Combine margarine and cracker crumbs in 9 x 13-inch baking pan. Press evenly over bottom of pan. Pour condensed milk over crumb layer. Layer chocolate chips, coconut and pecans over condensed milk. Press layers down firmly. Bake at 350 degrees for 25 to 30 minutes or until lightly browned. Cut into bars when cool. Yield: 24 servings.

Approx per serv: Cal 225; Prot 3.4 g; T Fat 14.0 g; Chl 8.1 mg; Car 24.2 g; Sod 127.1 mg; Pot 168.5 mg.

Amy Axford, Otsego

OATMEAL CARAMETTES

35 light caramels
5 tbsp. light cream
1 c. flour
1 c. quick-cooking oats
3/4 c. packed brown sugar
1/2 tsp. soda
1/4 tsp. salt
3/4 c. melted margarine
1 6-oz. package milk chocolate chips
1/2 c. chopped pecans

Melt caramels with cream in saucepan over low heat, stirring to blend well. Combine dry ingredients with margarine in bowl; mix well. Press 3/4 cup into 9 x 13-inch baking pan. Bake at 350 degrees for 10 minutes. Sprinkle with chocolate chips and pecans. Pour caramel mixture over top. Sprinkle remaining crumbs over all. Bake for 15 to 20 minutes longer or until golden brown. Chill for 1 to 2 hours. Cut into bars. Yield: 40 servings.

Approx per serv: Cal 142; Prot 1.4 g; T Fat 7.6 g; Chl 1.4 mg; Car 18.3 g; Sod 90.3 mg; Pot 69.5 mg.

Kathy Ives, Menominee

CORNFLAKE DREAM BARS

1/4 c. margarine, softened
1/2 c. packed light brown sugar
1 c. flour
2 eggs
1 c. packed light brown sugar
1 tsp. vanilla extract

1/4 tsp. salt
1 c. cornflakes
1 c. coconut
1 c. broken walnuts

Cream margarine and 1/2 cup brown sugar in mixer bowl until light and fluffy. Add flour; mix well. Press into greased 9 x 13-inch baking pan. Bake at 350 degrees for 15 minutes. Beat eggs in bowl until light. Add 1 cup brown sugar; mix well. Fold in remaining ingredients. Spread over baked layer. Bake for 20 to 25 minutes longer or until lightly browned. Cut into bars when cool. Yield: 36 servings.

Approx per serv: Cal 97; Prot 1.4 g; T Fat 4.5 g; Chl 14.0 mg; Car 13.5 g; Sod 48.5 mg; Pot 62.1 mg.

Cindy Brock, Delta

LEMON LOVE NOTES

1/2 c. butter
1 c. sifted flour
1/4 c. confectioners' sugar
1 c. sugar
2 tbsp. flour
1/2 tsp. baking powder
2 eggs, beaten
2 tbsp. lemon juice
2 tsp. grated lemon rind

Combine butter, 1 cup flour and confectioners' sugar in bowl; mix until crumbly. Press into 8 x 8-inch baking pan. Bake at 350 degrees for 8 minutes; cool. Combine sugar, 2 tablespoons flour and baking powder in bowl. Add remaining ingredients; mix well. Pour over baked layer. Bake for 25 minutes longer. Cut into squares when cool. Yield: 16 servings.
NOTE: Filling will puff up during baking and sink as it cools.

Approx per serv: Cal 147; Prot 1.7 g; T Fat 6.6 g; Chl 49.4 mg; Car 20.9 g; Sod 88.3 mg; Pot 21.2 mg.

Wanetta Webb, Kalkaska

NIKKI'S PUMPKIN SQUARES

2 c. sugar
2 c. canned pumpkin
4 eggs
3/4 c. oil
2 c. flour
2 tsp. soda
1/2 tsp. each cinnamon and salt

1 c. chopped pecans
1 3-oz. package cream cheese, softened
1 stick margarine, softened
2 c. confectioners' sugar
1 tsp. vanilla extract

Combine sugar, pumpkin, eggs and oil in mixer bowl. Beat until well blended. Add flour, soda, cinnamon and salt; mix well. Stir in pecans. Pour into greased and floured 10 x 15-inch baking pan. Bake at 350 degrees for 20 to 25 minutes or until golden brown. Combine remaining ingredients in bowl. Mix until smooth. Spread over cooled baked layer. Cut into squares to serve. Yield: 36 servings.

Approx per serv: Cal 195; Prot 1.9 g; T Fat 11.0 g; Chl 30.7 mg; Car 23.3 g; Sod 119.6 mg; Pot 67.6 mg.

Nikki Diehl, Isabella

PORTUGUESE WALNUT SQUARES

1/2 c. butter, softened
3/4 c. packed light brown sugar
1 egg
1/2 tsp. vanilla extract
2 tbsp. milk
2 tbsp. Port
6 tbsp. flour
1/2 tsp. baking powder
1 c. chopped walnuts
2 tbsp. Port
1 c. confectioners' sugar
1 tbsp. butter
Several drops of red food coloring
1 tbsp. (or more) Port
1/2 c. chopped walnuts

Cream 1/2 cup butter and brown sugar in mixer bowl until light and fluffy. Mix in egg, vanilla, milk and 2 tablespoons Port. Add flour and baking powder; mix well. Fold in 1 cup walnuts. Spoon into buttered and floured 9 x 9-inch baking pan. Bake at 350 degrees for 15 to 20 minutes or until toothpick inserted in center comes out clean. Brush top with 2 tablespoons Port. Combine confectioners' sugar, 1 tablespoon butter and food coloring with salt to taste in bowl. Add enough Port to make of spreading consistency. Spread on cooled cake. Sprinkle with 1/2 cup walnuts. Cut into squares when glaze is firm. Yield: 16 servings.

Approx per serv: Cal 219; Prot 2.5 g; T Fat 14.1 g; Chl 36.0 mg; Car 21.8 g; Sod 97.6 mg; Pot 102.1 mg.

Rosemary Publiski, Monroe

FRESH APPLE CHEWS

2 c. flour
3/4 c. packed brown sugar
1/2 c. butter, softened
1 egg
1 tsp. soda
1/2 tsp. salt
1 1/4 tsp. cinnamon
1 c. chopped walnuts
1 c. raisins
1 apple, peeled, finely chopped
30 green candied cherry halves

Combine first 7 ingredients and 3 tablespoons water in mixer bowl. Beat at low speed until well mixed, scraping bowl occasionally. Stir in walnuts, raisins and apple. Drop by heaping tablespoonfuls 2 inches apart on greased cookie sheet. Spread into 3-inch circles with spoon. Place cherry half in center of each. Bake at 375 degrees for 15 to 20 minutes or until lightly browned. Cool on wire rack. Yield: 30 servings.

Approx per serv: Cal 131; Prot 1.8 g; T Fat 6.0 g; Chl 17.9 mg; Car 18.6 g; Sod 105.6 mg; Pot 95.8 mg.

Gina Schmidt, Benzie

SAUCEPAN FUDGE CRACKLE COOKIES

1/4 c. butter
3 1-oz. squares semisweet chocolate
1 c. sugar
2 eggs
1 tsp. vanilla extract
1/2 c. chopped pecans
1 c. flour
1 tsp. baking powder
1/4 tsp. salt
3 tbsp. sugar

Melt butter and chocolate in saucepan over low heat, stirring until blended; cool. Combine with 1 cup sugar, eggs, vanilla and pecans in bowl; mix well. Stir in mixture of flour, baking powder and salt. Chill for 1 1/2 to 2 hours. Shape into 1 1/2-inch balls. Roll in 3 tablespoons sugar. Place on greased cookie sheet. Bake at 300 degrees for 20 minutes or until top has crackled appearance. Remove to wire rack to cool. Yield: 25 servings.

Approx per serv: Cal 111; Prot 1.4 g; T Fat 5.2 g; Chl 25.9 mg; Car 15.7 g; Sod 62.0 mg; Pot 36.0 mg.

Tammy Libby, Lapeer

DAD'S SPECIAL CHOCOLATE CHIP COOKIES

1 c. shortening
1 tbsp. butter, softened
2 c. packed brown sugar
2 eggs
2 tsp. vanilla extract
3 c. flour
1 tsp. soda
1/4 tsp. salt
1 6-oz. package miniature
chocolate chips
2 Heath bars, crushed

Cream shortening, butter and sugar in mixer bowl until light and fluffy. Add eggs and vanilla. Beat until smooth. Add dry ingredients; mix well. Stir in chocolate chips and crushed candy. Drop by spoonfuls onto ungreased cookie sheet. Bake at 350 degress for 10 minutes. Remove to wire rack to cool. Yield: 60 servings.

NOTE: May substitute 1/4 cup toffee chips for Heath bars.

Kesha Werstein, Monroe

WHOOPIE PIES

2/3 c. shortening
1 1/4 c. sugar
2 eggs
1 tsp. vanilla extract
1 c. milk
2 1/4 c. flour
1/2 c. cocoa
1 1/2 tsp. soda
1/4 tsp. cream of tartar
1/4 c. (heaping) flour
1 c. milk
1/2 c. shortening
1 c. butter
1 c. sugar
1/4 tsp. salt
1 tsp. vanilla extract

Cream 2/3 cup shortening and 1 1/4 cups sugar in mixer bowl until light and fluffy. Add eggs, 1 teaspoon vanilla and 1 cup milk; mix well. Blend in 2 1/4 cups flour, cocoa, soda and cream of tartar. Drop by teaspoonfuls onto lightly greased cookie sheet. Bake at 350 degrees for 10 to 12 minutes or until browned.

Remove to wire rack to cool. Blend 1/4 cup flour and 1 cup milk in saucepan. Cook over low heat until thick, stirring constantly. Add remaining ingredients. Beat until light and creamy. Spread over half the cookies. Top with remaining cookies. Yield: 36 servings.

Approx per serv: Cal 251; Prot 2.0 g; T Fat 18.6 g; Chl 47.5 mg; Car 20.4 g; Sod 185.6 mg; Pot 53.6 mg.

Jean Minner, Jackson

MOM'S MERINGUE COOKIES

2 egg whites
1/8 tsp. salt
1/8 tsp. cream of tartar
1 tsp. vanilla extract
3/4 c. sugar
1/4 c. chopped hickory nuts
1 6-oz. package chocolate chips

Combine egg whites, salt, cream of tartar and vanilla in mixer bowl. Beat until soft peaks form. Add sugar gradually, beating until stiff. Stir in hickory nuts and chocolate chips. Drop on baking parchment-lined cookie sheet. Bake at 300 degrees for 25 minutes. Remove to wire rack to cool. Yield: 24 servings.

Carolyn Sue Allen, Jackson

HONEY COOKIES

1/2 c. oil
1 c. honey
3/4 c. peanut butter
1/3 c. milk
1 1/2 c. whole wheat flour
2 tsp. baking powder
1 tsp. cinnamon
1/2 tsp. mace
1/4 tsp. cloves
3/4 c. oats
1/2 c. raisins

Heat oil and honey in saucepan. Add peanut butter and milk, stirring to blend well. Add remaining ingredients; mix well. Drop by teaspoonfuls on ungreased cookie sheet. Bake at 350 degrees for 12 minutes. Remove to wire rack to cool. Yield: 36 servings.

Approx per serv: Cal 117; Prot 2.4 g; T Fat 6.0 g; Chl 0.3 mg; Car 15.1 g; Sod 52.8 mg; Pot 81.4 mg.

Frances Burzynski, Otsego

JUMBO GINGERSNAPS

1/2 c. sugar
2 1/4 c. flour
1/4 c. dark molasses
2 tsp. soda
1/2 tsp. cinnamon
1/4 tsp. salt
3/4 c. oil
1/4 c. maple syrup
1 tsp. ginger
1/2 tsp. cardamom
1 egg
1/2 c. sugar

Combine first 11 ingredients in mixer bowl. Beat at low speed until well blended, scraping bowl occasionally. Shape by 1/4 cupfuls into balls; roll in remaining sugar. Place 3 inches apart on ungreased cookie sheet. Bake at 350 degrees for 15 minutes. Remove to wire racks to cool. Yield: 12 servings.

Approx per serv: Cal 292; Prot 3.1 g; T Fat 12.2 g; Chl 21.1 mg; Car 43.2 g; Sod 328.7 mg; Pot 105.4 mg.

Karen Derby, Oceana

MARY MALLAY'S MOLASSES COOKIES

1 c. butter, softened
1 c. sugar
2 eggs
1 c. molasses
4 c. flour
1 tsp. soda
1/2 tsp. salt
2 tsp. ginger
1 tsp. cinnamon
1 c. sour milk

Combine butter, sugar, eggs and molasses in mixer bowl. Mix until light and creamy. Add dry ingredients alternately with sour milk, mixing well after each addition. Shape into 1 1/2-inch balls; place on cookie sheet. Bake at 375 degrees for 10 to 12 minutes or until lightly browned. Remove to wire rack to cool.
Yield: 72 servings.

Approx per serv: Cal 75; Prot 1.0 g; T Fat 2.9 g; Chl 15.4 mg; Car 11.2 g; Sod 61.6 mg; Pot 55.9 mg.

Mary Mallay, Isabella

BANANA-OATMEAL COOKIES

3/4 c. shortening
3/4 c. sugar
1 egg
2 sm. bananas, mashed
1 1/2 c. flour
3/4 c. oats
1/2 tsp. soda
1/4 tsp. salt
1 tsp. each cinnamon, nutmeg
1/2 c. chopped pecans
1 12-oz. package chocolate chips

Cream shortening and sugar in mixer bowl until light and fluffy. Add egg and bananas; mix well. Add dry ingredients gradually, mixing well after each addition. Stir in pecans and chocolate chips. Drop by spoonfuls onto greased cookie sheet. Bake at 400 degrees for 8 to 10 minutes or until lightly browned. Remove to wire rack to cool. Yield: 36 servings.

Approx per serv: Cal 149; Prot 1.6 g; T Fat 9.6 g; Chl 7.0 mg; Car 16.1 g; Sod 28.3 mg; Pot 72.9 mg.

David Latham, Isabella

OATMEAL SCOTCHIES

1/2 c. butter, softened
3/4 c. packed brown sugar
1 egg
1 c. flour
1 tsp. baking powder
1/2 tsp. each soda and salt
3/4 c. quick-cooking oats
1 6-oz. package butterscotch chips
1/4 tsp. vanilla extract

Combine butter, brown sugar, egg and 1 1/2 teaspoons water in mixer bowl. Beat until light and creamy. Add mixture of next 4 ingredients; mix well. Stir in oats, butterscotch chips and vanilla. Drop by teaspoonfuls onto ungreased cookie sheet. Bake at 375 degrees for 10 to 12 minutes or until lightly browned. Remove to wire rack to cool.

Aaron Nadeau, Monroe

HELEN'S OATMEAL COOKIES

2 eggs
1 c. sugar
1 c. lard

1/2 c. sour cream
1 tsp. soda
1 tsp. cinnamon
2 c. flour
3 c. oats
1 c. raisins (opt.)
1 c. chopped pecans (opt.)
1 6-oz. package chocolate chips (opt.)

Combine eggs, sugar, lard and sour cream in mixer bowl. Beat until light and creamy. Add dry ingredients in order listed, mixing well after each addition. Stir in raisins, pecans and chocolate chips. Let stand for 30 minutes. Drop by spoonfuls onto ungreased cookie sheet. Bake at 350 degrees for 12 to 15 minutes or until lightly browned. Remove to wire rack to cool. Yield: 36 servings.

NOTE: This family recipe is at least 50 years old. May substitute margarine for lard and milk for sour cream.

Approx per serv: Cal 194; Prot 2.7 g; T Fat 11.4 g; Chl 20.9 mg; Car 21.8 g; Sod 29.4 mg; Pot 104.3 mg.

Helen Williams, Branch

ORANGE COOKIES

1 c. margarine, softened
2 c. sugar
2 eggs
1/2 tsp. salt
4 1/2 c. flour
2 tsp. baking powder
1 c. sour milk
1 tsp. soda
Juice and grated rind of 1 orange
2 1/4 c. confectioners' sugar
Juice and grated rind of 1 orange

Cream margarine and sugar in mixer bowl until light and fluffy. Mix in eggs and salt. Add flour and baking powder alternately with sour milk, mixing well after each addition. Add soda dissolved in juice of 1 orange. Stir in rind of 1 orange. Drop by spoonfuls onto greased cookie sheet. Bake at 375 degrees for 12 minutes. Remove to wire rack to cool. Combine confectioners' sugar and remaining juice and rind in bowl; mix well. Spread on cooled cookies.
Yield: 72 servings.

Approx per serv: Cal 93; Prot 1.2 g; T Fat 2.9 g; Chl 15.4 mg; Car 15.8 g; Sod 70.2 mg; Pot 20.8 mg.

Wendy St. John, Shiawassee

PEANUT BUTTER-CHOCOLATE CHIP COOKIES

2/3 c. shortening
1/2 c. sugar
1/2 c. packed brown sugar
1 egg
1/2 c. peanut butter
1 tsp. vanilla extract
1 1/2 c. flour
1/2 tsp. soda
1/2 tsp. salt
1 6-oz. package chocolate chips

Cream shortening, sugar and brown sugar in mixer bowl until light and fluffy. Add egg, peanut butter and vanilla. Beat until smooth and creamy. Blend in mixture of dry ingredients. Stir in chocolate chips. Drop by rounded teaspoonfuls onto ungreased cookie sheet. Bake at 375 degrees for 8 to 10 minutes or until lightly browned. Cool on cookie sheet for 5 minutes. Remove to wire rack to cool completely. Yield: 36 servings.

Approx per serv: Cal 125; Prot 1.8 g; T Fat 7.8 g; Chl 7.0 mg; Car 13.0 g; Sod 65.4 mg; Pot 55.0 mg.

Matt Donofrio, Monroe

PUMPKIN COOKIES

1/2 c. margarine, softened
1 c. packed brown sugar
2 eggs
1 c. mashed cooked pumpkin
1 tsp. vanilla extract
2 c. flour
1 tsp. each soda, baking powder
1/2 tsp. salt
1 tsp. cinnamon
1 c. chopped pecans (opt.)
1 c. chopped dates (opt.)
3 tbsp. margarine
1/2 c. packed brown sugar
2 tbsp. milk
1 c. confectioners' sugar
3/4 tsp. vanilla extract

Cream 1/2 cup margarine and 1 cup brown sugar in mixer bowl until light and fluffy. Mix in eggs, pumpkin and 1 teaspoon vanilla. Add next 5 ingredients; mix well. Stir in pecans and dates. Drop by spoonfuls onto greased cookie sheet. Bake at 350 degrees for 10 minutes.

Combine 3 tablespoons margarine, 1/2 cup brown sugar and milk in saucepan. Bring to a boil. Boil for 30 seconds. Stir in confectioners' sugar and 3/4 teaspoon vanilla. Spread on warm cookies. Yield: 48 servings.

Approx per serv: Cal 110; Prot 1.2 g; T Fat 4.7 g; Chl 10.6 mg; Car 16.6 g; Sod 83.5 mg; Pot 84.3 mg.

Stephanie Risner, Calhoun

PECAN KISSES

2 egg whites
2 c. confectioners' sugar
1 tsp. vinegar
1 tsp. vanilla extract
1 6-oz. package chocolate chips
1/2 c. chopped pecans
1/2 c. coconut

Beat egg whites in mixer bowl until soft peaks form. Add confectioners' sugar, vinegar and vanilla gradually, beating until stiff. Fold in chocolate chips, pecans or coconut as desired. Drop by teaspoonfuls 2 inches apart on greased cookie sheet. Bake at 300 degrees for 12 to 15 minutes or until firm. Remove to wire rack to cool. Yield: 42 servings.

Approx per serv: Cal 57; Prot 0.5 g; T Fat 2.8 g; Chl 0.0 mg; Car 8.6 g; Sod 4.5 mg; Pot 27.3 mg.

Michelle Crandall, Lapeer

SOUR CREAM COOKIES

2 c. packed brown sugar
1 c. sour cream
3 eggs
4 c. (scant) flour
2 tsp. each baking powder, soda
1/2 tsp. salt
2 tsp. vanilla extract

Combine brown sugar, sour cream and eggs in mixer bowl. Beat until smooth and creamy. Add mixture of dry ingredients; mix well. Stir in vanilla. Drop by spoonfuls onto greased cookie sheets. Bake at 400 degrees for 8 to 10 minutes or until lightly browned. Remove to wire racks to cool. Yield: 72 servings.

Approx per serv: Cal 58.4; Prot 1.1 g; T Fat 1.0 g; Chl 11.9 mg; Car 11.4 g; Sod 53.0 mg; Pot 35.0 mg.

Mary Kay Sweeney, Huron

BROWN SUGAR CUT-OUT COOKIES

1 c. shortening
2 c. packed brown sugar
2 eggs
1/4 c. cream
1 tsp. vanilla extract
4 1/2 c. flour
1 tsp. soda
1/2 tsp. each baking powder, salt
2 tsp. cinnamon
1 tsp. each nutmeg, cloves
1/2 c. chopped pecans

Cream shortening and brown sugar in mixer bowl until light and fluffy. Mix in eggs, cream and vanilla. Add dry ingredients and pecans; mix well. Roll out on floured surface. Cut out as desired. Place on greased cookie sheet. Bake at 350 degrees for 10 minutes or until lightly browned. Remove to wire rack to cool.
Yield: 72 servings.

Approx per serv: Cal 87; Prot 1.1 g; T Fat 3.9 g; Chl 7.0 mg; Car 12.1 g; Sod 32.9 mg; Pot 37.8 mg.

Scott Beaubien, Monroe

MELT-IN-YOUR-MOUTH SUGAR COOKIES

1 c. sugar
1 c. confectioners' sugar
1 c. butter, softened
1 c. oil
2 eggs
1 tsp. vanilla extract
1 tsp. each soda, salt
1 tsp. cream of tartar
4 1/2 c. flour

Combine first 4 ingredients in mixer bowl. Beat until smooth and well blended. Add eggs, vanilla, soda, salt and cream of tartar; mix well. Mix in flour. Drop by spoonfuls 2 to 3 inches apart on ungreased cookie sheet. Flatten with bottom of glass dipped in sugar. Bake at 350 degrees for 10 to 15 minutes or until lightly browned. Remove to wire rack to cool.
Yield: 72 servings.

Approx per serv: Cal 96; Prot 1.0 g; T Fat 5.8 g; Chl 14.9 mg; Car 10.1 g; Sod 76.9 mg; Pot 11.1 mg.

Shirley Stadler, Menominee

GRANDMOTHER'S WHITE COOKIES

1 c. shortening
2 1/2 c. sugar
1 c. sour cream
3 eggs
1 tsp. soda
6 c. flour
1 tsp. salt
1 tsp. nutmeg
1/2 c. (about) raisins
1/2 c. sugar

Cream shortening and 2 1/2 cups sugar in mixer bowl until light and fluffy. Add next 6 ingredients in order listed, mixing well after each addition. Roll out 1/4 inch thick on floured surface. Cut with round cookie cutter. Place on lightly greased cookie sheet. Place 1 raisin in center of each cookie. Sprinkle with 1/2 cup sugar. Bake at 350 degrees for 8 to 10 minutes or until lightly browned. Remove to wire rack to cool.
Yield: 96 servings.

NOTE: This recipe came from an old cookbook. The original called for chicken fat instead of shortening and gave no measurements for soda, salt or nutmeg.

Approx per serv: Cal 83; Prot 1.1 g; T Fat 3.1 g; Chl 9.0 mg; Car 12.9 g; Sod 34.4 mg; Pot 18.8 mg.

Theila Heinbokel, Montmorency

GRANDMA'S APPLE PIE

1 recipe 2-crust pie pastry
1/4 c. maple syrup
1/4 c. packed brown sugar
1/4 c. sugar
3 tbsp. flour
1/4 tsp. salt
1 tsp. cinnamon
1/4 tsp. nutmeg
1/8 tsp. ginger
7 c. thickly sliced peeled apples
1/4 c. coarsely chopped walnuts
2 tbsp. butter
2 tbsp. maple syrup

Line 10-inch pie plate with half the pastry. Combine next 8 ingredients in bowl; mix well. Stir in apples and walnuts. Pour into prepared pie plate. Dot with butter. Top with remaining pastry; seal edge and cut vents. Bake at 450 degrees for 40 minutes. Brush with 2 tablespoons maple syrup. Bake for 20 minutes longer. Yield: 8 servings.

NOTE: Use a combination of apples such as a tart variety with a sweet variety for an interesting flavor. Strips of aluminum foil around the edge of crust will prevent overbrowning. Nutritional information does not include pie pastry.

Approx per serv: Cal 211; Prot 1.1 g; T Fat 6.0 g; Chl 8.9 mg; Car 41.2 g; Sod 1065 mg; Pot 190.7 mg.

Paul Carey, Montmorency

BUTTERSCOTCH APPLE PIE

5 c. sliced peeled apples
1 6-oz. package butterscotch chips
1 unbaked 9-in. pie shell
Cinnamon to taste
1/4 c. sugar
1/4 c. light cream
1 tsp. salt
1 Oven Cooking Bag

Combine apples and butterscotch chips in bowl. Spoon into pie shell. Sprinkle with cinnamon. Combine sugar, cream and salt in bowl. Pour over apples. Place pie in Oven Cooking Bag. Bake at 375 degrees for 1 hour or until apples are tender and topping is brown. Remove pie from bag immediately. Yield: 6 servings.

Jodetta Aker, Eaton

NEVER-RUNNY BLUEBERRY PIES

1 c. shortening
3 c. flour
1/2 tsp. baking powder
9 c. fresh blueberries
1 1/2 c. sugar
1/3 c. flour

Combine shortening with 1/2 cup boiling water in bowl, stirring until shortening melts. Add mixture of sifted flour and baking powder; mix well. Divide into 4 portions. Press each into 9-inch pie plate. Prick sides and bottoms with fork. Bake at 350 degrees for 12 to 15 minutes or until lightly browned. Place 1/2 cup blueberries in each pie shell. Combine 6 cups blueberries, sugar and 1 cup water in saucepan. Bring to a boil, stirring to dissolve sugar. Cook

for 4 minutes. Stir in flour. Cook until thickened, stirring constantly; cool for several minutes. Pour into pie shells. Sprinkle remaining 1 cup blueberries over tops of pies. Chill for several hours. Serve with whipped cream or ice cream. Yield: 24 servings.

Approx per serv: Cal 150; Prot 2.2 g; T Fat 1.0 g; Chl 0.0 mg; Car 34.0 g; Sod 7.9 mg; Pot 61.0 mg.

Tanya Dostaler, Houghton

FREEZER BLUEBERRY PIE FILLING

1 1/3 c. sugar
1/3 c. quick-cooking tapioca
1/2 tsp. salt
8 c. blueberries
2 tbsp. lemon juice

Combine sugar, tapioca and salt in bowl. Add blueberries and lemon juice; toss to mix well. Spoon into two 4-quart freezer containers. Store in freezer for up to 6 months. Yield: 12 servings.

NOTE: Place 4 cups thawed berries in unbaked 9-inch pie shell. Bake at 425 degrees for 1 hour and 15 minutes.

Linda Schumacher, Huron

FRESH CHERRY PIE

1 to 1 1/2 c. sugar
1/3 c. flour
1/2 tsp. cinnamon
4 c. fresh pitted cherries
4 drops of almond flavoring
1 recipe 2-crust pie pastry
1 1/2 tsp. butter

Combine sugar, flour and cinnamon in bowl. Add cherries and almond flavoring, tossing to mix well. Spoon into pastry-lined 9-inch pie plate. Dot with butter. Top with remaining pastry; cut vents. Bake at 425 degrees for 35 to 45 minutes or until golden brown. Yield: 6 servings.

NOTE: This pie has won several first place awards at fairs.

Approx per serv: Cal 687; Prot 5.2 g; T Fat 25.0 g; Chl 3.0 mg; Car 78.1 g; Sod 382.0 mg; Pot 169.5 mg.

Marsha Snyder, Grand Traverse

FRENCH SILK PIE

1 1/3 c. graham cracker crumbs
1/3 c. melted butter
1 1/4 c. butter, softened
3/4 c. sugar
2 eggs, beaten
1 1/2 oz. semisweet chocolate, melted
1 tsp. vanilla extract

Mix cracker crumbs and melted butter in 9-inch pie plate. Press over bottom and side to form crust. Chill in refrigerator. Cream softened butter in mixer bowl. Add sugar gradually, beating until light and fluffy. Blend in remaining ingredients. Pour into prepared pie shell. Chill until serving time. Yield: 6 servings.

Approx per serv: Cal 678; Prot 4.7 g; T Fat 55.2 g; Chl 234.1 mg; Car 46.4 g; Sod 768.4 mg; Pot 148.5 mg.

Sylvia Fetter, Cass

POLKA DOT BLACK BOTTOM PIE

1 6-oz. package semisweet
*   chocolate chips*
1/2 c. milk
16 marshmallows
1 tsp. vanilla extract
1 1/2 c. whipping cream, whipped
1 baked 8-in. pie shell

Reserve 1 tablespoon chocolate chips. Combine remaining chocolate chips with milk and marshmallows in double boiler. Heat until melted, stirring to blend well. Stir in vanilla; cool. Fold 2/3 of the whipped cream gently into chocolate mixture. Spoon into pie shell. Spread remaining whipped cream over top. Press reserved chocolate chips pointed side down into whipped cream for a polka-dot effect. Yield: 6 servings.

Approx per serv: Cal 397; Prot 5.0 g; T Fat 20.9 g; Chl 3.0 mg; Car 52.4 g; Sod 253.7 mg; Pot 326.9 mg.

Alita Mae Jefferies, Huron

FRESH FRUIT PIE

1 1/2 c. flour
1/2 c. oil
2 tbsp. milk
1/8 tsp. salt
2 tsp. sugar
1 c. sugar
1 3-oz. package gelatin
3 1/2 tbsp. cornstarch
4 1/2 c. fresh fruit

Place flour in bowl; make well in center. Combine oil, milk, salt and 2 teaspoons sugar in well; mix with fork. Press over bottom and side of 9-inch pie plate. Bake at 350 degrees for 10 minutes; cool. Combine next 3 ingredients in saucepan. Blend in 1 1/2 cups water. Cook until thickened and clear, stirring constantly; cool completely. Stir in fruit. Spoon into prepared pie shell. Yield: 6 servings.

Gale Horn, Grand Traverse

FRESH PEACH CREAM PIE

6 peaches, peeled
1 unbaked 9-in. pie shell
1 c. sugar
2 tbsp. flour
1 c. coffee cream
Cinnamon to taste

Slice peaches 1 inch thick. Arrange in pie shell. Combine sugar, flour and cream in bowl; mix well. Pour over peaches. Sprinkle with cinnamon. Bake at 375 degrees for 45 minutes. Yield: 6 servings.

Approx per serv: Cal 410.6; Prot 3.9 g; T Fat 18.4 g; Chl 26.4 mg; Car 59.8 g; Sod 202.2 mg; Pot 269.3 mg.

Sandy Maynard, Shiawassee

PEAR PIE

1 recipe 2-crust pie pastry
7 med. Bartlett pears, peeled, sliced
1/3 c. flour
1/2 c. sugar
1/2 tsp. mace
2 tbsp. butter
1/2 tsp. cinnamon
2 tbsp. sugar

Line 9-inch pie plate with half the pastry. Arrange pears in pie shell. Sprinkle flour, 1/2 cup sugar and mace over pears; mix gently. Dot with butter. Top with remaining pastry; seal edge and cut vents. Sprinkle with cinnamon and 2 tablespoons sugar. Bake at 350 degrees for 45 to 60 minutes or until bubbly and lightly browned. Yield: 6 servings.

Approx per serv: Cal 556; Prot 5.8 g; T Fat 24.7 g; Chl 11.8 mg; Car 81.5 g; Sod 418.2 mg; Pot 286.4 mg.

Carol Holtrop, Huron

MARY'S RHUBARB CUSTARD PIE

1 recipe 2-crust pie pastry
1 egg white, lightly beaten
1 1/2 c. sugar
1/2 c. flour
1/4 tsp. nutmeg
1/8 tsp. salt
3 eggs
4 c. chopped rhubarb

Line 9 or 10-inch pie plate with half the pastry. Brush with egg white. Mix next 4 ingredients in bowl. Add eggs; beat until smooth. Stir in rhubarb. Pour into prepared pie shell. Cut remaining pastry into strips. Weave into lattice on top of pie; seal edges. Bake at 400 degrees for 50 minutes. Yield: 8 servings.

Approx per serv: Cal 440; Prot 6.8 g; T Fat 17.3 g; Chl 94.8 mg; Car 65.5 g; Sod 340.8 mg; Pot 214.0 mg.

Mary Rockwell, Ogemaw

KAREN'S STRAWBERRY PIE

4 c. fresh strawberries, sliced
1 baked 9-in. pie shell
3/4 c. sugar
2 tbsp. cornstarch
1 3-oz. package strawberry gelatin
1 8-oz. carton whipped topping

Place strawberries in pie shell. Combine sugar, cornstarch and 1 1/2 cups water in saucepan. Cook until thick and clear, stirring constantly. Add gelatin; stir until dissolved. Pour over strawberries. Chill until firm. Top with whipped topping. Yield: 6 servings.

Approx per serv: Cal 464; Prot 4.4 g; T Fat 19.9 g; Chl 0.0 mg; Car 69.8 g; Sod 238.9 mg; Pot 214.9 mg.

Karen Bodell, Ingham

STRAWBERRY CREAM PIE

2 c. milk, scalded
2/3 c. sugar
1/2 c. flour
1/2 tsp. salt
2 eggs, separated
2 tbsp. butter

1 tsp. vanilla extract
1 qt. fresh strawberries, sliced
1 baked pie shell
1 c. confectioners' sugar

Blend milk gradually into mixture of sugar, flour and salt in saucepan. Cook over low heat until mixture thickens, stirring constantly. Beat egg yolks in bowl. Stir a small amount of hot mixture into egg yolks; stir egg yolks into hot mixture. Cook for 1 minute longer. Stir in butter and vanilla; cool. Reserve 1 cup strawberries. Place remaining strawberries in pie shell. Spread cooled custard over top. Combine reserved berries, confectioners' sugar and egg whites in bowl. Beat until stiff. Spread over top of pie. Store in refrigerator. Yield: 8 servings.

Approx per serv: Cal 376; Prot 6.5 g; T Fat 14.4 g; Chl 80.6 mg; Car 56.8 g; Sod 352.8 mg; Pot 246.7 mg.

Judith See, Monroe

ZUCCHINI PIE

4 c. flour
2 c. sugar
1/2 tsp. salt
3 sticks margarine
6 to 8 c. sliced, seeded, peeled zucchini
2/3 c. lemon juice
1 c. sugar
1/4 tsp. nutmeg
1 tsp. cinnamon
1/2 tsp. cinnamon

Combine first 3 ingredients in bowl. Cut in margarine until crumbly. Press half the mixture over bottom of greased 9 x 13-inch baking pan. Bake at 375 degrees for 10 minutes. Cook zucchini in lemon juice in saucepan until tender. Add 1 cup sugar, nutmeg and 1 teaspoon cinnamon. Simmer for 1 minute. Stir in 1/2 cup crumb mixture. Simmer until mixture thickens, stirring constantly; cool. Pour over crust. Mix 1/2 teaspoon cinnamon with remaining crumb mixture in bowl. Sprinkle over pie. Bake at 375 degrees for 35 to 45 minutes or until lightly browned. Yield: 10 servings.

NOTE: This dessert tastes like apple crisp and will fool your family.

Approx per serv: Cal 680; Prot 6.8 g; T Fat 28.2 g; Chl 0.0 mg; Car 102.9 g; Sod 445.8 mg; Pot 290.1 mg.

Doris Burns, Washtenaw
Pam Pistor, Lenawee

BROWN SUGAR TARTS

2 1/2 c. flour
1 tbsp. sugar
1 tsp. salt
1 c. shortening
1 egg yolk, beaten
1/2 c. milk
1 stick butter, melted
2 c. packed brown sugar
2 eggs
1 tsp. vanilla extract

Combine flour, sugar and salt in bowl. Cut in shortening until crumbly. Stir in mixture of egg yolk and milk with fork. Roll out 1/4 inch thick on floured surface. Cut out; fit into muffin cups. Combine remaining ingredients in bowl; mix well. Fill pastry cups 1/2 full. Bake at 350 degrees for 20 minutes. Yield: 24 servings.

Approx per serv: Cal 247; Prot 2.2 g; T Fat 14.2 g; Chl 44.1 mg; Car 28.4 g; Sod 149.3 mg; Pot 90.0 mg.

Kathy Berden, Sanilac

BUTTER TARTS

1 recipe 1-crust pie pastry
1/2 c. butter, softened
1 c. sugar
3 egg yolks, beaten
1 egg white, stiffly beaten
1 c. raisins
1 c. chopped walnuts
1/2 tsp. vanilla extract

Line muffin tins with pastry. Cream butter and sugar in mixer bowl until light and fluffy. Add egg yolks; mix well. Fold in egg white, raisins, walnuts and vanilla. Pour into prepared muffin tins. Bake at 400 degrees for 15 minutes or until crust is lightly browned and filling is set. Yield: 8 servings.

Approx per serv: Cal 485; Prot 5.6 g; T Fat 30.6 g; Chl 129.8 mg; Car 51.3 g; Sod 292.7 mg; Pot 232.9 mg.

Gregory E. Givens, Oakland

FUDGE SWEET TARTS

1 c. flour
3/4 tsp. baking powder
1/4 tsp. salt
1/3 c. butter
1 egg, beaten
1 c. chocolate chips
1/3 c. sugar
1 tbsp. milk
1 tbsp. butter
1 tsp. vanilla extract
36 pecan halves

Combine flour, baking powder and salt in bowl. Cut in 1/3 cup butter until crumbly. Sprinkle with enough egg to form dough with fork. Roll out 1/16 inch thick on floured surface. Cut out into 3-inch circles; fit into small muffin cups. Melt chocolate chips in double boiler. Stir in remaining ingredients except pecan halves. Blend in any remaining egg. Spoon into prepared muffin cups. Place 1 pecan half on each. Bake at 350 degrees for 20 to 25 minutes or until crust is brown and filling is set.
Yield: 36 servings.

Approx per serv: Cal 74.1; Prot 0.9 g; T Fat 4.9 g; Chl 13.3 mg; Car 7.4 g; Sod 48.4 mg; Pot 30.2 mg.

Sue Lomasney, Macomb

MINIATURE SHOOFLY PIES

2 sticks margarine, softened
2 3-oz. packages cream cheese, softened
2 c. flour
2 eggs
1 1/2 c. packed brown sugar
2 tbsp. melted butter
1/4 tsp. vanilla extract
1 c. sugar
1 1/2 c. flour
1 stick margarine

Combine 2 sticks margarine, cream cheese and 2 cups flour in bowl; mix well to form dough. Shape into 16 balls. Press into muffin cups. Combine eggs, brown sugar, melted butter and vanilla in bowl; mix well. Spoon into prepared muffin cups. Combine sugar and 1 1/2 cups flour in bowl. Cut in 1 stick margarine until crumbly. Sprinkle over tart filling. Bake at 400 degrees for 20 minutes. Yield: 16 servings.

Approx per serv: Cal 440; Prot 4.7 g; T Fat 23.7 g; Chl 65.6 mg; Car 53.5 g; Sod 268.8 mg; Pot 118.6 mg.

Kathy Snyder, Grand Traverse

Microwave

See MICROWAVE TIPS
on page 148.

TACO POCKETS

1/2 lb. ground beef
1 lg. tomato, chopped
1/4 c. sliced green onions
1 tsp. garlic powder
1/4 tsp. salt
2 6-in. pita rounds
1 c. shredded lettuce
1/4 c. shredded Cheddar cheese

Place ground beef in hard plastic colander. Place over 4-cup glass measuring cup. Microwave on High for 2 minutes. Break ground beef apart with fork. Microwave for 1 to 2 minutes longer or until no longer pink. Stir with fork. Discard drippings. Place cooked ground beef in 4-cup glass measure. Add tomato, green onions, seasonings and 2 tablespoons water; mix well. Microwave on High for 5 to 6 minutes or until hot and bubbly, stirring once. Serve in pita-bread halves. Top with lettuce and cheese.
Yield: 4 servings.
NOTE: Nutritional information does not include pita-bread.

Approx per serv: Cal 47; Prot 2.7 g; T Fat 3.1 g; Chl 42.1 mg; Car 2.5 g; Sod 186.4 mg; Pot 121.0 mg.

 Deanna House, Kalamazoo

HOT BEEF DIP

1 2 1/2-oz. jar dried beef
1/2 c. Parmesan cheese
1/4 c. chopped green onions
1/4 c. sour cream
1/4 c. mayonnaise
1 8-oz. package cream cheese, softened
1 tbsp. parsley flakes

Cut dried beef into small pieces with kitchen shears. Combine with 1 cup cold water in 4-cup glass measure. Microwave for 4 minutes; drain well. Add remaining ingredients; mix well. Microwave for 4 to 5 minutes or until heated through, stirring once. Pour into serving dish. Serve with crackers, bread cubes or fresh vegetable sticks. Yield: 32 one-tablespoon servings.

Approx per serv: Cal 102; Prot 9.8 g; T Fat 6.5 g; Chl 27.5 mg; Car 0.8 g; Sod 1092.8 mg; Pot 81.2 mg.

Suzanne Threadgould, Ingham

WALNUT-CHEESE SPREAD

1 8-oz. package cream cheese
2 tbsp. milk
1/2 c. sour cream
1/2 c. chopped walnuts
2 tbsp. green pepper
2 tbsp. onion flakes
1/8 tsp. pepper
1 3-oz. package chipped ham
1/8 tsp. garlic salt

Microwave cream cheese in glass bowl on High for 45 to 60 seconds or until softened. Add remaining ingredients; mix well. Microwave, uncovered, on High for 3 1/2 to 4 1/2 minutes or until heated through, stirring once. Pour into serving dish. Serve hot or cold with crackers.
Yield: 48 one-tablespoon servings.

Approx per serv: Cal 36; Prot 1.0 g; T Fat 3.4 g; Chl 8.0 mg; Car 0.4 g; Sod 40.9 mg; Pot 18.0 mg.

Barbara Esquivel, Allegan

HEARTY BEEF SOUP

1 lb. lean ground beef, crumbled
1 8-oz. can tomato sauce
2 med. tomatoes, chopped
1 env. dry brown gravy mix
1 stalk celery, chopped
1/2 green pepper, coarsely chopped
1 tbsp. Worcestershire sauce
2 tsp. salt
Pepper to taste
1 c. uncooked macaroni

Microwave ground beef in large glass bowl on Medium-High for 6 minutes or until no longer pink, stirring once. Add tomato sauce, tomatoes, gravy mix and 5 cups water; mix well. Stir in vegetables and seasonings. Microwave, covered, on Medium-High for 20 minutes. Stir in macaroni. Microwave for 10 minutes longer or until macaroni is tender and soup is flavorful. Ladle into soup bowls. Garnish with shredded Cheddar cheese. Yield: 4 servings.

Nancy Juhl, Delta

GARDEN CASSEROLE

6 sm. unpeeled zucchini, sliced
2 tomatoes, peeled, chopped
1/2 c. chopped celery
1 sm. onion, sliced

1/2 tsp. oregano
3/4 c. chopped mozzarella cheese

Layer zucchini, tomatoes, celery and onion in glass casserole. Add oregano and salt and pepper to taste. Microwave, covered, on High until vegetables are tender-crisp. Add cheese. Microwave until cheese melts. Yield: 4 servings.

Approx per serv: Cal 124; Prot 8.0 g; T Fat 5.5 g; Chl 18.7 mg; Car 12.9 g; Sod 111.9 mg; Pot 644.0 mg.

Sally Sweeney, Huron

POTATOES BYRON

6 potatoes, baked
1/4 c. melted butter
1/2 tsp. salt
Dash of pepper
1/2 c. cream
1 can cream of mushroom soup
3/4 c. grated Cheddar cheese

Chop baked potatoes; place in 1 1/2-quart glass casserole. Add butter, seasonings, cream and soup; mix well. Microwave on High for 5 minutes. Top with cheese. Microwave for 1 to 2 minutes or until cheese melts. Yield: 6 servings.

Approx per serv: Cal 333; Prot 8.9 g; T Fat 16.3 g; Chl 41.6 mg; Car 39.6 g; Sod 788.4 mg; Pot 900.0 mg.

Barbara Esquivel, Allegan

VEGETABLE MEDLEY

1 20-oz. package frozen mixed vegetables
1 tsp. salt
1/4 tsp. minced garlic
2 tbsp. butter
1/3 c. flour
1/4 c. butter, melted
1 lg. can evaporated milk
1/3 c. milk
Nutmeg to taste
Thyme to taste
1/2 c. Parmesan cheese
2 tbsp. white wine (opt.)
2 c. toasted bread crumbs
3 tbsp. melted butter

Prepare mixed vegetables according to package directions; drain. Season with salt, garlic and 2 tablespoons butter. Pour into 3-quart glass casserole. Blend flour and 1/4 cup melted butter in

saucepan. Stir in mixture of evaporated milk and milk gradually. Cook until thickened, stirring constantly. Add nutmeg, thyme, cheese and wine; mix well. Pour over vegetables. Top with crumbs; drizzle with 3 tablespoons melted butter. Microwave on High for 20 minutes. Yield: 8 servings.

NOTE: Add 1 pound cooked ground beef for main dish casserole.

Approx per serv: Cal 304; Prot 9.8 g; T Fat 24.2 g; Chl 74.7 mg; Car 21.7 g; Sod 678.3 mg; Pot 298.4 mg.

Eileen Lienhart, Jackson

RED DOG SANDWICH

4 wieners, chopped
1/4 c. cubed sharp Cheddar cheese
6 stuffed olives, chopped
1 hard-boiled egg, chopped
1 tbsp. minced onion
1 tbsp. chili sauce
1 tbsp. (heaping) mayonnaise
6 hot dog buns, split

Combine first 7 ingredients in bowl; mix well. Spoon into buns; place on plates or paper towels. Microwave 1 sandwich on High for 45 seconds, 2 sandwiches for 1 minute and 15 seconds or 4 sandwiches for 2 minutes and 15 seconds. Yield: 6 servings.

Approx per serv: Cal 518; Prot 21.0 g; T Fat 33.2 g; Chl 117.7 mg; Car 32.3 g; Sod 1607.5 mg; Pot 317.6 mg.

Barbara Esquivel, Allegan

BEANS AND BEEF

1 lb. ground beef, crumbled
2 16-oz. cans pork and beans
1/2 tsp. garlic salt
4 slices process cheese

Microwave ground beef in 2-quart glass casserole on High until no longer pink, stirring once; drain. Add pork and beans and garlic salt; mix well. Microwave, covered, on High for 2 minutes. Top with cheese. Microwave, covered, on High for 1 minute longer. Yield: 6 servings.

Approx per serv: Cal 424; Prot 27.3 g; T Fat 20.0 g; Chl 71.5 mg; Car 33.6 g; Sod 1298.6 mg; Pot 547.5 mg.

Steve Thelen, Eaton

REUBEN CASSEROLE

1   16-oz. can sauerkraut,
    drained
1   12-oz. can corned beef,
    chopped
2 c. shredded Swiss cheese
1/4 c. Thousand Island
    dressing
1/2 c. salad dressing
2 med. tomatoes, sliced
3 tbsp. butter
2 slices rye bread, crumbled

Layer sauerkraut, corned beef and cheese in 1 1/2-quart casserole. Spread mixture of Thousand Island and salad dressing over cheese. Top with tomatoes. Microwave butter in small glass bowl on Medium-High for 1 minute or until melted. Stir in crumbs. Sprinkle over tomatoes. Microwave on Medium-High for 12 to 14 minutes or until heated through. Let stand for 5 minutes. Yield: 6 servings.

Approx per serv: Cal 508; Prot 28.3 g; T Fat 37.9 g; Chl 128.9 mg; Car 14.6 g; Sod 1744.6 mg; Pot 313.5 mg.

Marilyn VanDeVenne, Ionia

4-H is the youth component of the Cooperative Extension Service which disseminates knowledge from Michigan State University and the U.S. Department of Agriculture.

BEEF POT ROAST

1   3-lb. beef chuck roast,
    completely frozen
1 env. dry onion soup mix
4 sm. potatoes, peeled, quartered
2 c. 2-inch carrot sticks
1 c. chopped onion
1 clove of garlic, chopped

Place frozen roast in 4-quart glass casserole. Microwave, tightly covered, on Low for 30 minutes. Turn roast over. Sprinkle with half the soup mix. Microwave, tightly covered, on Low for 30 minutes. Turn roast over; sprinkle with remaining soup mix. Arrange vegetables around roast. Microwave, tightly covered, on Low for 20 to 30 minutes or until roast and vegetables are tender. Let stand for 10 minutes. Yield: 4 servings.

NOTE: May substitute 1 envelope brown gravy mix for soup mix or use Italian herbs to taste for a low salt pot roast.

Approx per serv: Cal 979; Prot 72.7 g; T Fat 54.2 g; Chl 247.2 mg; Car 47.1 g; Sod 904.5 mg; Pot 2130.0 mg.

Delenor Bell, Bay

CHICKEN AND DUMPLINGS

1   2 1/2 to 3 1/2-lb. chicken, cut up
1/2 c. chopped onion
1/2 c. chopped celery
4 med. carrots, sliced
2 tsp. salt
1/2 tsp. pepper
1/4 c. cornstarch
2 c. buttermilk baking mix
2/3 c. milk

Arrange chicken in 3-quart glass casserole. Add 2 cups hot water, vegetables, salt and pepper.

Microwave, covered, on Medium-High for 15 minutes. Blend cornstarch with 1/2 cup cold water. Stir into casserole. Microwave, covered, on Medium-High for 10 to 20 minutes or until chicken is tender. Combine baking mix and milk in bowl; mix well. Spoon around edge of casserole. Microwave, covered, for 5 to 6 minutes or until dumplings are puffed and cooked through. Yield: 4 servings.

Genny Wrubel, Otsego

APRICOT CHICKEN

5 chicken breasts
1 tbsp. (heaping) mayonnaise
1/2 env. dry onion soup mix
1/4 c. Russian salad dressing
1/2 c. apricot preserves

Arrange chicken breasts in 7 x 11-inch glass baking dish, placing meatiest portions toward outer edge. Combine remaining ingredients in small bowl; mix well. Spread over chicken, covering completely. Microwave, covered with waxed paper, on High for 7 minutes per pound, turning dish once. Yield: 5 servings.

Approx per serv: Cal 313; Prot 23.6 g; T Fat 12.7 g; Chl 70.1 mg; Car 26.0 g; Sod 449.6 mg; Pot 286.2 mg.

Barbara Esquivel, Allegan

CHICKEN-BROCCOLI SUPREME

6 8-oz. chicken breasts
1 egg, beaten
1/2 c. dry bread crumbs
1/2 c. Parmesan cheese
1/2 tsp. paprika
1/2 c. dry Sherry
2 10-oz. packages frozen broccoli spears
2 tbsp. butter
2 tbsp. flour
1/4 tsp. salt
1/2 c. milk
1/2 c. shredded Cheddar cheese

Bone and skin chicken breasts. Dip each in beaten egg; coat with mixture of crumbs, Parmesan cheese and paprika. Fold ends under to form rolls; place in 6 x 10-inch glass baking dish. Pour Sherry around rolls. Sprinkle with any remaining crumb mixture. Microwave, covered with waxed paper, on High for 16 to 18 minutes or until tender, turning dish once. Pour off and reserve pan juices. Microwave broccoli in packages on High for 10 to 12 minutes or until just tender, turning packages over once. Microwave butter in 2-cup glass measure on High for 45 seconds or until melted. Blend in flour and salt. Stir in milk and reserved pan juices gradually. Microwave on High for 1 1/2 to 2 1/2 minutes or until thickened, stirring twice. Stir in Cheddar cheese until melted. Arrange chicken breasts and broccoli on large microwave-proof serving plate. Pour cheese sauce over top. Microwave, uncovered, on High for 2 to 3 minutes or to serving temperature. Yield: 6 servings.

NOTE: Chicken without broccoli and cheese sauce is delicious cold.

Approx per serv: Cal 556; Prot 48.8 g; T Fat 17.1 g; Chl 165.6 mg; Car 21.8 g; Sod 434.7 mg; Pot 810.4 mg.

Jean Chilcote, Benzie

SWEET AND SOUR PORK

1 8-oz. can pineapple chunks
1 1/2 lb. pork, cut into 1-in. cubes
1 tbsp. instant minced onion
1 tbsp. soy sauce
1 tsp. Kitchen Bouquet
3 tbsp. cornstarch
1/4 c. packed brown sugar
1/4 c. cider vinegar
1 5-oz. can sliced water
   chestnuts, drained
1 med. green pepper, cut into
   1/2-in. strips
1 med. tomato, coarsely chopped

Drain pineapple, reserving juice. Combine juice with next 4 ingredients in 2-quart glass casserole; mix well. Microwave, covered, on Medium for 30 minutes, stirring once. Blend cornstarch, brown sugar, vinegar and 1 cup water in small bowl. Add to casserole with pineapple and water chestnuts; mix well. Microwave, covered, on Medium-High for 8 minutes. Add green pepper; mix well. Microwave for 7 to 12 minutes longer or until sauce is clear and thickened. Fold in tomato. Let stand, covered, for 10 minutes. Serve over rice or crisp noodles. Yield: 6 servings.

Approx per serv: Cal 466; Prot 21.0 g; T Fat 28.5 g; Chl 70.3 mg; Car 31.4 g; Sod 297.4 mg; Pot 543.7 mg;

Robert Lang, Jr., Isabella

FISH FILLETS WITH MUSHROOMS

1 lb. fish fillets
2 tbsp. butter
1/2 tsp. lemon juice
2 green onions, sliced
1/2 c. sliced mushrooms
1 tomato, peeled, chopped
1/2 tsp. salt

Arrange fillets in 7 x 12-inch glass baking dish, placing thickest portion around outer edge. Dot with butter; sprinkle with mixture of lemon juice and 2 tablespoons water. Top with remaining ingredients. Microwave, covered with waxed paper, on High for 5 minutes. Let stand for 5 minutes. Yield: 3 servings.

Approx per serv: Cal 323; Prot 29.6 g; T Fat 20.2 g; Chl 106.8 mg; Car 4.6 g; Sod 531.3 mg; Pot 648.7 mg.

Joyce M. Freeman, Eaton

MUNCHING PEANUT BRITTLE

1 c. sugar
1/2 c. light corn syrup
1 c. roasted salted peanuts
1 tsp. butter
1 tsp. vanilla extract
1 tsp. soda

Microwave sugar and corn syrup in 1 1/2-quart glass casserole on High for 4 minutes. Stir in peanuts. Microwave for 3 to 5 minutes or until brown. Add butter and vanilla; mix well. Microwave for 1 to 2 minutes longer or until peanuts are lightly browned. Add soda; mix until light. Pour onto lightly greased baking sheet. Cool for 30 to 60 minutes. Break into small pieces. Store in airtight container. Yield: 60 servings.

NOTE: May substitute raw peanuts by combining with sugar and syrup before microwaving and adding 1/8 teaspoon salt.

Approx per serv: Cal 35; Prot 0.6 g; T Fat 1.3 g; Chl 0.2 mg; Car 5.8 g; Sod 26.4 mg; Pot 16.4 mg.

Jamie Lang, Isabella

CHERRY COBBLER

4 c. cherries
1 c. sugar
1/4 tsp. almond flavoring
1 c. flour
2/3 c. sugar
1 1/4 tsp. baking powder
1/4 c. oil
1 egg

Microwave cherries in glass casserole on High until boiling. Stir in 1 cup sugar and flavoring. Combine flour, 2/3 cup sugar, baking powder, oil and egg in bowl; mix until crumbly. Sprinkle over hot cherries. Microwave on High for 10 to 15 minutes. Yield: 8 servings.

NOTE: May substitute peaches, adding nutmeg to taste; raspberries, adding a small amount of butter; apples prepared as for pie filling, omitting thickener or rhubarb prepared as for pie filling, omitting thickener. This is a quick dessert — just cobble it up.

Approx per serv: Cal 334; Prot 3.4 g; T Fat 7.9 g; Chl 31.6 mg; Car 64.7 g; Sod 61.3 mg; Pot 172.9 mg.

Jane White, Antrim

The H's in 4-H stand for Head, Heart, Hands, and Health.

NUTRITION BALLS

1 stick margarine, melted
3/4 c. packed brown sugar
1 1/2 c. oats
1 c. coconut
1 c. chopped walnuts
1/2 c. wheat germ
1/3 c. sesame seed
1/2 c. raisins
1/2 c. sunflower seed
1/3 c. honey
1 tsp. cinnamon

Combine all ingredients in large glass casserole; mix well. Microwave on High for 6 minutes, stirring every 2 minutes. Shape into small balls with buttered hands; place on waxed paper. Let stand until cool. Yield: 50 servings.

Approx per serv: Cal 90; Prot 1.6 g; T Fat 5.4 g; Chl 0.0 mg; Car 9.7 g; Sod 28.6 mg; Pot 78.3 mg.

Patrick Esper, Livingston

Holiday Specialties & Food Gifts

HOLIDAY APPLE SALAD

2 c. sugar
1 c. cinnamon candies
Several drops of red food coloring (opt.)
8 med. Jonathan apples, peeled, cored
1 8-oz. package cream cheese, softened
1/2 c. finely chopped pecans

Combine sugar, candies, food coloring and 1 cup water in saucepan. Cook until sugar and candies are dissolved. Place apples in saucepan. Pour syrup over apples. Cook over low heat until tender, basting frequently with syrup. Cool. Place each apple on lettuce-lined salad plate. Fill centers with mixture of cream cheese and pecans. Yield: 8 servings.

NOTE: Serve on spotless linen with carefully arranged silver and topped with a generous serving of "Peace on Earth, good will to all." Submitted in memory of Ethelmary Ebers.

Approx per serv: Cal 581; Prot 3.4 g; T Fat 17.5 g; Chl 31.5 mg; Car 109.7 g; Sod 82.6 mg; Pot 300.8 mg.

 Nellie Jost, Kent

4-H CLOVER JELLY

1 qt. clover blossoms
3 drops of red food coloring
2 tbsp. lemon juice
1 pkg. Sure-Jel
3 to 4 c. sugar

Rinse clover blossoms. Trim off stems and leaves. Simmer blossoms in water to cover in saucepan for 5 minutes; remove from heat. Steep for 15 minutes. Strain liquid through cheesecloth into bowl. Add food coloring and lemon juice. Stir in Sure-Jel. Add 1 cup sugar for each cup liquid. Pour into saucepan. Bring to a boil. Boil for 1 minute; skim. Pour into hot sterilized jelly jars. Seal with 2-piece lids. Process in boiling water bath for 5 minutes.

NOTE: Gather red or white clover blossoms on a sunny summer day. Look carefully — you might find a lucky 4-H clover.

CHRISTMAS PARTY TREE

3 heads curly lettuce
2 1-pt. boxes cherry tomatoes
2 to 4 bunches celery hearts, cut into
*   1-in. pieces*

2 green peppers, cut into 1/2-in. strips
2 red sweet peppers, cut into
*   1/2-in. strips*
1 bunch green onions, cut into pieces
1 lb. small mushrooms
1 bunch baby carrots, peeled
1 1-lb. package radishes
2 cucumbers, scored, sliced 1/2-in. thick
1 head cauliflower, broken into flowerets
1 bunch broccoli, cut into flowerets
1 6-oz. can ripe olives
1 6-oz. jar green olives
1 lb. cooked ham, cubed (opt.)
1 lb. cheese, cubed (opt.)

Cover 36-inch styrofoam cone with green foil. Cover with curly lettuce, securing with toothpicks and rubber bands. Arrange vegetables, olives, ham and cheese as desired in colorful juxtaposition on cone, securing with toothpicks. Place on large serving platter. Serve with assorted dips.

NOTE: This makes a great and tasty centerpiece instead of flowers.

Chris Dernay, Oakland

CHARLES SILM'S FRUITCAKE

1 18-oz. jar prepared mincemeat
1 c. chopped walnuts

6 oz. mixed candied fruit
1 can sweetened condensed milk
1 egg, beaten
3/4 c. flour
3/4 tsp. soda
1 c. grape wine

Combine first 5 ingredients in bowl; mix well. Add mixture of flour and soda; mix well. Spoon into greased loaf pans lined with greased waxed paper. Bake at 350 degrees for 1 1/2 hours or until golden brown on top. Cool in pans. Remove from pans. Wrap in cheesecloth soaked in wine. Place in plastic bag; seal. Store in cool place for 1 to 2 weeks.
Yield: 30 servings.

Charles Silm, Clinton

PETITS FOURS

1/4 c. butter, softened
1/4 c. shortening
1 c. sugar
1/2 tsp. vanilla extract
1/4 tsp. almond extract
2 c. sifted cake flour
1 tbsp. baking powder
1/4 tsp. salt
3/4 c. milk
6 egg whites
1/4 c. sugar
Cooked Petis Fours Icing

Cream butter and shortening in bowl until light and fluffy. Add 1 cup sugar gradually, beating until fluffy. Stir in flavorings. Sift flour, baking powder and salt together. Add to creamed mixture alternately with milk, beating well after each addition. Beat egg whites until foamy. Add 1/4 cup sugar gradually, beating until soft peaks form. Fold into batter. Spread in greased and lightly floured 9 x 13-inch cake pan. Bake at 350 degrees for 35 minutes or until cake tests done. Cool. Cut into desired shapes. Spoon Cooked Petits Fours Icing over cakes. Let stand until icing is firm. Decorate as desired. Yield: 35 servings.

COOKED PETITS FOURS ICING

3 c. sugar
1/4 tsp. cream of tartar
1 tsp. vanilla extract
2 1/2 c. confectioners' sugar
Food coloring

Bring sugar, cream of tartar and 1 1/2 cups hot water to a boil in covered saucepan; uncover. Cook to 226 degrees on candy thermometer. Cool to 110 degrees. Beat in remaining ingredients, tinting as desired.

Approx per serv: Cal 181; Prot 1.2 g; T Fat 3.5 g; Chl 4.8 mg; Car 37.4 g; Sod 72.2 mg; Pot 23.1 mg.

Julie McCarty, Monroe

WALDORF ASTORIA RED VELVET CAKE

1/2 c. shortening
1 1/2 c. sugar
2 eggs
2 1-oz. bottles of red food coloring
2 tbsp. cocoa
2 1/2 c. sifted cake flour
1 tsp. salt
1 c. buttermilk
1 tbsp. vanilla extract
1 tsp. soda
1 tsp. vinegar
Red Velvet Cake Icing

Cream shortening, sugar and eggs in bowl until light and fluffy. Blend in mixture of food coloring and cocoa. Sift flour and salt together. Add to creamed mixture alternately with buttermilk, beating well after each addition. Blend in vanilla and mixture of soda and vinegar. Pour into 2 greased and floured 9-inch cake pans. Bake at 350 degrees for 25 minutes or until cake tests done. Turn onto wire rack to cool. Split layers if desired. Spread Red Velvet Cake Icing between layers and over top and side of cake. Yield: 16 servings.

RED VELVET CAKE ICING

5 tbsp. flour
1 c. milk
1 c. butter
1 c. sugar
1 tsp. vanilla extract

Blend flour and milk in saucepan. Cook over low heat until smooth and thickened. Cool. Cream butter, sugar and vanilla in bowl until light and fluffy. Add cooked mixture gradually, beating until of whipped cream consistency.
NOTE: Double Icing recipe if layers are split.

Approx per serv: Cal 375; Prot 3.5 g; T Fat 20.0 g; Chl 69.5 mg; Car 46.9 g; Sod 360.6 mg; Pot 82.8 mg.

Cindy Smalley, Ingham

ALICE'S COFFEE CAKES

1 pkg. yeast
1/4 c. sugar
1 c. lukewarm milk
1 tsp. salt
1 tbsp. vanilla extract
1/4 tsp. nutmeg
3 eggs, beaten
1 c. margarine
4 c. flour
1/2 c. (about) butter, softened
1 can cherry pie filling

Dissolve yeast and sugar in milk in bowl. Stir in salt, vanilla, nutmeg and eggs. Let stand until bubbly. Cut 1 cup margarine into flour in large bowl. Add yeast mixture; mix well. Refrigerate for 3 hours to overnight. Divide into 3 portions. Roll each into rectangle on lightly floured surface. Spread with softened butter. Top with pie filling. Roll as for jelly roll. Shape into circle on lightly greased baking sheet. Cut 1/4-inch deep slashes around top; pull or twist gently to open slashes. Bake at 350 degrees for 30 to 35 minutes. Glaze as desired. Garnish with almonds. Yield: 24 servings.

Approx per serv: Cal 176; Prot 3.6 g; T Fat 13.1 g; Chl 43.3 mg; Car 25.4 g; Sod 242.3 mg; Pot 53.1 mg.

Alice M. Edwards, Eaton

GRANDMOTHER'S HOT CROSS BUNS

1 c. milk, scalded
2 pkg. dry yeast
1 egg, beaten
1/4 c. shortening
1/4 c. sugar
1 tsp. salt
1/2 tsp. cinnamon
1/2 tsp. nutmeg
4 1/2 c. flour
1 c. raisins

Pour scalded milk and 1 cup water into large bowl. Cool to lukewarm. Add yeast, egg, shortening, sugar, salt and spices; mix well. Add 2 cups flour; beat well. Let rise in warm place for 1 hour. Mix in remaining flour gradually. Add raisins. Knead on floured surface until smooth and elastic. Let rise for 1 hour or until doubled in bulk. Roll on floured surface; cut with biscuit cutter. Place on greased baking sheet. Let rise until doubled in bulk. Bake at 400 degrees for 20 to 25 minutes or until golden brown. Garnish each bun with cross of confectioners' sugar frosting. Yield: 26 servings.

NOTE; Made during lent and especially on Ash Wednesday and Good Friday.

Approx per serv: Cal 134; Prot 3.2 g; T Fat 2.9 g; Chl 11.0 mg; Car 24.0 g; Sod 91.5 mg; Pot 95.8 mg.

Mary Ann Mehne, Muskegon

CHRISTMAS STOLLEN

2 pkg. dry yeast
1 tsp. sugar
1/4 c. lukewarm milk
1/2 c. butter
3/4 c. milk
2 eggs
1 tsp. salt
1/2 c. sugar
4 c. flour
1 1/2 slices candied pineapple, chopped
1/3 lb. candied red cherries, chopped

Dissolve yeast and 1 teaspoon sugar in lukewarm milk. Heat butter and 3/4 cup milk in saucepan until butter melts. Cool slightly. Beat eggs with salt and 1/2 cup sugar in large bowl. Stir in yeast mixture. Add flour and milk mixture alternately, mixing well after each addition. Add candied fruit; mix well. Let rise, covered, until doubled in bulk. Divide into 9 portions. Roll each into 10-inch rope on floured surface. Braid 3 ropes at a time, sealing ends. Place on greased baking sheets. Let rise until doubled in bulk. Bake at 350 degrees until golden brown. Cool. Decorate with confectioners' sugar glaze, additional candied cherries and pecan halves. Yield: 12 servings.

Approx per serv: Cal 648; Prot 63.1 g; T Fat 22.5 g; Chl 252.0 mg; Car 44.4 g; Sod 466.4 mg; Pot 785.6 mg.

Dianne M. Bieneman, Kent

TOFFEE BUTTER CRUNCH

1 c. butter, melted
1 1/3 c. sugar
1 tbsp. light corn syrup
1 c. coarsely chopped toasted almonds
18 oz. milk chocolate, melted
1 c. finely chopped toasted almonds

Blend first 3 ingredients and 3 tablespoons water in saucepan. Cook over medium heat to hard-crack stage or 300 degrees on candy thermometer, stirring occasionally. Stir in coarsely chopped almonds. Pour into well-greased 9 x 13-inch pan. Cool completely. Spread with half the melted chocolate; sprinkle with half the finely chopped almonds. Invert on waxed paper. Spread with remaining chocolate; sprinkle with remaining almonds. Chill until firm. Break into pieces. Yield: 48 servings.

Approx per serv: Cal 140; Prot 1.7 g; T Fat 9.9 g; Chl 14.0 mg; Car 12.8 g; sod 57.2 mg; Pot 79.1 mg.

Rosalind Lehman, Midland

FRENCH FUDGE

3 c. semisweet chocolate chips
1 c. sweetened condensed milk
1 1/2 tsp. vanilla extract
1/8 tsp. salt
1/2 c. chopped pecans

Melt chocolate chips in double boiler over hot water, stirring occasionally. Add remaining ingredients. Mix just until smooth. Pour into waxed paper-lined 8-inch square pan; smooth surface. Chill for 2 hours. Turn onto cutting board; remove waxed paper. Cut into squares. Yield: 36 servings.

Approx per serv: Cal 110; Prot 1.4 g; T Fat 7.0 g; Chl 2.9 mg; Car 12.9 g; Sod 16.8 mg; Pot 82.6 mg.

Mary Harvell, Monroe

MICHIGAN POTATO NEVER-FAIL FUDGE

3 oz. unsweetened chocolate
3 tbsp. butter
1/3 c. cooled mashed potatoes
1/4 tsp. vanilla extract
1/8 tsp. salt
1 16-oz. package confectioners' sugar

Melt chocolate and butter in double boiler over hot water. Add potatoes, vanilla and salt; blend well. Add confectioners' sugar; mix well. Knead until smooth. Press into buttered 8-inch square pan. Cool. Cut into squares. Yield: 48 servings.

Approx per serv: Cal 55; Prot 0.2 g; T Fat 1.7 g; Chl 2.2 mg; Car 10.7 g; Sod 18.8 mg; Pot 19.0 mg.

Mary Densmore, Kalkaska

CANDIED FRUIT SQUARES

6 tbsp. butter, melted
1 1/2 c. graham cracker crumbs
1 c. shredded coconut
2 c. chopped mixed candied fruit
1 c. chopped dates
1 c. chopped pecans
1 15-oz. can sweetened condensed milk

Combine butter and graham cracker crumbs in bowl; mix well. Pat into 10 x 15-inch baking pan. Layer coconut, candied fruit, dates and pecans over crust; press lightly. Pour condensed milk over layers. Bake at 350 degrees for 25 to 30 minutes or until firm. Cool. Cut into bars. Cover tightly with foil to store. Yield: 48 srevings.

Shirley Towns, Barry

4-H is learning to be a leader.

DATE CRUMBLES

1 16-oz. package dates, chopped
1/2 c. sugar
1 c. packed brown sugar
1 c. shortening
1/2 c. butter
1/2 c. melted shortening
1 egg
2 c. flour
2 1/2 c. oats
1 tsp. salt
1 tsp. soda
1 tsp. vanilla extract

Combine dates, sugar and 1/2 cup water in saucepan. Cook until thickened. Combine brown sugar and remaining ingredients in bowl; mix well. Pat half the oats mixture into 9 x 14-inch baking pan. Spread with date mixture. Sprinkle with remaining oats mixture. Bake at 375 degrees for 45 minutes or until brown. Cool. Cut into squares. Yield: 24 servings.

NOTE: This recipe has been made by my family for Christmas for 4 generations.

Approx per serv: Cal 323; Prot 2.9 g; T Fat 18.9 g; Chl 22.4 mg; Car 37.4 g; Sod 175.6 mg; Pot 170.8 mg.

James Rund, Gogebic

MARASCHINO CHERRY BARS

2 c. flour
1/3 c. sugar
3/4 c. butter, softened
2 eggs, lightly beaten
1 c. packed brown sugar
1/3 c. flour
1 1/2 tsp. baking powder
1/2 tsp. salt
1/2 tsp. vanilla extract
1/2 c. chopped pecans
1   10-oz. jar maraschino cherries,
    drained, chopped
3 tbsp. cherry juice
2 tbsp. margarine, softened
2 1/2 c. confectioners' sugar
3 tbsp. flaked coconut

Combine first 3 ingredients in bowl; mix until crumbly. Press into 9 x 13-inch baking pan. Bake at 350 degrees for 12 to 15 minutes or until light brown. Combine eggs, brown sugar, flour, baking powder, salt, vanilla, pecans and cherries in bowl; mix well. Pour over baked layer. Bake at 350 degrees for 20 to 25 minutes or until set. Cool. Cream cherry juice, margarine and confectioners' sugar in bowl until light and fluffy. Spread over cooled layer. Sprinkle with coconut. Cut into bars. Yield: 36 servings.

Approx per serv: Cal 181; Prot 1.5 g; T Fat 6.2 g; Chl 25.9 mg; Car 30.8 g; Sod 104.2 mg; Pot 45.4 mg.

Jeremy Nadeau, Monroe

CREAM CHEESE COOKIES

1 c. confectioners' sugar
1 c. butter, softened
2 1/2 c. flour
1/2 tsp. salt
1/2 tsp. vanilla extract
2   3-oz. packages cream cheese, softened
2 c. confectioners' sugar
1/4 c. flour
2 tsp. vanilla extract
1 c. chopped walnuts
1 c. milk chocolate chips
1/4 c. butter
1 c. confectioners' sugar

Cream first 2 ingredients in bowl until light and fluffy. Add 2 1/2 cups flour, salt and 1/2 teaspoon vanilla; mix well. Shape into small balls. Place on ungreased cookie sheet. Make indentation in each with thumb. Bake at 350 degrees for 8 to 10 minutes or until light brown. Combine cream cheese, 2 cups confectioners' sugar, 1/4 cup flour, 2 teaspoons vanilla and walnuts in bowl; mix well. Spoon into hot cookies. Cool until filling is set. Melt chocolate chips and 1/4 cup butter in 1/4 cup water in saucepan. Stir in confectioners' sugar. Spoon over cookies. Yield: 48 servings.

Approx per serv: Cal 154; Prot 1.6 g; T Fat 9.1 g; Chl 18.7 mg; Car 17.9 g; Sod 89.8 mg; Pot 33.9 mg.

Jan Weber, Macomb

EASTER BUNNY COOKIES

1 c. butter, softened
1 1/2 c. confectioners' sugar
1 egg
1 tsp. vanilla extract
1 1/2 c. oats
2 1/4 c. flour
1 tsp. soda

Cream butter and confectioners' sugar in bowl until light and fluffy. Blend in egg and vanilla. Process oats in blender container for 1 minute or until ground. Combine with flour and soda. Add to creamed mixture gradually, mixing well after each addition. Chill, covered, for 1 hour. Roll 1/8 inch thick on lightly floured surface. Cut with bunny-shaped cookie cutter. Place on cookie sheet. Bake at 375 degrees for 7 minutes or until edges are light golden brown. Cool completely. Decorate with frosting glaze and cinnamon candies for eyes. Yield: 36 servings.

NOTE: Nutritional information does not include glaze or candies for decorating.

Approx per serv: Cal 108; Prot 1.5 g; T Fat 5.6 g; Chl 22.8 mg; Car 13.2 g; Sod 87.1 mg; Pot 22.6 mg.

Gwen Barker, Leelanau

CANDY CANE COOKIES

1 1/4 c. butter, softened
1 c. confectioners' sugar
1 egg
1 tsp. vanilla extract
1/2 tsp. almond extract (opt.)
3 1/2 c. flour
1/2 tsp. salt
Several drops of red food coloring
1 egg white, lightly beaten
1/4 c. red sugar (opt.)

Cream butter and confectioners' sugar in bowl until light and fluffy. Add egg and flavorings; beat well. Stir in mixture of flour and salt. Divide into 2 portions. Tint 1 portion light red. Chill in refrigerator. Roll by teaspoonfuls into 4-inch strips. Twist 1 red and 1 white strip together lightly. Repeat with remaining dough. Shape into candy canes on cookie sheet. Brush with egg white. Sprinkle with red sugar. Bake at 350 degrees for 10 to 12 minutes or until very lightly browned. Cool on wire racks. Store in airtight container. Yield: 48 servings.

Approx per serv: Cal 91; Prot 1.2 g; T Fat 5.0 g; Chl 20.1 mg; Car 10.5 g; Sod 83.1 mg; Pot 12.4 mg.

Chad Pendell, Isabella

4-H is fun.

GUMDROP GEMS

1 c. butter, softened
1 1/2 c. sifted confectioners' sugar
1 tsp. vanilla extract
1 egg
2 1/2 c. sifted flour
1 tsp. soda
1 tsp. cream of tartar
1/4 tsp. salt
1 c. small gumdrops, sliced

Cream first 3 ingredients in bowl until light and fluffy. Add egg; beat well. Stir in mixture of dry ingredients. Shape into 2 x 12-inch log. Chill, wrapped, for several hours to overnight. Cut into 1/4-inch slices. Place on ungreased cookie sheet. Decorate with gumdrops. Bake at 375 degrees for 12 minutes. Yield: 48 servings.

Approx per serv: Cal 57; Prot 0.8 g; T Fat 0.5 g; Chl 6.0 mg; Car 12.4 g; Sod 38.5 mg; Pot 9.7 mg.

Shiela Digue, Monroe

FRESH PEACH BUTTER

6 lb. peaches, peeled, mashed
1/4 c. lemon juice
1 tsp. cinnamon
3 1/4 c. sugar

Process peaches in blender or food processor 3 cups at a time until pureed. Measure 11 cups peaches into Crock·Pot. Add lemon juice and cinnamon; mix well. Cook, uncovered, on High for 7 hours, stirring twice. Add sugar; mix well. Cook for 2 hours longer, stirring occasionally. Pour into hot sterilized 8-ounce jars, leaving 1/2-inch headspace. Seal with 2-piece lids. Process in boiling water bath for 10 minutes. Yield: 112 one-tablespoon servings.

Approx per serv: Cal 31; Prot 0.15 g; T Fat 0.0 g; Chl 0.0 mg; Car 7.8 g; Sod 0.25 mg; Pot 43.7 mg.

Beverly Zurface, Barry

TOMATO BUTTER

4 c. chopped peeled ripe tomatoes
4 c. sugar
1 6-oz. package lemon gelatin

Bring tomatoes and sugar to a boil in saucepan, stirring constantly. Simmer for 15 minutes, stirring constantly. Remove from heat; stir in gelatin until dissolved. Pour into hot sterilized jars, leaving 1/2-inch headspace. Seal with 2-piece lids. Process in boiling water bath for 10 minutes. Yield: 64 one-tablespoon servings.

Approx per serv: Cal 60; Prot 0.3 g; T Fat 0.0 g; Chl 0.0 mg; Car 15.1 g; Sod 8.8 mg; Pot 24.7 mg.

Frances Hazelton, Shiawassee

CRANBERRY MOUSSE

1 c. cranberry juice cocktail
1 3-oz. package raspberry gelatin
1 16-oz. can cranberry sauce
1 c. whipped topping

Bring cranberry juice to a boil in saucepan. Add gelatin; stir until dissolved. Add cranberry sauce; mix well. Pour into serving dish. Chill until thickened. Fold in whipped topping. Chill until firm. Garnish with additional whipped topping just before serving. Yield: 6 servings.

Approx per serv: Cal 249; Prot 1.6 g; T Fat 2.9 g; Chl 0.0 mg; Car 56.5 g; Sod 49.1 mg; Pot 63.6 mg.

Mary Pat Wiser, Branch

BLUEBERRY FREEZER JAM

1/4 c. Sure-Jel
2 tbsp. sugar
1 c. blueberries, mashed
3/4 c. sugar
2 tbsp. corn syrup
2 tbsp. lemon juice

Combine Sure-Jel and 2 tablespoons sugar. Stir into blueberries in mixer bowl. Add remaining ingredients. Beat at low speed for 7 minutes. Pour into jelly jars; cover. Let stand at room temperature overnight. Store in freezer.

Irene Haas, Arenac

MINT JELLY

2 1/2 c. apple juice
1 tbsp. white vinegar
1/2 c. (or more) packed mint leaves
4 c. sugar
Several drops of green food coloring
1/2 bottle of pectin

Combine apple juice, vinegar and mint in saucepan. Cook for 10 minutes. Remove and discard mint. Add sugar and food coloring. Cook for 2 minutes. Stir in pectin; remove from heat. Pour into 7 hot sterilized 4-ounce jelly jars; seal with 2-piece lids. Process in boiling water bath for 5 minutes.

Marilyn Irrer, Clinton

QUEEN ANNE'S LACE JELLY

15 lg. Queen Anne's Lace flowers
5 drops of yellow food coloring
1 drop of red food coloring
2 tbsp. lemon juice
1 box Sure-Jel
3 to 4 c. sugar

Select open blossoms only; if small, use 30 flowers. Rinse flowers well; clip off stems completely. Simmer in 4 cups water in large saucepan for 5 minutes. Strain through muslin. Measure into saucepan. Add food coloring and lemon juice. Prepare mixture according to Sure-Jel package directions, using 1 cup sugar per cup of liquid. Pour into hot sterilized jelly glasses, leaving 1/4-inch headspace. Seal. Process in boiling water bath for 5 minutes. Jelly tastes like apple and honey.

Cristy Wareham, Benzie

SPICY TOMATO RELISH

20 med. tomatoes, peeled, chopped
1 1/2 c. chopped onions
3/4 c. sugar
1/2 c. packed brown sugar
2 tsp. celery seed
2 tsp. noniodized salt
3/4 tsp. cinnamon
3/4 tsp. cloves
3/4 tsp. ginger
3/4 tsp. allspice
1 c. cider vinegar

Combine all ingredients in large heavy saucepan. Simmer until consistency of applesauce, stirring frequently. Pour into 4 hot sterilized 1-pint jars, leaving 1/4-inch headspace. Seal with 2-piece lids. Process in boiling water bath for 35 minutes.
Yield: 64 two-tablespoon servings.

Approx per serv: Cal 26; Prot 0.5 g; T Fat 0.1 g; Chl 0.0 mg; Car 6.3 g; Sod 80.3 mg; Pot 108.8 mg.

Nancy M. Hoover, Alcona

HOMEMADE DOG BISCUITS

1 pkg. dry yeast
1 c. warm chicken broth
2 tbsp. molasses
1 c. all-purpose flour
1 1/2 c. whole wheat flour
1 c. bran cereal
1/2 c. yellow cornmeal
1/2 c. dry nonfat milk powder
2 tsp. garlic powder
2 tsp. salt
3/4 to 1 c. all-purpose flour
1 egg, beaten
1 tbsp. milk

Dissolve yeast in 1/4 cup warm water. Stir in next 9 ingredients. Knead in flour on floured surface. Roll out to 3/8-inch thickness; cut as desired. Place on ungreased baking sheet. Brush with mixture of egg and milk. Bake at 300 degrees for 45 minutes. Turn off oven. Let stand in closed oven overnight.
Yield: 42 servings.

NOTE: These are good bazaar sellers. Our dog Barney gave these as Christmas gifts.

Approx per serv: Cal 53; Prot 2.0 g; T Fat 0.3 g; Chl 6.3 mg; Car 10.7 g; Sod 135.7 mg; Pot 55.3 mg.

Kathy Brown, Berrien

Low Salt, Low Sugar & Special Needs

Flavor Makers...

SPICE/HERB	MEAT/DAIRY	FISH/EGGS/ POULTRY	VEGETABLES	FRUIT	BREADS/ SWEETS
Allspice	Ground beef Ham Roasts Sausage Stews	Clam chowder Oysters	Beets Red cabbage Spinach Sweet potatoes Tomatoes	Apples Bananas Cherries Citrus fruit Peaches	Cookies Fruit pies Mincemeat Pumpkin pie Spice cake
Basil	Beef Cheese dishes Liver Pork Veal	Duck Egg dishes Goose Seafood Turkey	Carrots Green beans Peas Summer squash Tomatoes		
Caraway Seed	Cheese dip Cottage cheese Liver Pork	Fish salads Stuffed eggs Tuna casserole	Cauliflower Cucumbers Potatoes Sauerkraut	Apples Applesauce	Biscuits Corn bread Rye bread

Celery (seed, salt, flakes)	Cheese mixtures
	Ham spread
	Meat loaf
	Roasts
	Stews
		Chicken
		  casseroles
		Chowders
		Deviled eggs
		Seafood
			Coleslaw
			Corn
			Potatoes
			Sauerkraut
			Tomatoes
				Fruit salad
				  dressings
				Fruit salads
					Bread

Cinnamon	Ham Lamb Pork	Chicken Duck Fish	Artichokes Beans Beets Carrots Pumpkin Sweet potatoes	Apples Cranberries Dates Grapefruit Peaches Pineapple	Cakes Cheesecake Chocolate Cookies Pies Waffles
Cloves	Beef Ham Pork Sausage	Chicken Duck Fish	Beans Beets Onions Sweet potatoes Tomatoes Winter squash	Apples Bananas Citrus fruit Cranberries Peaches Pears	Cookies Fruitcake Gingerbread Mincemeat Steamed pudding Sweet breads
Cumin	Beef Cheese dishes Chicken Indian dishes Mexican dishes	Chicken soup Chili powder Curry powder Deviled eggs Fish	Beans Cabbage Pea soup Rice Sauerkraut	Chutney	Rye bread
Curry "A mix of spices & herbs"	Beef Veal	Chicken Clam chowder Egg dishes Seafood	Carrots Lentils Rice Tomatoes	Apples Bananas Pineapple	Biscuits
Ginger	Barbecue Corned beef Meat loaf Pot roast Veal	Chicken Poultry stews Turkey	Beets Carrots Pumpkin Sweet potatoes Winter squash	Apples Bananas Figs Pears Pineapple	Cookies Gingerbread Indian pudding Pies Spice cake

Herb & Spice Chart

SPICE/HERB	MEAT/DAIRY	FISH/EGGS/ POULTRY	VEGETABLES	FRUIT	BREADS/ SWEETS
Marjoram	Beef Cheese dishes Game Ham	Chicken Creamed eggs Goose Seafood	Mushrooms Peas Salad Greens Zucchini		

Mustard	Beef and Veal
	Cheese spread
	Ham and Pork
	Sausage
		Chicken
		Deviled eggs
		Omelets
		Seafood
			Any vegetable,
			  when mixed
			  in butter or
			  sauce
				Fruit salad
				  dressings
					Biscuits

Nutmeg	Cheese fondue Ground meat Sausage	Chicken Oysters	Carrots Cauliflower Chinese peas Green beans Spinach Summer squash	Bananas Cherries Peaches Pears Prunes Rhubarb	Cakes Cookies Custard pie Doughnuts Muffins Puddings
Oregano	Beef and veal Italian dishes Mexican dishes Pork	Eggs Fish Game birds Turkey	Bean salads Green beans Guacamole Mushrooms		

Paprika	Beef
	Cheese mixture
	Pork
	Sour cream
	  mixes
	Veal
		Fish
		Omelets
		Poultry
			Beans
			Cabbage
			Cauliflower
			Corn
			Potatoes
				Fruit salad
				  dressings
				Fruit salads	

Rosemary	Beef Italian dishes Pork Veal	Chicken Rabbit Salmon	Broccoli Brussels sprouts Cabbage Potatoes	Fruit cocktail Jam Jelly	Ham biscuits
Saffron	Sausage Veal	Chicken Curry Seafood Spanish dishes	Rice		Cakes Fancy rolls

Tarragon	Game
	Meat marinades
	Steak
	Sweetbreads
	Veal
		Chicken
		Duck
		Eggs
		Squab
		Turkey
			Marinades for:
			  Artichokes
			  Asparagus
			  Cauliflower		

Thyme	All meats Cheese mixtures Game Liver	Duck Poultry Scrambled eggs Shellfish	Beans Spinach Tomatoes Zucchini		

BEEF ORIENTAL STIR FRY

1 1/2 lb. beef sirloin
1 green pepper, cut into strips
1 c. sliced zucchini
1 stalk broccoli, sliced
2 stalks celery, sliced
1 sm. onion, sliced
2 tbsp. oil
1/2 tsp. ginger
1/4 tsp. white pepper
1 1/2 tbsp. cornstarch
1 10-oz. can chicken broth
2 tbsp. oil
Soy sauce
3 c. cooked rice

Cut sirloin cross grain into 1/8 x 2-inch strips. Stir-fry vegetables 1 at a time in 2 tablespoons oil in skillet over medium-high heat until tender-crisp. Place each vegetable in second skillet when cooked. Add ginger and white pepper. Stir in mixture of cornstarch and broth. Cook until thickened, stirring constantly. Add 2 tablespoons oil to first skillet. Stir-fry sirloin to desired degree of doneness. Season with soy sauce to taste. Mix sirloin with vegetables. Serve over rice. Serve with soy sauce. (Omit for low-salt diet.) Yield: 4 servings.
NOTE: May substitute chicken breast for sirloin and use vegetables of choice.

Approx per serv: Cal 674; Prot 41.6 g; T Fat 35.8 g; Chl 117.0 mg; Car 41.0 g; Sod 1003.3 mg; Pot 1077.4 mg.

 Betty Bonofiglio, Eaton

NUTBURGERS

1 c. ground walnuts
1 c. shredded Cheddar cheese
1/2 c. bread crumbs
1/4 c. wheat germ
1/2 c. chopped onion
2 tbsp. sesame seed
1 tbsp. chopped parsley
1 tsp. soy sauce
2 cloves of garlic, minced
1/4 tsp. thyme
2 tbsp. nonfat dry milk powder
4 eggs, lightly beaten
1/4 c. (about) oil

Combine first 11 ingredients in bowl; mix well. Add eggs; mix well. Shape into patties. Fry in oil in skillet over medium heat. Drain.
Yield: 5 servings.

Approx per serv: Cal 505; Prot 19.2 g; T Fat 40.9 g; Chl 225.8 mg; Car 18.6 g; Sod 389.1 mg; Pot 359.1 mg.

Sandy Gill, Menominee

SPINACH SALAD

1 16-oz. package fresh spinach
1 c. bean sprouts
3 hard-boiled eggs, sliced
1 tbsp. bacon bits
1/3 c. oil
Artificial sweetener to equal 3/4 c. sugar
1/3 c. catsup
1 tbsp. Worcestershire sauce
1 tbsp. dehydrated onion flakes

Rinse and drain spinach and bean sprouts. Tear spinach into bite-sized pieces. Combine spinach and sprouts in salad bowl. Layer eggs over top. Sprinkle with bacon bits and salt to taste. Combine remaining ingredients in small bowl; mix well. Pour over salad just before serving.
Yield: 6 servings.

Approx per serv: Cal 196; Prot 7.2 g; T Fat 15.5 g; Chl 126.4 mg; Car 8.9 g; Sod 327.0 mg; Pot 516.5 mg.

Beverly Barrett, Eaton

MOLASSES CAKE

1/2 c. molasses
1/2 c. lard
1 1/2 c. flour
1 tsp. cloves
1 tsp. cinnamon
1 tsp. soda
1/2 c. raisins

Cream molasses and lard in bowl. Add mixture of flour and spices with soda dissolved in 1 cup boiling water; mix well. Stir in raisins. Pour into greased and floured 8 x 12-inch baking pan. Bake at 350 degrees for 40 to 50 minutes or until cake tests done. Cool. Cut into squares.
Yield: 12 servings.

Approx per serv: Cal 187; Prot 1.8 g; T Fat 8.8 g; Chl 8.2 mg; Car 25.5 g; Sod 72.4 mg; Pot 186.3 mg.

Elsie G. Sundling, Delta

MAYO CAKE

3 c. flour
3/4 tsp. salt
1 tbsp. soda
6 tbsp. cocoa
1 1/2 c. sugar
1 1/2 c. cold coffee
1 c. mayonnaise
1 1/2 tsp. vanilla extract
2 c. confectioners' sugar
1/2 c. butter, softened
3 tbsp. cocoa
1 tsp. vanilla extract
1 to 2 tbsp. warm milk
2 tbsp. shortening

Combine first 8 ingredients in mixer bowl; beat until well blended. Pour into 2 greased and floured 8-inch cake pans. Bake at 350 degrees for 30 minutes. Cool on wire rack. Combine confectioners' sugar, butter and cocoa in mixer bowl; beat until well blended. Add vanilla and enough milk to make of spreading consistency. Add shortening; beat until fluffy. Spread between layers and over top and side of cake. Yield: 16 servings.

Approx per serv: Cal 386; Prot 3.5 g; T Fat 19.8 g; Chl 28.7 mg; Car 51.2 g; Sod 412.7 mg; Pot 95.4 mg.

Julie D. Fedore, Cass

DEPRESSION CAKE

1 c. raisins
1/2 c. shortening
1 c. sugar
2 c. flour
2 tsp. baking powder
1 tsp. soda
1 tsp. cinnamon
1/2 tsp. cloves
1/2 tsp. salt

Combine raisins, shortening, sugar and 1 cup water in saucepan. Bring to a boil; cool. Combine remaining ingredients in bowl. Add raisin mixture; mix well. Pour into greased and floured 8-inch square baking pan. Bake at 350 degrees for 1 hour or until cake tests done. Cool. Cut into squares. Yield: 10 servings.

Approx per serv: Cal 310; Prot 3.0 g; T Fat 11.5 g; Chl 0.0 mg; Car 50.3 g; Sod 259.0 mg; Pot 135.9 mg.

Holly Steiner, Barry

RICH NO-EGG CHOCOLATE CAKE

1/2 c. margarine
2 tsp. vinegar
2 tsp. vanilla extract
3 c. flour
2 c. sugar
6 tbsp. cocoa
2 tsp. soda
2 tsp. salt

Melt margarine in saucepan over medium heat; remove from heat. Add vinegar, vanilla and 2 cups water. Combine remaining ingredients in bowl. Add margarine mixture; stir with fork until well mixed. Pour into 2 greased and floured 8-inch cake pans. Bake at 350 degrees for 35 to 40 minutes or until cake tests done. Cool in pan for 20 minutes. Turn onto wire rack to cool completely. Frost as desired. Yield: 15 servings.

Approx per serv: Cal 254; Prot 3.0 g; T Fat 6.8 g; Chl 0.0 mg; Car 46.7 g; Sod 414.6 mg; Pot 59.2 mg.

Pete Hopkins, Ingham

4-H is 200,000 Michigan youths.

WHOLE WHEAT CHOCOLATE CHIP COOKIES

2/3 c. shortening
2/3 c. margarine, softened
3/4 c. packed brown sugar
3/4 c. sugar
2 eggs
1 tsp. vanilla extract
1 3/4 c. all-purpose flour
1 1/2 c. whole wheat flour
1 tsp. soda
1 c. chopped pecans (opt.)
2 c. chocolate chips

Cream first 6 ingredients in bowl until light and fluffy. Mix flours and soda. Add to creamed mixture; mix well. Stir in pecans and chocolate chips. Drop by rounded teaspoonfuls onto ungreased cookie sheets. Bake at 350 degrees for 10 minutes. Cool slightly before removing from pan. Yield: 60 servings.

Approx per serv: Cal 128; Prot 1.4 g; T Fat 8.9 g; Chl 8.4 mg; Car 13.7 g; Sod 41.7 mg; Pot 57.1 mg.

Marcia Leavitt, Bay

RAISIN COOKIES

2/3 c. prune juice
1 c. raisins
1/4 c. margarine
1 egg, beaten
1 tsp. liquid sweetener
1 c. flour
1 tsp. soda
1/8 tsp. salt

Combine first 3 ingredients in saucepan. Bring to a boil; cool. Combine egg, sweetener and sifted dry ingredients in bowl; mix well. Add raisin mixture; mix well. Drop by teaspoonfuls onto ungreased baking sheet. Bake at 350 degrees for 8 minutes. Remove to wire rack to cool. Yield: 24 servings.

NOTE: Add ground nuts or finely chopped apple for variety.

Approx per serv: Cal 62; Prot 1.0 g; T Fat 2.2 g; Chl 10.5 mg; Car 10.0 g; Sod 73.0 mg; Pot 71.1 mg.

Nellie Cronk, Hillsdale

BONNIE'S ICE CREAM

*2 10-oz. packages frozen
   strawberries, thawed*
1 6-oz. package strawberry gelatin
1 1/2 c. sugar
2 16-oz. bottles of strawberry soda
2 32-oz. bottles of ginger ale

Puree strawberries in blender or food processor. Dissolve gelatin in 1/2 cup boiling water in bowl. Add sugar, pureed strawberries and strawberry soda; mix well. Pour into 1-gallon ice cream freezer. Add enough ginger ale to fill. Freeze using manufacturer's instructions. Yield: 20 servings.

NOTE: This recipe is good for those with milk and dairy product allergies. It is similar to sherbet. Try varying the flavors of fruit and gelatin.

Approx per serv: Cal 119; Prot 0.9 g; T Fat 0.1 g; Chl 0.0 mg; Car 30.0 g; Sod 27.3 mg; Pot 49.7 mg.

Bonnie Wickerham, Clinton

MILK-FREE ICE CREAM

1 8-oz. carton whipped topping
1/4 c. sugar
1 tsp. vanilla extract
1 egg (opt.)
1 banana, mashed

Whip topping in mixer bowl. Mix in sugar, vanilla, beaten egg yolk and banana. Fold in stiffly beaten egg white. Freeze for 30 minutes. Beat for 1 minute. Pour into freezer container; cover. Freeze until firm. Yield: 4 servings.

NOTE: May substitute 1 cup strawberries, blueberries or other fruit.

Approx per serv: Cal 267; Prot 2.6 g; T Fat 15.7 g; Chl 63.2 mg; Car 30.8 g; Sod 29.7 mg; Pot 114.7 mg.

Marcia Leavitt, Bay

MICROWAVE BREAD PUDDING

1 egg, beaten
1/2 c. milk
1 slice bread, crumbled
2 tbsp. raisins
1/8 to 1/4 tsp. cinnamon
Artificial sweetener to taste

Combine egg, milk, bread, raisins and cinnamon in 2-cup glass casserole. Microwave on High for 3 to 5 minutes or until thickened, stirring occasionally. Add sweetener. Yield: 1 serving.

Approx per serv: Cal 223; Prot 11.5 g; T Fat 10.2 g; Chl 270.0 mg; Car 22.6 g; Sod 141.7 mg; Pot 387.2 mg.

Elizabeth F. Beyne, Marquette

MICROWAVE RICE PUDDING

1 egg, beaten
1/2 c. milk
1/2 c. cooked rice
2 tbsp. raisins
1/8 tsp. cinnamon
Artificial sweetener to taste

Combine egg, milk, rice, raisins and cinnamon in 2-cup glass casserole. Microwave on High for 3 to 5 minutes or until thickened, stirring occasionally. Stir in sweetener. Cool. Yield: 1 serving.

Approx per serv: Cal 327; Prot 13.3 g; T Fat 10.2 g; Chl 269.9 mg; Car 45.8 g; Sod 510.6 mg; Pot 412.9 mg.

Elizabeth F. Beyne, Marquette

Kids Cook

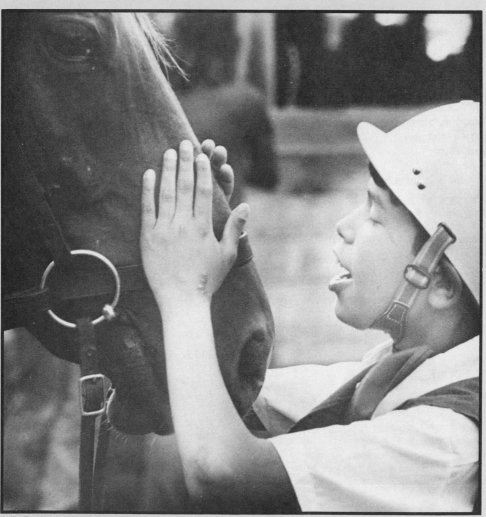

Credit: Port Huron Times Herald

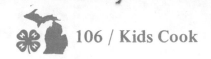

FROZEN SLUSH

1   3-oz. package strawberry gelatin
1   c. sugar
1   46-oz. can pineapple juice
2   qt. ginger ale

Combine gelatin and sugar in bowl. Add 3 cups boiling water. Stir until gelatin dissolves. Cool. Add pineapple juice. Freeze until firm. Thaw for 2 hours. Scoop into glasses. Add enough ginger ale to fill. Yield: 20 servings.
NOTE: May place slush in punch bowl and pour in ginger ale.

Approx per serv: Cal 124; Prot 0.7 g; T Fat 0.1 g; Chl 0.0 mg; Car 31.2 g; Sod 14.3 mg; Pot 116.3 mg.

Wendy Haeussler, Washtenaw

MAMBO SHAKE

1/4 c. milk
4 ripe bananas, mashed
2 tbsp. lemon juice
1/2 tsp. cinnamon
3 tbsp. sugar
3 3/4 c. milk
1 pt. vanilla ice cream

Stir 1/4 cup milk into bananas; beat until smooth. Add lemon juice, cinnamon and sugar; mix well. Stir in 3 3/4 cups milk and ice cream. Pour into glasses. "Hope you like it."
Yield: 6 servings.

Approx per serv: Cal 308; Prot 7.9 g; T Fat 13.8 g; Chl 50.9 mg; Car 41.2 g; Sod 98.5 mg; Pot 582.0 mg.

Courtney Moraski, Menominee

MUSHROOM CHICKEN

1 chicken, cut up
1 can cream of mushroom soup

Rinse chicken with cold water. Pat dry with paper towels. Place in single layer in baking pan. Spoon soup over chicken. Bake at 300 degrees for 2 hours. The gravy in the bottom of the pan is delicious on rice or noodles.
Yield: 4 servings.

Approx per serv: Cal 203; Prot 22.4 g; T Fat 9.3 g; Chl 82.7 mg; Car 6.3 g; Sod 650.5 mg; Pot 302.8 mg.

Monica Siebarth, Lenawee

CHICKEN WITH RICE

1 c. rice
1 chicken, cut up
1 can cream of mushroom soup
1 can cream of chicken soup
1 env. dry onion soup mix

Sprinkle rice in 9 x 13-inch baking dish. Arrange chicken over rice. Mix canned soups and 1/2 soup can water in bowl. Pour over chicken. Sprinkle dry soup mix over top. Bake at 350 degrees for 1 hour. Yield: 5 servings.

Approx per serv: Cal 374; Prot 23.0 g; T Fat 11.4 g; Chl 83.7 mg; Car 43.4 g; Sod 1578.5 mg; Pot 363.1 mg.

Jenny Kimball, Isabella

HOBO DINNER

1 lb. ground beef
2 potatoes, sliced
2 carrots, sliced
1 onion, sliced
2 c. green beans

Shape ground beef into 4 patties. Place each patty on large piece of heavy foil. Season with salt and pepper to taste. Layer potatoes, carrots, onion and green beans on top. Add a small amount of water to each. Seal foil. Place on grill or campfire. Cook until vegetables are tender, turning packets over once.
Yield: 4 servings.

Approx per serv: Cal 423; Prot 24.2 g; T Fat 24.4 g; Chl 77.1 mg; Car 26.7 g; Sod 254.3 mg; Pot 960.1 mg.

Marcia Leavitt, Bay

IMPOSSIBLE CHEESEBURGER PIE

1 lb. ground beef
1 1/2 c. chopped onions
3 eggs
1 1/4 c. milk
3/4 c. buttermilk baking mix
1/8 tsp. salt
3/4 tsp. pepper
2 tomatoes, sliced
1 c. shredded Cheddar cheese

Preheat oven to 400 degrees. Grease 10-inch pie plate. Brown ground beef and onions in skillet, stirring frequently; drain. Spoon into pie plate.

Combine eggs, milk, baking mix, salt and pepper in blender container. Process on High for 15 seconds. Pour into pie plate. Bake for 25 minutes. Remove from oven. Arrange tomato slices on top. Sprinkle with cheese. Bake for 5 to 8 minutes longer or until knife inserted near center comes out clean. Yield: 6 servings.

Approx per serv: Cal 393; Prot 25.1 g; T Fat 23.8 g; Chl 203.2 mg; Car 19.0 g; Sod 466.7 mg; Pot 446.9 mg.

Kristy Powers, Macomb

MICROWAVE HASH AND EGG NESTS

> 1   15 1/2-oz. can hash
> 4 eggs

Grease four 6-ounce glass custard dishes. Spread hash evenly over bottom and up side of each dish. Break 1 egg into each dish. Pierce yolk with fork. Cover with plastic wrap. Place dishes in circle on plate. Microwave on Medium-High for 4 1/2 to 5 minutes or until eggs are cooked as desired. "Fun to make and eat too."
Yield: 4 servings.

Brenda Allen, Jackson

POLKA DOT MACARONI AND CHEESE

> 1 can Cheddar cheese soup
> 1/2 c. milk
> 1/2 tsp. salt
> 1   7-oz. package macaroni, cooked
> 2 oz. Cheddar cheese, cubed
> 2 frankfurters, cooked, sliced
> Paprika to taste

Combine soup, milk and salt in bowl; mix well. Add macaroni and cheese; mix well. Spread in baking dish. Arrange frankfurter slices over top; push down gently. Sprinkle with paprika. Bake at 375 degrees for 25 minutes.
Yield: 4 servings.

Cheryl Yalch, Macomb

TUNABURGERS

> 1   7-oz. can tuna, drained
> 1 c. chopped celery
> 1/2 c. shredded mozzarella cheese

> 1 sm. onion, minced
> 1/4 c. mayonnaise
> 1/4 c. butter
> 4 slices bread

Combine tuna, celery, cheese and onion in bowl; mix well. Add mayonnaise. Season with salt and pepper to taste; mix well. Spoon onto slices of buttered bread. Place on baking sheet. Cover loosely. Bake at 350 degrees for 15 minutes. Yield: 4 servings.

Approx per serv: Cal 469; Prot 17.5 g; T Fat 36.5 g; Chl 83.9 mg; Car 18.1 g; Sod 833.5 mg; Pot 322.4 mg.

Cathy Purdy, Livingston

CORN SPOON BREAD

> 1   16-oz. can cream-style corn
> 1   16-oz. can whole kernel corn, drained
> 1   6-oz. package corn muffin mix
> 1 stick margarine, melted
> 1 c. sour cream
> 2 eggs, beaten

Combine all ingredients in bowl; mix well. Pour into buttered 8 x 8-inch baking dish. Bake at 350 degrees for 40 to 45 minutes or until browned and set. Yield: 6 servings.

Approx per serv: Cal 480; Prot 8.5 g; T Fat 29.5 g; Chl 101.1 mg; Car 50.2 g; Sod 745.8 mg; Pot 238.8 mg.

Kari Gracey, St. Joseph

DANNY'S MONKEY BREAD

> 4 cans refrigerator biscuits
> 3/4 c. sugar
> 1 1/2 tsp. cinnamon
> 3/4 c. margarine
> 1 c. sugar
> 1 tsp. vanilla extract
> 1 1/2 tsp. cinnamon

Cut each biscuit into quarters. Mix 3/4 cup sugar and 1 1/2 teaspoons cinnamon in bowl. Coat each biscuit piece with cinnamon sugar. Place in well-greased bundt pan. Combine margarine, 1 cup sugar, vanilla and 1 1/2 teaspoons cinnamon in saucepan. Bring to a boil. Cook for 5 minutes. Pour over biscuits. Bake at 350 degrees for 30 minutes. Invert on serving plate immediately. Yield: 12 servings.

Approx per serv: Cal 522; Prot 6.8 g; T Fat 20.3 g; Chl 0.9 mg; Car 78.5 g; Sod 1059.9 mg; Pot 113.8 mg.

Danny Petrie, Branch

SOFT PRETZELS

1 loaf frozen bread dough, thawed
Salt

Cut bread dough lengthwise into 8 strips. Let rise, covered, for 10 minutes. Roll each strip into 1/2 x 18-inch rope. Shape into pretzels on greased baking sheet. Brush with lukewarm water. Sprinkle with salt. Let rise, uncovered, for 15 to 20 minutes. Place shallow pan of water on bottom shelf of oven. Preheat oven to 425 degrees. Bake pretzels on center shelf over hot water for 15 to 20 minutes or until golden brown. Yield: 8 servings.

Michelle Leavitt, Bay

BANANA BOATS

4 lg. unpeeled bananas
1 4-oz. carton whipped topping
1/4 c. salted peanuts
4 maraschino cherries

Wash unpeeled bananas. Slit each peel lengthwise to within 1-inch of end. Cut away about 1/2-inch peel on either side of slit. Scoop out banana with spoon. Fold into whipped topping. Spoon banana mixture into banana peel shells. Sprinkle with peanuts. Top with maraschino cherries. Serve immediately or chill for up to 1 hour. Yield: 4 servings.

Approx per serv: Cal 252; Prot 4.0 g; T Fat 11.8 g; Chl 0.0 mg; Car 37.0 g; Sod 45.8 mg; Pot 506.0 mg.

Brenda Allen, Jackson

SHERBET CUPS

1 1/2 c. vanilla wafer crumbs
1/4 c. chopped pecans
1 env. whipped topping mix, prepared
1 pt. sherbet

Fold vanilla wafer crumbs and pecans into whipped topping. Spread mixture over bottoms and sides of paper-lined muffin cups to form shells. Fill each shell with 1 rounded scoop sherbet. Freeze until firm. Yield: 8 servings.

Approx per serv: Cal 190; Prot 2.2 g; T Fat 7.6 g; Chl 7.4 mg; Car 29.2 g; Sod 53.2 mg; Pot 67.8 mg.

Colleen Rottier, Newaygo

SNOW ICE CREAM

1 c. evaporated milk
1 c. sugar
2 eggs
1 tbsp. vanilla extract
2 1/2 to 3 qt. clean fresh snow

Combine first 4 ingredients in bowl. Beat until smooth. Add snow. Beat until blended. Serve immediately. Yield: 8 servings.

Approx per serv: Cal 160; Prot 3.8 g; T Fat 3.9 g; Chl 73.0 mg; Car 28.0 g; Sod 52.7 mg; Pot 112.4 mg.

Bernice Rath, Monroe

STRAWBERRY-PEANUT YUM-YUM

1 3-oz. package strawberry gelatin
1 c. whipping cream, whipped
1/3 c. crunchy peanut butter
8 ice cream cones
1 4-oz. carton whipped topping
8 animal crackers

Prepare gelatin in mixer bowl according to package directions. Chill until thickened. Beat with electric mixer until soft peaks form. Fold in whipped cream and peanut butter. Chill until firm. Spoon into ice cream cones. Top with whipped topping. Place animal cracker upright on top of each cone. Yield: 8 servings.

Elaine Warner, Branch

FRESH APPLE CAKE

1 3/4 c. sugar
1 c. oil
3 eggs
2 c. flour
1 tsp. baking powder
1 tsp. cinnamon
1 tsp. vanilla extract
1/2 tsp. salt
4 apples, peeled, chopped
1/2 c. chopped pecans
1/2 c. raisins

Combine all ingredients in bowl; mix well. Pour into greased 9 x 13-inch cake pan. Bake at 350 degrees for 45 minutes. Cool. Sprinkle with confectioners' sugar. Yield: 12 servings.

Approx per serv: Cal 461; Prot 4.5 g; T Fat 23.7 g; Chl 63.2 mg; Car 60.7 g; Sod 134.5 mg; Pot 190.6 mg.

Guy Bunyea, Jr., Washtenaw

SARAH'S WACKY CHOCOLATE CAKE

3 c. flour
2 c. sugar
2 tsp. soda
6 tbsp. cocoa
1/2 c. oil
1 tbsp. vinegar
1/2 tsp. vanilla extract

Combine flour, sugar, soda and cocoa in sifter. Sift into ungreased 9 x 13-inch baking pan. Combine oil, vinegar, 2 cups water and vanilla in bowl. Add to dry ingredients; mix well. Bake at 350 degrees for 45 minutes or until toothpick inserted in center comes out clean. Yield: 10 servings.

Approx per serv: Cal 396; Prot 4.5 g; T Fat 11.9 g; Chl 0.0 mg; Car 70.1 g; Sod 165.6 mg; Pot 87.6 mg.

Sarah Billie, Gogebic

LINDA'S QUICK CAKE

1 can cherry pie filling
1 8-oz. can crushed pineapple
1 2-layer pkg. yellow cake mix
1 stick margarine, melted

Grease 9 x 13-inch cake pan generously. Spread pie filling in pan. Spoon pineapple over pie filling. Sprinkle dry cake mix over top. Drizzle with margarine. Bake at 400 degrees for 30 to 35 minutes or until golden brown. Yield: 16 servings.

Approx per serv: Cal 240; Prot 1.6 g; T Fat 8.0 g; Chl 0.0 mg; Car 39.6 g; Sod 373.2 mg; Pot 16.9 mg.

Bobbi Jo Gustman, Newaygo

PEANUT BUTTER CREAMS

1/4 c. confectioners' sugar
1 6-oz. package chocolate chips
1/2 c. sweetened condensed milk
1 c. peanut butter

Combine confectioners' sugar and chocolate chips in bowl. Stir in condensed milk. Add peanut butter; mix well. Shape into acorn-sized balls. Place on waxed paper-lined plate. Chill in refrigerator. Yield: 48 servings.

Approx per serv: Cal 72; Prot 2.0 g; T Fat 4.5 g; Chl 2.2 mg; Car 7.1 g; Sod 39.5 mg; Pot 65.0 mg.

Austin Zurface, Barry

WONDER FUDGE

1/4 c. margarine
1 6-oz. package chocolate chips
1/4 c. corn syrup
1 tsp. vanilla extract
1 1/2 c. sifted confectioners' sugar
2 c. crisp rice cereal

Combine the margarine, chocolate chips, corn syrup and vanilla in saucepan. Cook over low heat until chocolate melts, stirring constantly. Remove from heat. Stir in confectioners' sugar and cereal. Press into buttered 8 x 8-inch dish. Chill until firm. Cut into squares. Yield: 36 servings.

Approx per serv: Cal 68; Prot 0.3 g; T Fat 3.0 g; Chl 0.0 mg; Car 10.8 g; Sod 33.0 mg; Pot 17.5 mg.

Michelle Kempf, Newaygo

NO-BAKE PEANUT BUTTER BARS

2 c. graham cracker crumbs
3 1/2 c. confectioners' sugar
2 sticks margarine, melted
1 c. creamy peanut butter
1 tsp. vanilla extract
2 c. chocolate chips, melted

Combine crumbs, confectioners' sugar, margarine, peanut butter and vanilla in bowl; mix well. Press into 9 x 13-inch dish. Spread chocolate over top. Cool. Cut into squares. Yield: 36 servings.

Approx per serv: Cal 203; Prot 2.7 g; T Fat 12.6 g; Chl 0.0 mg; Car 22.6 g; Sod 144.7 mg; Pot 99.5 mg.

Jodi Zeno, Menominee

COCONUT CHIP BARS

1/2 c. melted margarine
1 1/2 c. graham cracker crumbs
1 6-oz. package chocolate chips
1 6-oz. package butterscotch chips
1 c. chopped walnuts
1 c. flaked coconut
1 can sweetened condensed milk

Combine margarine and crumbs in 9 x 12-inch baking dish; mix well. Press evenly over bottom of pan. Sprinkle chocolate and butterscotch chips, walnuts and coconut over crust. Pour condensed milk over top. Bake at 350 degrees for 20 to 25 minutes or until set. Yield: 24 servings.

Amanda Whitty, Baraga

MONKEY BARS

3/4 c. margarine, softened
2/3 c. sugar
2/3 c. packed brown sugar
1 egg
1 tsp. vanilla extract
1 c. mashed banana
2 1/4 c. flour
2 tsp. baking powder
1/2 tsp. salt
1   6-oz. package semisweet
    chocolate chips

Cream margarine and sugars in bowl until light and fluffy. Add egg and vanilla; mix well. Add banana; mix well. Stir in flour, baking powder and salt. Fold in chocolate chips. Press into 10 x 15-inch baking pan. Bake at 350 degrees for 25 minutes. Cool completely. Cut into bars. Roll in confectioners' sugar or frost with butter frosting. Yield: 30 servings.
NOTE: Nutritional information does not include confectioners' sugar or frosting.

Approx per serv: Cal 149; Prot 1.6 g; T Fat 6.9 g; Chl 8.4 mg; Car 21.3 g; Sod 117.4 mg; Pot 75.9 mg.

Jodi Burak, Delta

SAUCEPAN BROWNIES

1 stick margarine
1/4 c. cocoa
1 c. sugar
1/2 tsp. vanilla extract
2 eggs, slightly beaten
3/4 c. flour
1/4 tsp. salt
3/4 c. chopped pecans (opt.)

Melt margarine in saucepan over low heat. Add cocoa; blend well. Remove from heat. Add sugar and vanilla; mix well. Stir in eggs. Sift flour and salt together. Stir into chocolate mixture. Mix in pecans. Pour into greased 8-inch square baking pan. Bake at 350 degrees for 20 to 25 minutes. Cool. Cut into squares. Yield: 20 servings.
NOTE: May substitute 2 squares chocolate for cocoa.

Approx per serv: Cal 138; Prot 1.8 g; T Fat 8.6 g; Chl 25.3 mg; Car 14.8 g; Sod 89.1 mg; Pot 55.7 mg.

Barbara Knochel, Bay

GINGERBREAD COOKIES

1/2 c. butter, softened
3/4 c. sugar
1 egg
3/4 c. light molasses
3 1/2 c. flour
1 1/2 tsp. cloves
1 1/2 tsp. cinnamon
1 tsp. ginger
1 tsp. soda
1/4 tsp. salt
1/2 c. sugar (opt.)

Cream butter, 3/4 cup sugar and egg in bowl until light and fluffy. Blend in molasses. Stir in flour, spices, soda and salt. Chill overnight. Roll out 1/8 inch thick on lightly floured surface. Cut out with cookie cutters. Place on greased cookie sheets. Sprinkle with sugar. Bake at 375 degrees for 6 to 8 minutes or until light brown. May decorate cooled cookies with icing if desired. Yield: 72 servings.

Approx per serv: Cal 57; Prot 0.7 g; T Fat 1.4 g; Chl 7.5 mg; Car 10.3 g; Sod 35.9 mg; Pot 38.5 mg.

Angela Edwards, Branch

OLD-FASHIONED SUGAR COOKIES

1/2 c. shortening
1 c. sugar
1 egg
1 tsp. vanilla extract
2 1/2 c. sifted flour
1/2 tsp. cream of tartar
1/4 tsp. salt
1/2 tsp. soda
1/3 c. milk

Cream shortening, sugar and egg in bowl until light and fluffy. Blend in vanilla. Sift flour, cream of tartar, salt and soda together. Add to creamed mixture alternately with milk, mixing well after each addition. Roll out 1/4 inch thick. Cut out with cookie cutters. Bake at 350 degrees for 6 to 10 minutes or until light brown. Do not overbake. Frost and decorate as desired. Yield: 24 servings.

Approx per serv: Cal 122.7; Prot 1.6 g; T Fat 5.1 g; Chl 11.0 mg; Car 17.6 g; Sod 48.1 mg; Pot 21.4 mg.

Linda Kiesling, Shiawassee

NO-BAKE OATMEAL COOKIES

1/4 c. cocoa
2 c. sugar
1 1/2 c. milk
1/2 c. margarine
4 c. oats
1 tsp. butter
1/2 c. peanut butter
1 tsp. vanilla extract

Combine cocoa, sugar, milk and margarine in saucepan. Bring to a boil. Boil for 1 minute. Remove from heat. Stir in oats, butter, peanut butter and vanilla. Drop by spoonfuls onto waxed paper. Cool. Yield: 48 servings.

Approx per serv: Cal 98; Prot 2.0 g; T Fat 4.2 g; Chl 1.3 mg; Car 14.0 g; Sod 44.5 mg; Pot 58.8 mg.

Alysa Krueger, Shiawassee

NO-BAKE CHOCOLATE COOKIES

2 c. sugar
1/2 c. milk
1 stick margarine
1 tsp. salt
1/2 c. chopped pecans
1 tbsp. (heaping) peanut butter
1 6-oz. package chocolate chips
1 c. coconut
3 c. oats

Combine sugar, milk, margarine and salt in large saucepan. Bring to a boil; mix well. Remove from heat. Stir in remaining ingredients. Drop by teaspoonfuls onto waxed paper. Let stand until firm. Yield: 48 servings.

Amber Nethaway, Shiawassee

CHOCOLATE-COVERED WORMS

1 8-oz. package semisweet chocolate chips
1 8-oz. package butterscotch chips
1 3-oz. can Chinese noodles

Melt chocolate and butterscotch chips in saucepan over low heat; mix well. Remove from heat. Add noodles. Stir until noodles are completely coated. Drop by teaspoonfuls onto waxed paper. Cool and eat. Yield: 30 servings.

Ryan Dittmar, Washtenaw

STRAWBERRY GELATIN DESSERT

1/2 angel food cake, broken into small pieces
2 3-oz. packages strawberry gelatin
1 pkg. whipped topping mix, prepared
2 c. miniature marshmallows
1 12-oz. can crushed pineapple
1 10-oz. package frozen strawberries, thawed
3/4 c. chopped pecans

Place cake pieces in 9 x 13-inch pan. Dissolve gelatin in 2 cups boiling water in bowl. Chill until partially set. Fold in whipped topping, marshmallows, pineapple and strawberries. Pour over cake. Sprinkle with pecans. Chill for 3 hours to overnight. Yield: 12 servings.

Approx per serv: Cal 323; Prot 7.5 g; T Fat 22.7 g; Chl 17.8 mg; Car 49.2 g; Sod 542.1 mg; Pot 223.1 mg.

Lori Anger, Midland

4-H is 4 million youths in America.

TURTLE CAKE

1 2-layer pkg. German chocolate cake mix
2 tbsp. butter
1 14-oz. package caramels
7 oz. sweetened condensed milk
1 1/2 c. chopped pecans
1 6-oz. package chocolate chips

Prepare cake mix using package directions. Pour half the batter into greased and floured 9 x 13-inch cake pan. Bake at 350 degrees for 15 minutes. Combine butter, caramels and condensed milk in saucepan. Heat until butter and caramels melt, mixing well; cool slightly. Pour over baked cake layer. Sprinkle with pecans and chocolate chips. Spread remaining cake batter carefully over top. Bake at 350 degrees for 20 to 25 minutes. Cool. Cut into squares. Serve with whipped topping. Yield: 15 servings.

NOTE: Nutritional information does not include ingredients used in preparing cake mix.

Approx per serv: Cal 459; Prot 5.7 g; T Fat 20.6 g; Chl 11.3 mg; Car 66.2 g; Sod 421.8 mg; Pot 215.2 mg.

Michelle Root, Washtenaw

BANANA DESSERT

1 1-layer pkg. white cake mix
1 sm. package vanilla instant pudding mix
1 c. cold milk
1 8-oz. package cream cheese, softened
4 bananas, sliced
1 8-oz. carton whipped topping

Prepare and bake cake mix, using package directions. Cool. Combine pudding mix, milk and cream cheese in bowl; mix well. Spread over cake. Arrange sliced bananas over pudding layer. Top with whipped topping. Store in refrigerator. Yield: 8 servings.

Pam Smith, Branch

NACHOS

1 8-oz. package tortilla chips
8 oz. Cheddar cheese, shredded

Arrange tortilla chips in single layer on baking sheet. Sprinkle cheese over top. Bake at 350 degrees for about 5 minutes or until cheese melts. Cool "until you cannot wait any longer!" Yield: 4 servings.

Approx per serv: Cal 534; Prot 18.0 g; T Fat 39.0 g; Chl 74.1 mg; Car 30.4 g; Sod 800.9 mg; Pot 92.5 mg.

Lori Ovink, Marquette

POPCORN MUNCHIES

6 c. popped popcorn
1 c. dry roasted peanuts
1/3 c. shredded coconut
1/4 c. honey
2 tbsp. butter, melted
3/4 c. chopped dried apricots
3/4 c. raisins

Combine popcorn, peanuts and coconut in 9 x 13-inch baking pan. Drizzle mixture of honey and butter over popcorn; mix gently. Bake at 300 degrees for 20 minutes, stirring several times. Cool. Stir popcorn to break into pieces. Add apricots and raisins; mix gently.
Yield: 8 one-cup servings.

Approx per serv: Cal 170; Prot 2.0 g; T Fat 5.7 g; Chl 8.9 mg; Car 31.3 g; Sod 48.4 mg; Pot 260.8 mg.

Jesse Skinner, Isabella

MINI PIZZAS

4 English muffins, split
4 tsp. oil
1 8-oz. can tomato sauce
2 tsp. oregano
1 tsp. basil
8 tsp. grated mozzarella cheese
8 tsp. Parmesan cheese

Spread each muffin half with 1/2 teaspoon oil and 2 tablespoons tomato sauce. Sprinkle with seasonings and cheeses. Arrange on baking sheet. Bake at 400 degrees for 8 to 10 minutes or until cheese melts. Yield: 8 servings.

Jacob Koch, Wayne

POPCORN CRUNCH

1 1/3 c. sugar
1/2 c. light corn syrup
1 c. margarine
8 c. popped popcorn
1 1/2 c. pecan halves (opt.)
2/3 c. whole almonds (opt.)

Combine sugar, corn syrup and margarine in large saucepan. Bring to a boil. Cook for 10 to 15 minutes or until light golden brown, stirring constantly. Remove from heat. Add popcorn and nuts; mix well. Spread on lightly greased baking sheet. Cool completely. Break into pieces. Yield: 10 one-cup servings.

Approx per serv: Cal 539; Prot 5.0 g; T Fat 38.9 g; Chl 0.0 mg; Car 47.9 g; Sod 236.4 mg; Pot 235.5 mg.

Amy Jahn, Huron

FINGER GELATIN

3 3-oz. packages any flavor gelatin
4 env. unflavored gelatin

Combine flavored and unflavored gelatin in bowl; mix well. Add 4 cups boiling water. Stir until gelatin dissolves. Pour into 9 x 13-inch dish. Let stand for 15 minutes. Chill until firm. Cut into squares or shapes as desired.
Yield: 64 servings.

Approx per serv: Cal 16; Prot 0.7 g; T Fat 0.0 g; Chl 0.0 mg; Car 3.5 g; Sod 13.1 mg; Pot 8.5 mg.

Angela Schumacher, Huron

Snacks

THIMBLEBERRY JAM

1 c. thimbleberries
1 c. sugar
1 tsp. butter

Bring thimbleberries to a boil in saucepan. Add sugar and butter. Bring to a boil. Boil for 1 minute. Pour into hot sterilized jars; seal. Process in boiling water bath for 5 minutes.

NOTE: Thimbleberries have their own pectin. The butter prevents foam and eliminates the need to skim. Thimbleberries are a type of raspberry that grows wild and are unique to the Upper Peninsula.

Agnes Ahola, Houghton

THIMBLEBERRY FRUIT AND NUT GRANOLA

1/2 c. butter
1/3 c. sugar
1/3 c. thimbleberry jam
1/3 c. chopped dried apricots
1/2 c. chopped dates
1/2 c. coarsely flaked coconut
3 tbsp. sesame seed
1/4 c. sunflower seed
2 tbsp. wheat germ
1/2 c. coarsely chopped cashews
3 c. oats
1/2 c. raisins

Combine butter, sugar and jam in large saucepan. Cook over low heat until melted, stirring constantly. Add remaining ingredients except raisins; stir to coat evenly. Spread in ungreased 9 x 13-inch baking pan. Bake at 325 degrees for 35 to 45 minutes or until golden brown, stirring occasionally. Stir in raisins. Spread on cookie sheet to cool. Store in airtight container in cool dry place. Yield: 6 servings.

NOTE: Other jams may be substituted for thimbleberry.

Kimberly Passerello, Houghton

GRANOLA

12 c. oats
2 c. almonds
2 c. pecans

1 c. soy flour (opt.)
1 c. sunflower seed
1/2 c. unsweetened coconut
1/2 c. sesame seed
2 c. nonfat dry milk powder
2 1/2 c. olive oil
2 1/2 c. honey
2 c. raisins

Combine first 8 ingredients in large bowl; mix well. Beat olive oil and honey in bowl until blended. Pour over dry ingredients; mix well. Pour into lightly greased baking pan. Bake at 275 degrees for 50 minutes, stirring occasionally. Stir in raisins. Cool completely. Store cooled Granola in plastic bags.
Yield: 56 one-half cup servings.

Approx per serv: Cal 308; Prot 6.4 g; T Fat 18.3 g; Chl 0.9 mg; Car 32.9 g; Sod 26.8 mg; Pot 289.1 mg.

Shawna Hughes, Tina Hughes, Marquette

HONEY CRUNCH

1 c. Corn Chex
1 c. Wheat Chex
1 c. Rice Chex
1 c. quick-cooking oats
1 c. chopped pecans
1 tsp. cinnamon
1/4 tsp. salt
1/2 c. butter
1/3 c. honey
1/4 c. packed brown sugar
1/2 c. raisins

Mix cereals, oats, pecans, cinnamon and salt in large bowl. Combine butter, honey and brown sugar in saucepan. Cook over low heat until melted, stirring constantly. Pour over cereal mixture; stir to coat evenly. Spread in 10 x 15-inch baking pan. Bake at 325 degrees for 20 to 25 minutes or until golden brown, stirring occasionally. Stir in raisins. Spread on waxed paper-covered racks to cool. Store in tightly covered container in cool dry place.
Yield: 14 one-half-cup servings.

Sharon Shumaker, Antrim

TOASTED CEREAL SNACK

2 c. Kix
2 c. Cheerios

2 1/2 c. pretzel sticks
1 1/2 c. mixed nuts
1/3 c. butter, melted
1 tbsp. Worcestershire sauce
1/2 tsp. garlic salt
1/2 tsp. celery salt

Mix cereals, pretzels and nuts in 9 x 13-inch baking pan. Blend butter with Worcestershire sauce, garlic salt and celery salt. Stir into cereal mixture. Bake at 250 degrees for 15 minutes; stir gently. Bake for 15 minutes longer. Yield: 8 one-cup servings.

Sarah O'Henley, Huron

GOAT'S MILK SOFT CHEESE

1 gal. goat's milk
2 tbsp. buttermilk
2 drops of cheese rennet
1 tbsp. (about) salt

Heat goat's milk in saucepan over low heat to 72 degrees. Add buttermilk and cheese rennet diluted with 1/4 cup water. Stir for 1 to 2 minutes. Let stand at 72 degrees for 18 to 20 hours. Pour into muslin bag. Hang in cool place to drain whey from curd. Let drain for 12 to 24 hours or until reduced to slightly less than half the original weight. Add salt to taste (about 2 teaspoons per pound); mix well. Store, tightly covered, in refrigerator for up to 2 weeks. Yield: 1 1/2 pounds.

NOTE: The lower the temperature of the cheese, the shorter the draining time.

Denise Bretzke, Benzie

SCOTCH EGGS

1/2 c. sour cream
2 tsp. prepared horseradish
1/2 tsp. dried dillweed
1/4 tsp. salt
12 oz. pork sausage
8 hard-boiled eggs
1 egg, lightly beaten
1/2 c. fine dry bread crumbs
Oil for frying

Combine sour cream, horseradish, dillweed and salt in small bowl; mix well. Chill until serving time. Divide sausage into 8 portions. Peel hard-boiled eggs; pat dry. Press 1 portion sausage

around each egg to enclose completely. Dip in beaten egg; roll in bread crumbs to coat. Fry in 1/2-inch deep 375-degree oil for 5 to 6 minutes or until golden brown, turning frequently. Drain on paper towels. Serve with sour cream sauce. Yield: 4 servings.

NOTE: These pack well for picnics and camping trips.

Larry Taylor, Don Jones, Jr.
Anjeanette Taylor, Formici Dean, Ingham

BEEF JERKY

Lean beef or venison
Steak sauce
Worcestershire sauce
Garlic salt
Pepper (opt.)

Trim fat from beef or venison. Cut into 1/2-inch strips. Place in large dish. Cover with mixture of steak sauce and Worcestershire sauce. Sprinkle with garlic salt and pepper. Marinate, covered, overnight. Drain. Place strips on rack on baking sheet. Bake at 200 degrees for 6 to 8 hours or until dry but not brittle. Store in sealed plastic bags in freezer.

NOTE: May use food dryer, according to manufacturer's directions.

Anne Westlund, Antrim

GOAT JERKY

1 1/2 to 2 lb. boneless goat brisket
   or steak
1/3 c. soy sauce
1 tbsp. Worcestershire sauce
1 tsp. garlic salt
1/2 tsp. seasoned pepper

Trim fat completely. Slice into long 1/8 to 1/4-inch thick strips. Combine soy sauce, Worcestershire sauce, garlic salt and seasoned pepper in large bowl. Add goat meat, stirring to coat evenly. Marinate for 2 hours to overnight. Drain. Place strips in single layer on oven rack or rack in broiler pan. Bake at 150 to 200 degrees for 5 to 12 hours or until dark brown but not brittle. Yield: 8 servings.

NOTE: Beef may be substituted for goat. Jerky can be cooked over open fire or wood stove.

Denise Bretzke, Benzie

BAKED CARAMEL CORN

2 sticks margarine, melted
2 c. packed brown sugar
1/2 c. corn syrup
1 tsp. salt
1/2 tsp. soda
1 tsp. vanilla extract
6 qt. popped popcorn

Bring margarine, brown sugar, corn syrup and salt to a boil in saucepan, stirring constantly. Cook for 5 minutes. Do not stir. Remove from heat. Stir in soda and vanilla. Pour over popcorn in large baking pan; mix well. Bake at 250 degrees for 1 hour, stirring every 15 minutes. Break apart when cool. Yield: 24
Yield: 24 one-cup servings.

Approx per serv: Cal 180; Prot 0.8 g; T Fat 8.0 g; Chl 0.0 mg; Car 27.4 g; Sod 209.7 mg; Pot 80.9 mg.

Helen Potter, Shiawassee

4-H is a family-oriented program.

RICHARD'S GOAT'S MILK ICE CREAM

9 egg yolks
3 c. sugar
3/4 tsp. salt
6 c. goat's milk, scalded
6 c. cream
1 tsp. vanilla extract

Beat egg yolks, sugar and salt in saucepan. Pour goat's milk over mixture. Cook until mixture coats spoon, stirring constantly. Cool completely. Stir in cream and vanilla. Pour into ice cream freezer. Freeze according to manufacturer's instructions. Yield: 15 servings.

Approx per serv: Cal 300; Prot 6.2 g; T Fat 7.0 g; Chl 164.6 mg; Car 55.1 g; Sod 228.9 mg; Pot 489.9 mg.

Richard G. Anders, St. Joseph

DENISE'S GOAT'S MILK ICE CREAM

4 c. goat's milk
1/3 c. honey
3 tbsp. flour
1/4 tsp. salt
3 eggs, beaten
1 1/2 tsp. vanilla extract

Pour goat's milk into saucepan. Stir in honey, flour and salt gradually. Cook over low heat until thickened, stirring constantly. Stir a small amount of hot mixture into eggs; stir eggs into hot mixture. Cook for 1 minute, stirring constantly. Chill. Stir in vanilla. Pour into ice cream freezer container. Freeze according to manufacturer's instructions. Yield: 6 servings.

Approx per serv: Cal 221; Prot 8.9 g; T Fat 9.4 g; Chl 149.2 mg; Car 26.1 g; Sod 175.7 mg; Pot 338.4 mg.

Denise Bretzke, Benzie

PEANUT BUTTER BALLS

1/2 c. carob powder
1/2 c. (or less) honey
1/2 c. natural peanut butter
1/2 c. raw sunflower seed
1/2 c. sesame seed
1/4 c. raw wheat germ
1/2 c. (or more) unsweetened coconut
Nonfat dry milk powder (opt.)

Combine first 7 ingredients in order listed in bowl, mixing well after each addition. Add additional coconut or a small amount of dried milk powder if necessary to make of desired consistency. Shape into small balls; place on waxed paper. Let stand until firm.
Yield: 48 servings.

Sandi Timlin, Clare

GOAT'S MILK YOGURT

1 qt. goat's milk
1 c. instant nonfat dry milk powder
1/4 c. plain yogurt

Mix goat's milk and dry milk powder in saucepan. Heat to 180 degrees. Do not boil. Remove from heat. Cool to 100 degrees. Stir in yogurt. Incubate at 90 degrees for 3 hours for mild taste. Incubate longer for tart taste, tasting every 30 minutes. Refrigerate to use as desired. May add honey, jam or pie filling for flavor.
Yield: 6 one-cup servings.

Approx per serv: Cal 171; Prot 11.4 g; T Fat 6.6 g; Chl 26.6 mg; Car 16.4 g; Sod 146.5 mg; Pot 591.8 mg.

Sandra Bell-Zorkot, Bay

Heritage Foods

MAPLE SUGAR CAKE

2 eggs, well beaten
1 c. packed brown sugar
1 c. maple syrup
1 tsp. baking powder
1 tsp. soda
1 c. sour cream
1 tsp. vanilla extract (opt.)
2 c. (about) flour

Combine eggs and brown sugar in large bowl; mix well. Stir in syrup, baking powder, soda and sour cream. Add vanilla and flour; mix well. Pour into greased 9 x 13-inch cake pan. Bake at 325 degrees for 40 to 50 minutes or until cake tests done. Cool. Cut into squares. Does not require icing. Yield: 24 servings.

This recipe was used only on special occasions such as reunions, holidays, birthdays and days of grief.

Approx per serv: Cal 133; Prot 1.9 g; T Fat 2.6 g; Chl 25.3 mg; Car 25.8 g; Sod 62.3 mg; Pot 83.9 mg.

Martha W. Warner
Liberty Hyde Bailey Birthsite Museum
South Haven, Van Buren County

MINTADE

1/2 c. chopped fresh mint
2 c. sugar
1 c. grapefruit juice
1 c. lemon juice
1 c. loganberry juice

Combine mint, sugar and 4 cups water in saucepan. Boil for 5 minutes. Cool. Strain into pitcher. Add remaining ingredients; mix well. Chill until serving time. Yield: 8 servings.
NOTE: May substitute grape juice for loganberry juice.

My grandmother always made this in summer from mint that we picked at our cottage on Long Lake.

Judy Huynh, Ionia

BARA BRITH BREAD

2/3 c. buttermilk
1/4 c. packed light brown sugar
1/4 c. butter
1/2 tsp. salt
1 1/4 c. flour

1 pkg. dry yeast
1/4 tsp. cinnamon
1/8 tsp. nutmeg
1/8 tsp. cloves
1 egg
2/3 c. raisins
1 to 1 1/4 c. flour

Combine first 4 ingredients in saucepan. Heat to 115 degrees, stirring constantly. Add to mixture of 1 1/4 cups flour, yeast and spices in mixer bowl. Add egg. Beat at low speed for 30 seconds. Beat at high speed for 3 minutes. Stir in raisins and as much flour as possible with spoon. Turn onto floured surface. Knead in enough remaining flour to make moderately stiff dough. Knead for 6 to 8 minutes or until smooth and elastic. Place in greased bowl, turning to grease surface. Let rise, covered, until doubled in bulk. Shape into loaf; place in greased loaf pan. Bake at 375 degrees for 15 to 20 minutes. Cover with foil. Bake for 20 minutes longer. Remove from pan. Cool on wire rack. Yield: 12 servings.

Bara Brith means speckled in Welsh. Raisins or currants are the speckling today, but fresh blueberries used to be commonly used.

Approx per serv: Cal 183; Prot 4.2 g; T Fat 4.6 g; Chl 33.2 mg; Car 31.5 g; Sod 162.8 mg; Pot 139.6 mg.

Penny S. Pearson, Huron

FINNISH BISCUIT
(COFFEE BREAD)

1 cake yeast
1 c. plus 2 tbsp. sugar
1 tsp. salt
3 c. milk, scalded
4 1/4 c. flour
5 eggs
5 c. flour
1/2 c. melted butter
9 to 12 cardamom seed, crushed
1/2 c. confectioners' sugar
1/4 c. milk
2 tbsp. butter

Dissolve yeast in 1/2 cup lukewarm water. Combine sugar, salt, milk and 4 1/4 cups flour in bowl; beat well. Add yeast; beat well. Let stand for 10 minutes. Add eggs; mix well. Stir in 5 cups flour, melted butter and cardamom. Knead on floured surface until smooth and elastic. Place in greased bowl, turning to grease surface. Let rise for 1 hour. Fill and shape as desired. Place in 5 loaf pans or pie plates. Let rise for 1 hour or until doubled in bulk. Bake at 350 degrees for 30 minutes. Blend remaining ingredients in bowl. Drizzle over warm breads. Yield: 50 servings.

NOTE: Fill with almond or poppy seed filling or cinnamon sugar for coffee breads or braid into loaves.

Approx per serv: Cal 145; Prot 3.7 g; T Fat 34.6 g; Chl 34.6 mg; Car 24.2 g; Sod 85.3 mg; Pot 54.9 mg.

Vernice Johnson, Menominee

GERMAN CHRISTMAS PEPPER BUNS

3 pkg. dry yeast
Flour
2 c. milk
1 c. honey
1 c. dark molasses
3/4 tsp. pepper
3/4 c. butter

Dissolve yeast in 2 cups warm water in large bowl. Add enough flour to make of pancake batter consistency. Let rise until doubled in bulk. Heat milk in saucepan until warm. Add honey, molasses, pepper and butter. Stir until butter melts. Add to yeast mixture; mix well. Stir in enough flour to make soft dough. Place in greased bowl, turning to grease surface. Let rise until doubled in bulk. Spoon into greased muffin cups. Let rise until doubled in bulk. Bake at 350 degrees for 20 to 30 minutes or until brown. Yield: 72 servings.

NOTE: Arrange buns on baking sheets in Christmas tree shape. Decorate as desired for gifts.

My German grandmother made these only at Christmas. It isn't Christmas without them.

Anna Butterfield, Lapeer

RAISED POTATO DOUGHNUTS

2 pkg. dry yeast
2 c. milk, scalded
2 c. potato water
3/4 c. sugar
2/3 c. butter
4 c. flour
4 eggs, beaten
1 3/4 c. warm mashed cooked potatoes

2 tsp. salt
6 to 8 c. flour
Oil for deep frying

Dissolve yeast in 1/2 cup warm water. Combine milk, potato water, sugar and butter in saucepan. Heat until butter melts. Cool to lukewarm. Combine with yeast and 4 cups flour in large bowl; mix well. Add eggs, potatoes and salt; mix well. Add 6 to 8 cups flour or enough to make soft dough. Let rise until doubled in bulk. Roll 1/4 inch thick on floured surface. Cut with doughnut cutter. Let rise until doubled in bulk. Deep-fry until brown. Drain on paper towels. Yield: 80 servings.

This recipe was my great-grandmother's.

Daniel Schneirla, Saginaw

ERIC'S INDIAN FRY BREAD

4 1/2 c. flour
2 tbsp. sugar
2 tbsp. baking powder
4 tsp. salt
1/2 stick butter
2 c. milk
Oil for deep frying

Combine first 6 ingredients in bowl; mix well. Knead on floured surface for 5 minutes. Shape into ball. Place in greased bowl. Let stand in warm place for 10 minutes. Pat into small round cakes. Deep-fry until golden brown on both sides. Drain on paper towel.

Eric Dearman, Calhoun

MIRIAM'S INDIAN FRY BREAD

4 c. flour
1/2 tsp. salt
1 1/2 tsp. baking powder
Oil for deep frying

Sift dry ingredients into bowl. Stir in 1 cup water. Knead on floured surface. Divide into 12 portions. Roll; shape as for doughnut. Deep-fry in hot oil until brown on both sides. Drain on paper towel. Spread with jam or confectioners' sugar if desired. May make into larger rounds and layer with meat, lettuce, tomatoes and cheese for Indian tacos. Yield: 12 servings.

This recipe comes from Indian elders and is served at many festivals.

Miriam Rund, Gogebic

KRUSCZCIKI (CRULLERS)

12 egg yolks, beaten
1 tsp. vanilla extract
1 tbsp. Brandy
1/4 c. sour cream
1 tbsp. vinegar
1/2 tsp. salt
2 c. flour
Oil for deep frying
Confectioners' sugar

Combine first 5 ingredients; mix well. Add salt and half the flour; mix well. Stir in remaining flour gradually. Knead until well mixed. Roll on floured surface. Cut into strips. Make slit in center of each strip. Pull end through slit to make bow shape. Deep-fry several at a time until brown. Drain on paper towel. Sprinkle with confectioners' sugar.

This old Polish recipe belonged to my great-grandmother, and has been handed down for generations.

Michelle Conrod, St. Joseph

ITALIAN ANISE TOAST

2 eggs
2/3 c. sugar
1 tsp. aniseed
1 c. sifted flour

Beat eggs and sugar in bowl until light. Add aniseed and flour; mix well. Press into greased and floured loaf pan. Bake at 375 degrees for 20 minutes or until bread tests done. Pan will be only half filled. Remove from pan. Cut into 1/2-inch slices. Place on greased baking sheet. Bake for 5 minutes on each side.
Yield: 16 servings.

Approx per serv: Cal 71; Prot 1.6 g; T Fat 0.8 g; Chl 31.6 mg; Car 14.3 g; Sod 7.9 mg; Pot 15.8 mg.

Kelly Liles, Macomb

GERMAN PANCAKES

4 eggs
1/3 c. sugar
2 c. milk
2 c. flour
1 tsp. salt
1 tsp. vanilla extract
1/4 c. margarine, softened

Beat eggs in bowl until light. Add sugar and milk; mix well. Add flour, salt and vanilla; beat well. Spread margarine in shallow 12-inch round casserole. Pour in batter. Bake at 350 degrees for 40 minutes or until puffed and golden brown. Remove from pan. Fill with fruit; garnish with confectioners' sugar.
Yield: 6 servings.

NOTE: May reduce sugar to 2 tablespoons and fill with cheese and meat sauce for main dish.

This is an old-country favorite which is easy to prepare, showy to serve, and best to eat.

Approx per serv: Cal 369; Prot 11.5 g; T Fat 14.8 g; Chl 179.9 mg; Car 46.9 g; Sod 530.7 mg; Pot 200.2 mg.

Neil P. Kentner, St. Joseph

PANNUKAAKKU (FINNISH OVEN PANCAKE)

1/2 c. butter
4 eggs
2 tbsp. sugar
1 tsp. salt
4 c. milk
2 c. flour
2 tbsp. sugar

Melt butter in 9 x 13-inch baking pan. Do not brown. Beat eggs, 2 tablespoons sugar and salt in bowl until lemon colored. Add milk; mix well. Stir in flour gradually. Pour in butter; beat well. Pour batter into buttered pan. Bake in preheated 400-degree oven for 30 to 40 minutes or until golden brown. Sprinkle 2 tablespoons sugar on top. Serve warm.
Yield: 12 servings.

Approx per serv: Cal 240; Prot 7.2 g; T Fat 12.6 g; Chl 119.3 mg; Car 24.2 g; Sod 332.6 mg; Pot 160.8 mg.

Virginia Rintala, Houghton

FINNISH PANNUKAAKKU

1 stick margarine
3 eggs
3 tbsp. sugar
3 c. milk
1/2 tsp. vanilla extract
1 c. flour
3 tbsp. melted margarine

Melt 1 stick margarine in 9 x 13-inch baking pan. Combine eggs, sugar and milk in bowl; beat well. Add vanilla, flour and 3 tablespoons

melted margarine; mix well. Pour into prepared pan. Bake in preheated 400-degree oven for 15 to 20 minutes or until light brown. Serve warm with fresh fruit or cinnamon.
Yield: 12 servings.

Pannukaakku means pancake in Finnish. It has been in the Liimatta family for generations.

Approx per serv: Cal 204; Prot 4.9 g; T Fat 14.2 g; Chl 71.7 mg; Car 14.2 g; Sod 174.5 mg; Pot 117.0 mg.

Diane Trudgeon-Fontana, Keweenaw

ARAB POCKET BREAD

1 env. dry yeast
2 tbsp. sugar
1 tbsp. salt
6 c. (about) whole wheat flour

Dissolve yeast and sugar in 2 1/2 cups warm water in large bowl. Let stand until bubbly. Add salt and 4 cups flour; mix well. Add enough additional flour to make stiff dough. Knead on floured surface until smooth and elastic. Place in greased bowl, turning to grease surface. Let rise until doubled in bulk. Divide and shape into 30 balls. Let rest, covered, for 20 minutes. Roll each 1/4 to 1/8 inch thick. Let rest for 20 minutes. Remove racks from oven. Be sure each loaf has no creases; slide several at a time directly onto bottom of preheated 450-degree oven. Bake for 3 to 4 minutes or until completely puffed. Cool on wire rack. Store, tightly wrapped, in refrigerator for several days only or freeze. Toast lightly for fresh-baked flavor. Yield: 30 servings.

Approx per serv: Cal 84; Prot 3.3 g; T Fat 0.5 g; Chl 0.0 mg; Car 18.0 g; Sod 214.0 mg; Pot 93.5 mg.

Kimberly Passerello, Houghton

PITA BREAD

1 pkg. dry yeast
2 tsp. sugar
4 1/2 c. flour
1 1/2 tsp. salt
3 tbsp. olive oil

Dissolve yeast and sugar in 1/4 cup warm water. Combine flour, salt, oil, yeast and 1 3/4 cups water in bowl. Beat with wooden spoon until well mixed. Knead on floured surface for 5 to 10 minutes or until smooth and elastic. Place in greased bowl, turning to grease surface. Let rise, covered, in warm place for 1 1/4 hours or until doubled in bulk. Knead lightly. Roll into 12-inch rectangle. Cut into 12 pieces. Shape each piece into ball. Roll into 1/2 x 6 1/2-inch circles. Preheat greased baking sheet on lowest rack of 500-degree oven. Bake rolls 2 at a time on hot baking sheet for 4 minutes; turn. Bake for 1 minute longer. Place on towel; cover with damp towel. Stuff with favorite fillings.
Yield: 12 servings.

Approx per serv: Cal 205; Prot 5.1 g; T Fat 3.9 g; Chl 0.0 mg; Car 36.6 g; Sod 267.7 mg; Pot 56.2 mg.

Judy Utrup, Osceola

SWEDISH RYE BREAD

3 c. medium rye flour
1/2 c. dark molasses
1/4 c. shortening
1 tbsp. salt
1 env. dry yeast
1 tbsp. caraway seed
3 1/2 to 4 c. all-purpose flour

Combine first 4 ingredients and 2 1/2 cups hot water in bowl. Cool to lukewarm. Stir in yeast. Add caraway seed and enough all-purpose flour to make stiff dough. Knead on floured surface for 10 minutes. Place in greased bowl. Let rise, covered, in warm place for 2 hours or until doubled in bulk. Punch dough down. Let rise for 30 minutes. Shape into 3 balls. Let rest for 10 minutes. Shape each into round loaf in greased 8-inch round baking pan. Let rise, covered, for 1 to 1 1/2 hours or until very light. Bake at 375 degrees for 30 minutes or until bread tests done. Yield: 36 servings.

Approx per serv: Cal 100; Prot 2.4 g; T Fat 1.8 g; Chl 0.0 mg; Car 18.6 g; Sod 182.5 mg; Pot 165.3 mg.

Annette L. Dedic, Delta

SWEDISH LIVER PAULT

2 c. ground liver
3 c. ground potatoes
1/3 c. milk
1 1/2 tbsp. salt
3 c. flour
1/2 tsp. baking powder (opt.)

Combine all ingredients in bowl; mix well. Shape into hand-sized dumplings. Place in boiling salted water in large kettle. Cook for 1 hour. Drain. Serve hot with butter and a glass of milk. May cool completely, slice and fry in butter in skillet until brown. Yield: 8 servings.

Ellen Wiltzer, Missaukee

SIKOTAKI YAHNI
(GREEK LIVER CASSEROLE)

3 med. onions, chopped
3 tbsp. olive oil
1 lb. liver, cut into 1-in. cubes
1/2 c. flour
2 tbsp. tomato paste
1/2 c. beef stock
3/4 c. red wine
Oregano to taste
12 pitted green olives

Saute onions in olive oil in Dutch oven; remove onions. Coat liver with flour. Brown in Dutch oven. Add tomato paste, stock, wine, oregano, salt and pepper to taste and sauteed onions. Bring to a boil. Bake, covered, at 350 degrees for 30 minutes. Add olives. Bake, covered, for 10 minutes longer. Serve over hot cooked rice. Yield: 4 servings.

Betty L. Horrocks, Presque Isle

The 4-H emblem is a green 4-leaf clover with 4 white H's.

PASTIES

1 recipe 2-crust pie pastry
5 potatoes, chopped
1 onion, chopped
3/4 to 1 lb. round steak, diced
1 c. chopped rutabaga (opt.)
1/4 c. butter

Roll dough into four 1/4-inch thick circles on lightly floured surface. Arrange potatoes, onion, steak and rutabaga over half of each circle. Add salt and pepper to taste. Dot with butter. Fold dough over to enclose filling; roll edge to seal. Place on baking sheet. Bake at 400 degrees for 45 minutes. Serve hot or cold with catsup. Good for picnics. Yield: 4 servings.

My great-grandmother brought this Cornish recipe to the Upper Peninsula in the 1800's. Miners would carry them in dinner buckets to have a filling meal.

Approx per serv: Cal 986; Prot 34.5 g; T Fat 55.8 g; Chl 112.6 mg; Car 87.2 g; Sod 784.3 mg; Pot 1518.7 mg.

Jon Rund, Gogebic

MEAT AND POTATO PIIRAKKA

1/2 tsp. salt
2 tbsp. oil
1 1/2 c. all-purpose flour
1 1/2 c. rye flour
2 c. mashed cooked potatoes
1/4 c. hot milk
2 tbsp. melted butter
2 c. cooked ground roast beef
1/4 c. milk

Combine 1 cup water, salt and oil in bowl. Add all-purpose flour. Beat until smooth. Mix in rye flour. Knead on floured surface for 3 minutes. Divide into 12 portions. Roll each into 6 to 8-inch circle on floured surface. Beat potatoes, hot milk and butter in bowl until fluffy. Place 2 tablespoons potato mixture and 2 tablespoons beef on half of each circle. Fold dough over to enclose filling; crimp edge. Place on greased baking sheet. Brush with milk. Bake at 450 degrees for 15 minutes or until lightly browned. Brush with milk. Yield: 6 servings.

A variation of this recipe was used in Karelia, Finland to let a boy know he was liked by the girl's family.

Approx per serv: Cal 514; Prot 16.1 g; T Fat 26.1 g; Chl 58.2 mg; Car 53.3 g; Sod 481.5 mg; Pot 340.6 mg.

Tanya Dostaler, Houghton

SAUERBRATEN

1   8 to 10-lb. top sirloin roast
1 c. vinegar
1 lg. onion, sliced
1 c. sliced carrots
1/2 clove of garlic
1/2 c. sugar
1 tbsp. salt
1   6-oz. can tomato paste
1 bay leaf
1/4 tsp. chopped parsley
1/4 tsp. chopped celery
1 tsp. marjoram
2 tsp. salt
1 tsp. pepper
Flour
1/4 to 1/2 c. Burgundy

Marinate roast in mixture of vinegar and next 5 ingredients in refrigerator for 3 days. Drain, reserving marinade. Remove and chop 1 tablespoon onion and 1 tablespoon carrot. Strain marinade; set aside. Roast sirloin as desired, turning occasionally. Combine 2 cups water, 2 cups reserved marinade, chopped onion and carrot, tomato paste and next 6 ingredients in saucepan. Boil for 30 minutes. Stir in mixture of enough flour to thicken to desired consistency and a small amount of water. Cook until thickened, stirring constantly. Add Burgundy. Slice roast; arrange on serving platter. Top with sauce. Yield: 12 servings.

Michelle Schluckebier, Saginaw

HULPCHES

1 head cabbage
1 1/2 lb. ground beef
1 c. uncooked rice
1 c. grated potato
1/4 c. grated onion
4 c. (or more) sauerkraut

Core cabbage; place in boiling water in saucepan. Remove and drain leaves as each becomes wilted. Trim center vein. Combine ground beef, rice, potato, onion and salt and pepper to taste in bowl; mix well. Place 1 tablespoon mixture on each leaf; roll to enclose filling, tucking in ends. Arrange in roasting pan lined with half the sauerkraut. Top with remaining sauerkraut and juice. Bake at 300 degrees for 2 to 3 hours or until rice is tender. Yield: 6 servings.

NOTE: Cabbage is easily prepared by microwaving cored cabbage on High, removing leaves as wilted.

Approx per serv: Cal 560; Prot 28.9 g; T Fat 12.5 g; Chl 77.1 mg; Car 85.5 g; Sod 1258.9 mg; Pot 882.1 mg.

Joan M. Kuhne, Saginaw

LaVONNE'S ENCHILADA CASSEROLE

1/2 lb. ground beef
1/2 c. chopped onion
1 can cream of mushroom soup
1 can cream of chicken soup
1/2 c. chopped green chilies
1 can mild enchilada sauce
2 1/2 c. pinto beans
12 corn tortillas
8 oz. Cheddar cheese, grated

Brown ground beef and onion in skillet, stirring frequently; drain. Add soups, green chilies, enchilada sauce and pinto beans; mix well. Layer tortillas and ground beef mixture 1/2 at a time in 9 x 13-inch baking dish. Top with cheese. Bake at 350 degrees for 30 minutes. Yield: 8 servings.

NOTE: May substitute 1/2 can spaghetti sauce mixed with 1/2 package enchilada sauce mix for enchilada sauce.

LaVonne Cadeau, Baraga

SWEDISH MEATBALLS

2 lb. ground beef
1 env. dry onion soup mix
1 egg
1/2 c. quick-cooking oats
1/2 tsp. nutmeg
2 to 4 tbsp. shortening
1 can cream of chicken soup
1 soup can beef broth

Combine first 5 ingredients in bowl; mix well. Shape by teaspoonfuls into balls. Brown in shortening in skillet; remove meatballs. Add soup and broth to pan drippings; mix well. Return meatballs to skillet. Simmer for 1 hour. Yield: 8 servings.

Approx per serv: Cal 456; Prot 24.2 g; T Fat 32.4 g; Chl 127.6 mg; Car 11.8 g; Sod 1097.8 mg; Pot 434.5 mg.

Helene Svinicki, Menominee

PANCID (FILIPINO RICE NOODLE DISH)

1 lb. chopped pork
1 c. sliced celery
1 1/2 c. sliced carrots
1 1/2 c. sliced mushrooms
1   10-oz. package frozen small shrimp
8 oz. pancid noodles
Garlic powder and pepper to taste

Stir-fry pork in skillet over medium heat until brown. Add celery and carrots. Stir-fry until tender-crisp. Add mushrooms and shrimp. Simmer until heated through. Soak noodles in hot water for 3 to 4 minutes; drain. Combine vegetable mixture and noodles in large bowl. Add seasonings; mix gently. Yield: 4 servings.

NOTE: Pancid noodles are also called rice sticks or rice vermicelli. This recipe can also be prepared with beef or sausage instead of shrimp.

Sara Hutchings, Cass

SAUCIJZEBROODJES
(PIGS IN A BLANKET)

2 c. flour
1 tbsp. baking powder
1/2 tsp. salt
1 tbsp. butter
1 tbsp. lard
2/3 c. milk
1 1/2 lb. ground lean shoulder pork
1/2 c. cracker crumbs
1/2 c. milk
1 egg

Combine first 3 ingredients in bowl. Cut in butter and lard until crumbly. Add milk; mix well. Roll on floured surface until slightly thicker than pie crust. Cut into 3-inch squares. Combine remaining ingredients and salt and pepper to taste in bowl; mix well. Shape into 2-inch long rolls. Place on pastry squares; wrap pastry to enclose filling; seal ends. Place on baking sheet. Bake at 350 degrees for 30 minutes or until brown. Yield: 20 servings.

Approx per serv: Cal 164; Prot 7.7 g; T Fat 9.3 g; Chl 38.0 mg; Car 11.6 g; Sod 417.9 mg; Pot 125.7 mg.

Maryann Springett, Van Buren

POPPERKOSH

1 lg. green pepper, sliced
1 lg. onion, sliced
1 to 2 tbsp. butter
1 to 2 tbsp. oil
2 to 3 qt. tomato juice
4 c. chopped peeled potatoes
1 lb. frankfurters, cut into 2-in. pieces
Paprika to taste

Saute green pepper and onion in mixture of butter and oil in 8-quart Dutch oven until tender. Add tomato juice. Bring to a simmer over medium heat. Add potatoes. Cook until almost tender. Add cut frankfurters. Simmer until frankfurters puff. Season with salt and pepper to taste. Sprinkle with paprika. Yield: 8 servings.
NOTE: Use home-canned tomato juice if possible for improved flavor and texture.

Approx per serv: Cal 308; Prot 10.3 g; T Fat 20.9 g; Chl 45.7 mg; Car 20.5 g; Sod 846.6 mg; Pot 690.7 mg.

Joanne K. Atkinson, Midland

KALA MOJAKKA (FISH SOUP)

4 or 5 med. potatoes, peeled,
  coarsely chopped
1 med. onion, sliced
3 carrots, cut into 1-in. pieces (opt.)
1 bay leaf (opt.)
1 1/2 to 2 lb. trout
1/4 c. (about) flour
1/4 tsp. allspice (opt.)
1 to 2 tbsp. butter

Combine potatoes, onion and carrots in large saucepan; add water to cover. Cook until almost tender. Add bay leaf, salt and pepper to taste and trout cut into large pieces. Cook until fish flakes easily. Blend enough flour to make soup of desired consistency with a small amount of water. Stir into soup. Cook until thickened, stirring constantly. Pour into soup tureen. Sprinkle with allspice; top with butter. Yield: 4 servings.

The weekly visit of the fish man with his fresh catch of walleye, white fish or trout made this a special summer treat.

Helen Walker, Delta

LUTEFISK

Lutefisk
Salt

Cut lutefisk into serving portions. Wrap in cheesecloth; tie securely. Place in cold water in large kettle; add a generous amount of salt. Bring to boiling point over low heat. Do not overcook. Drain; remove cheesecloth and place on serving plate. Serve hot with white sauce or drawn butter.

This Scandinavian recipe was prepared in the old days by purchasing dried lutefisk and processing for 2 to 3 days in a lye mixture. Today the stores in our area have done the work, and we buy the whitened fish ready to prepare. It is always served at Christmas.

Clayton Rund, Gogebic

SALSA ALLE VONGOLE
(WHITE CLAM SAUCE)

2 cloves of garlic, minced
1/4 c. olive oil
1 tbsp. chopped parsley
1/2 tsp. salt

1/4 tsp. oregano
1/4 tsp. pepper
1 c. littleneck clams
8 oz. linguine
1 egg, lightly beaten

Saute garlic in olive oil in skillet until lightly browned. Add 1/4 cup water, parsley, seasonings and clams with liquid. Cook until heated through. Do not overcook. Cook linguine according to package directions; drain almost all water. Add egg; toss lightly. Add clam sauce; toss lightly. Serve with Parmesan cheese. Yield: 3 servings.

Approx per serv: Cal 531; Prot 22.4 g; T Fat 22.3 g; Chl 122.1 mg; Car 58.7 g; Sod 405.3 mg; Pot 367.4 mg.

Patricia Dresch, Macomb

BARLEY SOUP

1 c. pearl barley
2 onions, chopped
1/2 c. thinly sliced cabbage
1/2 c. chopped rutabaga
1 med. potato, peeled, chopped
1/2 c. chopped celery
1/2 c. chopped carrot

Combine all ingredients with 2 to 3 cups water and salt and pepper to taste in 4-quart saucepan. Cook until barley and vegetables are tender.

This was a survival food of the Scottish family when times were bad. If a venison, beef or lamb bone was available it was oven-roasted for the fat and flavor and cracked for marl. It was added with accumulated pan drippings and haggis when available. The soup was served with hard thin breads much like today's crackers or with bread toasted over fireplace coals. If the mixture was thick and stiff, it was worked into a biscuit-like dough, rolled into plate-sized circles, folded over, crimped with fork and baked.

Marcia Potts-Vande Vusse, Eaton

MAPLE-BAKED BEANS

8 c. cooked navy beans
1 c. catsup
2 tsp. salt
1 1/2 to 2 c. maple syrup
1/4 tsp. pepper
1/2 lb. bacon, chopped

Combine beans, 1 cup water and remaining ingredients in 3-quart casserole; mix well. Bake at 300 degrees for 4 hours or until thickened. Yield: 20 servings.

We made maple syrup for many years on our centennial farm.

Approx per serv: Cal 257; Prot 7.1 g; T Fat 8.4 g; Chl 7.9 mg; Car 39.7 g; Sod 423.8 mg; Pot 429.9 mg.

Florence Linebaugh, Ionia

POLISH NOODLES AND CABBAGE

1/2 c. chopped onion
1/4 c. margarine
4 c. chopped cabbage
1/2 tsp. salt
1/8 tsp. pepper
1 tsp. caraway seed
1 8-oz. package egg noodles, cooked
1/2 c. sour cream

Saute onion in margarine in skillet until tender. Add cabbage. Saute for 5 minutes or until tender-crisp. Add salt, pepper and caraway seed. Stir in noodles and sour cream. Cook for 5 minutes, stirring frequently. Spoon into serving bowl. Yield: 6 servings.

Approx per serv: Cal 391; Prot 6.5 g; T Fat 13.9 g; Chl 44.0 mg; Car 62.3 g; Sod 287.0 mg. Pot 201.0 mg.

Sally Lichota, St. Clair

FRESH MUSTARD GREEN PATTIES

2 lb. fresh mustard greens
1/2 tsp. salt
3 eggs, beaten
1/4 c. grated Parmesan cheese
1/4 c. flour
2 tbsp. finely chopped onion
1/8 tsp. pepper
1/4 tsp. salt
1/2 c. fine dry bread crumbs
2 tbsp. oil

Cook mustard greens in 1 cup boiling water with 1/2 teaspoon salt in covered saucepan until tender; drain and chop finely. Stir in eggs, cheese, flour, onion and seasonings. Shape into 12 patties. Coat with crumbs. Brown in oil in skillet. Yield: 6 servings.

Approx per serv: Cal 200; Prot 11.2 g; T Fat 9.9 g; Chl 131.5 mg; Car 19.2 g; Sod 443.5 mg; Pot 633.0 mg.

Clara Shepherd, Muskegon

CINDY'S PIEROGI

1 c. flour
1/4 tsp. salt
1 egg
1/2 c. dry cottage cheese
1 egg yolk
1 tsp. butter
1/2 c. (about) mashed cooked potatoes

Combine first 3 ingredients in bowl. Stir in 1/4 cup water. Knead on floured surface. Roll out thin. Cut into squares. Mix remaining ingredients in bowl. Spoon 1 teaspoon onto each square. Fold into triangles; pinch edges to seal. Drop into boiling salted water in large saucepan. Cook until dumplings rise to surface. Cook for 5 minutes longer. Drain. Rinse with cold water; drain. Serve with lightly browned butter. May saute in butter in skillet and serve with sour cream. Yield: 50 dumplings.

Approx per serv: Cal 16; Prot 0.7 g; T Fat 0.4 g; Chl 10.7 mg; Car 2.2 g; Sod 24.2 mg; Pot 10.3 mg.

Cindy Cotter, Isabella

SALLY'S PIEROGI (DUMPLINGS)

2 c. flour
1 egg
1/4 tsp. salt
5 or 6 med. potatoes, cooked, mashed
1 c. grated Cheddar cheese
1/2 c. finely chopped onion

Sift flour onto bread board. Add egg and salt; mix well. Add 1/2 cup hot water in fine stream, mixing well. Knead several times; divide into 2 portions. Let rest, covered with moist towel, for 15 to 20 minutes. Roll thinly on lightly floured surface; cut with biscuit cutter. Mix remaining ingredients in bowl. Place 1 teaspoonful mixture on each circle; fold over to enclose filling, sealing edge. Place several at a time in boiling salted water in large saucepan. Do not crowd. Cook for 5 minutes or until pierogi float to surface. Serve with melted butter, buttered bread crumbs or sour cream. Yield: 8 servings.

Approx per serv: Cal 291; Prot 10.7 g; T Fat 5.7 g; Chl 45.6 mg; Car 49.1 g; Sod 179.0 mg; Pot 638.4 mg.

Sally Lichota, St. Clair

WARM GERMAN POTATO SALAD

4 slices bacon, chopped
1/2 c. vinegar
6 tbsp. sugar
2 tsp. salt
1/4 tsp. pepper
1 tbsp. (about) flour
6 c. chopped cooked potatoes
1 med. onion, chopped
2 hard-boiled eggs, chopped
1 c. chopped celery

Fry bacon in skillet until crisp. Add 1/3 cup water, vinegar, sugar, salt and pepper. Bring to a boil. Add flour mixed with a small amount of water. Cook until thickened, stirring constantly. Boil for 1 minute. Pour over mixture of potatoes and remaining ingredients in serving bowl; mix well. Yield: 8 servings.

Approx per serv: Cal 237; Prot 6.1 g; T Fat 5.6 g; Chl 67.2 mg; Car 41.9 g; Sod 612.4 mg; Pot 799.4 mg.

Kenneth Schneirla, Saginaw

POLISH-BAKED SAUERKRAUT

1 med. onion, chopped
1 med. green pepper, chopped
1 8-oz. can sliced mushrooms, drained
2 tbsp. butter
4 c. sauerkraut, rinsed, drained
1 28-oz. can tomatoes
2 tbsp. (or more) sugar

Saute onion, green pepper and mushrooms in butter in skillet. Combine with remaining ingredients in 3-quart casserole. Bake at 350 degrees for 1 hour. Yield: 8 servings.

Approx per serv: Cal 93; Prot 3.0 g; T Fat 3.4 g; Chl 8.9 mg; Car 14.8 g; Sod 1047.3 mg; Pot 497.8 mg.

Jane Wade, Muskegon

BUNJACOUDA

2 pt. half and half
1 6-oz. can anchovies, chopped
3 or 4 sticks butter
2 to 4 cloves of garlic, minced

Combine all ingredients in electric skillet. Cook over low heat until slightly thickened, stirring constantly. Serve with Italian bread and bite-sized pieces of cabbage, cauliflower, celery, green pepper and curly lettuce for dipping. Yield: 10 servings.

Approx per serv: Cal 480; Prot 6.0 g; T Fat 49.4 g; Chl 162.3 mg; Car 5.0 g; Sod 604.0 mg; Pot 220.3 mg.

Clayton Rund, Gogebic

BUTTERMILKPAAP

1 qt. buttermilk
1 c. pearl barley
1/2 c. raisins
1 tbsp. salt

Combine all ingredients in 2-quart saucepan. Cook over low heat until milk is absorbed. Spoon into serving bowls. Serve with cream, sugar and honey. Yield: 6 servings.

My husband's grandmother prepared this for her great-grandchildren to show them the foods she ate as a girl.

This breakfast recipe from the Netherlands was prepared by mixing the ingredients in a kettle and hanging it overnight in the fireplace. It was then available all day for people who worked outside in the cold.

Approx per serv: Cal 210; Prot 8.9 g; T Fat 0.5 g; Chl 3.3 mg; Car 43.9 g; Sod 1282.4 mg; Pot 374.3 mg.

Marcia L. Potts-Vande Vusse, Eaton

HOMEMADE SWEET PICKLES

3 to 4-in. cucumbers
2 c. coarse salt
1 tbsp. (heaping) alum
2 qt. cider vinegar
12 c. sugar
2 tbsp. pickling spice
1 tbsp. celery seed
Several drops of green food coloring (opt.)

Cut enough cucumbers lengthwise into quarters to fill 2-gallon crock. Dissolve salt in 4 quarts boiling water. Pour over cucumbers. Let stand in cool place for 1 week. Drain; discard brine and soft cucumbers. Fill crock with clear cold water. Let stand for 24 hours. Drain. Dissolve alum in 4-quarts boiling water. Pour over cucumbers. Let stand for 24 hours. Drain. Combine vinegar, sugar and seasonings in saucepan. Bring to a boil. Pour over cucumbers. Let stand for 24 hours. Drain liquid into saucepan. Bring to a boil; pour over cucumbers. Let stand for 24 hours. Repeat 2 times. Drain liquid into saucepan. Bring to a boil. Pack cucumbers vertically into hot sterilized pint jars, adding food coloring. Pour boiling liquid over cucumbers. Seal with 2-piece lids; shake jars. Process in boiling water bath for 5 minutes. Yield: 10 pints.

Carolyn Sue Allen, Jackson

RIFFLES

1 egg, lightly beaten
Pinch of salt
Flour

Fill egg shell half with water. Add to egg with salt; beat well. Add enough flour to make stiff batter. Pour into boiling liquid gradually, cutting into small pieces with knife. Cook for several minutes.

NOTE: Riffles taste like tiny dumplings and are especially good in homemade soups and stews.

Sally Richardson, Kalkaska

SPECIAL TURKEY DRESSING

2 c. dry bread crumbs
2 lg. onions, finely chopped
2 c. finely chopped celery
2 1/2 lb. ground beef
1   16-oz. box seedless raisins
2 tbsp. sage
2 tsp. poultry seasoning
4 c. mashed cooked potatoes
1 can cream of mushroom soup

Soak bread crumbs in water; squeeze dry. Saute onions and celery in skillet until tender. Brown ground beef lightly in skillet; drain. Combine all ingredients in large bowl; mix well. Use as stuffing for up to 24-pound turkey.

This recipe was my great-grandmother's.

Michelle L. Conrod, St. Joseph

DUTCH ST. NICK CAKE

1 c. packed brown sugar
1 c. molasses
1 1/2 c. cold coffee
2 tsp. aniseed
2 c. flour
1 tsp. soda
1 tsp. cinnamon

Combine first 3 ingredients in bowl; mix well. Add aniseed. Combine remaining ingredients. Add to molasses mixture; mix well. Pour into ungreased 9 x 13-inch cake pan. Bake at 350 degrees for 1 hour. Cool in pan. Yield: 18 servings.

This recipe originated in the Netherlands.

Approx per serv: Cal 142; Prot 1.5 g; T Fat 0.1 g; Chl 0.0 mg; Car 34.2 g; Sod 52.5 mg; Pot 229.5 mg.

Grace Hoekwater, Missaukee

BLACK WALNUT CAKE

1 c. butter, softened
3 c. sifted confectioners' sugar
1 tsp. vanilla extract
4 eggs, separated
2 3/4 c. flour
1 tbsp. baking powder
1/2 tsp. cinnamon
1/4 tsp. salt
1 1/3 c. milk
1 c. chopped black walnuts
1/4 c. confectioners' sugar

Cream butter, confectioners' sugar and vanilla in bowl until light and fluffy. Add egg yolks 1 at a time, beating well after each addition. Combine flour, baking powder, cinnamon and salt. Add to creamed mixture alternately with milk, beating well after each addition. Fold in walnuts. Fold stiffly beaten egg whites gently into batter. Pour into greased and floured 10-inch bundt pan. Bake at 350 degrees for 50 minutes or until cake tests done. Cool in pan for 10 minutes. Turn onto wire rack to cool completely. Dust with 1/4 cup confectioners' sugar. Yield: 16 servings.

Approx per serv: Cal 297; Prot 6.2 g; T Fat 18.5 g; Chl 101.5 mg; Car 27.7 g; Sod 261.3 mg; Pot 105.5 mg.

Donna Sobcralski, Mason

GREAT-GRANDMOTHER'S GOLD CAKE

1 c. butter, softened
1 c. sugar
3 eggs
1 tbsp. vanilla extract
3 c. flour
1 tbsp. baking powder
1 c. milk
1/4 to 1/2 c. finely chopped pecans
1 oz. chocolate, melted (opt.)

Cream butter and sugar in bowl until light and fluffy. Add eggs 1 at a time, beating well after each addition. Add vanilla; mix well. Sift flour and baking powder together. Add to creamed mixture alternately with milk, beating well after each addition. Sprinkle pecans in bottom of greased and floured 8 or 9-inch tube pan. Spoon 2/3 of the batter into 3 portions in prepared pan. Blend chocolate into remaining batter. Spoon chocolate batter between portions of yellow batter. Cut lightly with spatula to

marbleize. Bake at 350 degrees for 1 hour. Cool in pan for 10 minutes. Turn onto wire rack to cool completely. Do not frost.
Yield: 16 servings.

This recipe was imported from Germany in 1880 by my grandmother and translated into modern measurements by my mother.

Approx per serv: Cal 295; Prot 4.8 g; T Fat 16.9 g; Chl 85.0 mg; Car 32.4 g; Sod 221.5 mg; Pot 97.8 mg.

Jane M. Trembath, Luce

WILD BLUEBERRY UPSIDE-DOWN CAKE

2 tbsp. butter
1 c. packed brown sugar
2 c. fresh blueberries
3 eggs, separated
1 c. sugar
1/3 c. milk
1 c. sifted flour
1 tsp. baking powder
1/2 tsp. salt

Melt butter in 9 x 9-inch cake pan. Sprinkle brown sugar and blueberries evenly over bottom of prepared pan. Combine beaten egg yolks, sugar, milk, flour, baking powder and salt in bowl; mix well. Fold in stiffly beaten egg whites gently. Spoon over blueberries. Bake at 350 degrees for 45 minutes. Loosen edges with knife. Invert on serving plate. Let stand, covered with cake pan, for 1 minute. Remove pan. Cut into squares. Serve warm with whipped cream. Yield: 9 servings.

Approx per serv: Cal 299; Prot 4.1 g; T Fat 5.1 g; Chl 93.4 mg; Car 61.0 g; Sod 219.1 mg; Pot 158.7 mg.

Charles Kinsey, Montmorency

HICKORY NUT CAKE

2/3 c. butter, softened
1 2/3 c. sugar
3 eggs
1 1/3 c. chopped hickory nuts
2 3/4 c. cake flour
2 tbsp. baking powder
1 c. milk
1 tsp. vanilla extract
1 16-oz. package light brown sugar
1/2 c. cream
1/4 c. butter
1 tsp. vanilla extract

Cream butter and sugar in bowl until light and fluffy. Add eggs; beat well. Coat nuts with a small amount of flour. Sift remaining flour and baking powder together. Add to creamed mixture alternately with milk, mixing well after each addition. Fold in vanilla and nuts. Grease and flour bottoms of 2 layer or one 9 x 13-inch cake pan. Spoon in batter. Bake at 425 degrees for 20 minutes or until cake tests done. Cool on wire rack. Combine brown sugar and cream in saucepan. Cook over medium heat to soft-ball stage. Remove from heat. Beat until cooled. Add butter and vanilla. Beat until of spreading consistency. Frost cooled cake.
Yield: 12 servings.

This recipe was brought from France in 1880.

Wilma Harp, Cass

GRANDMA SYPE'S PORK CAKE

1 lb. ground pork
1 c. molasses
2 c. sugar
5 c. flour
2 tsp. soda
1 tsp. salt
2 tsp. cinnamon
1/2 tsp. allspice
1/2 tsp. cloves
1 lb. raisins
1 c. chopped pecans

Combine pork with 2 cups boiling water in bowl. Cool. Combine remaining ingredients in bowl; mix well. Add pork mixture; mix well. Spoon into loaf pan. Bake at 350 degrees for 45 to 50 minutes or until cake tests done. Cool in pan for 10 minutes. Turn onto wire rack to cool completely. Yield: 12 servings.

This cake has been a traditional Christmas treat in our family for almost 80 years.

Approx per serv: Cal 674; Prot 13.8 g; T Fat 17.0 g; Chl 23.4 mg; Car 120.6 g; Sod 352.5 mg; Pot 746.0 mg.

Debbra Lefcheck, Linda Lefcheck
Jennifer Lefcheck, Monroe

BAKLAVA

Rind of 1 lemon
1 c. sugar
1 tsp. cinnamon
1/2 tsp. cloves
1 1/2 c. honey
1 1/2 tsp. lemon juice
3 c. chopped walnuts
1/2 c. sugar
1 1/2 tsp. cinnamon
1 c. melted butter
2 8-oz. packages phyllo dough

Combine first 4 ingredients in saucepan. Simmer for 25 minutes or to 230 degrees on candy thermometer. Stir in honey and lemon juice. Cool. Combine walnuts, 1/2 cup sugar and 1 1/2 teaspoons cinnamon in bowl; mix well. Brush bottom of 9 x 13-inch baking dish with butter. Fold 2 sheets phyllo in half; place in prepared pan. Brush with butter. Repeat layers. Sprinkle with 1/2 cup walnut mixture. Place 2 folded sheets phyllo over walnuts. Brush with butter; sprinkle with 1/2 cup walnuts. Repeat layers 4 times. Top with remaining phyllo, brushing butter between every other sheet and over top. Sprinkle with 1 tablespoon water. Score top layer only into squares. Bake at 325 degrees for 50 minutes or until golden. Cut through score lines; separate squares slightly. Pour cooled syrup over hot Baklava. Cool in pan on wire rack. Let stand, covered with foil, at room temperature overnight.
Yield: 42 servings.

Tonya Simmons, Gratiot

JAN HAGEL

1 c. margarine, softened
1 c. sugar
1 egg, separated
2 c. sifted flour
1/8 tsp. salt
1/2 tsp. cinnamon
1/2 tsp. vanilla extract

Cream margarine, sugar and egg yolk in bowl until light and fluffy. Add sifted dry ingredients to creamed mixture gradually, mixing well after each addition. Blend in vanilla. Knead lightly. Press evenly over greased 12 x 15-inch baking sheet. Brush with mixture of beaten egg white and a small amount of water. Bake at 300 degrees for 20 minutes. Cut into squares; cool.
Yield: 96 servings.

This recipe came from the Netherlands.

Approx per serv: Cal 35.2; Prot 0.3 g; T Fat 2.0 g; Chl 2.9 mg; Car 4.1 g; Sod 26.3 mg; Pot 3.3 mg.

Emma Ridderbos, Van Buren

ROSENMUNNAR
(SWEDISH COOKIES)

1/2 lb. butter, softened
1/2 c. sugar
2 c. flour
1/2 c. (about) strawberry jam

Cream butter and sugar in bowl until light and fluffy. Add flour; mix well. Shape into walnut-sized balls. Place on cookie sheet. Make indentation in center of each with finger. Fill indentations with jam. Bake at 325 degrees for 15 to 20 minutes or until light brown.
Yield: 30 servings.

Approx per serv: Cal 112; Prot 1.0 g; T Fat 6.2 g; Chl 18.9 mg; Car 13.4 g; Sod 75.6 mg; Pot 14.5 mg.

Karen Bell, Genesee

4-H is over 40 million alumni in U.S.

RHUBARB SPICE PIES

8 c. chopped rhubarb
4 c. sugar
2/3 c. flour
1 c. raisins
1/2 stick margarine
2 tbsp. lemon juice
1 tsp. pumpkin pie spice
1 tsp. cloves
3 unbaked 8-in. pie shells

Cook rhubarb in a small amount of water in saucepan until tender. Add sugar, flour, raisins, margarine, lemon juice and spices; mix well. Pour into pie shells. Bake at 425 degrees for 20 minutes. Reduce temperature to 350 degrees. Bake for 15 minutes longer. Yield: 18 servings.

Approx per serv: Cal 393; Prot 2.9 g; T Fat 12.7 g; Chl 0.0 mg; Car 69.3 g; Sod 218.6 mg; Pot 221.3 mg.

Mary Scherzer, Bay

WHITE CHRISTMAS PIE

1/2 c. sugar
1/4 c. flour
1 env. unflavored gelatin
1/2 tsp. salt
1 3/4 c. milk
3/4 tsp. vanilla extract
1/4 tsp. almond flavoring

3 egg whites
1/4 tsp. cream of tartar
1/2 c. sugar
1/2 c. whipping cream, whipped
1 c. shredded coconut
1 baked 9-in. pie shell

Combine first 4 ingredients in saucepan. Add milk gradually. Bring to a boil over medium heat, stirring constantly. Cook for 1 minute, stirring constantly. Cool until mixture mounds from spoon. Blend in flavorings. Beat egg whites and cream of tartar in bowl until soft peaks form. Add 1/2 cup sugar gradually, beating until stiff. Fold in gelatin mixture gently. Fold in whipped cream and coconut. Spoon into pie shell. Chill for several hours. Garnish with additional coconut if desired.
Yield: 6 servings.

Approx per serv: Cal 411; Prot 8.4 g; T Fat 17.3 g; Chl 10.0 mg; Car 57.7 g; Sod 451.3 mg; Pot 247.7 mg.

Lisa Locke, Eaton

COTTAGE CHEESE CREPES

1 c. flour
1 1/2 c. milk
2 eggs
1 tbsp. oil
1/4 tsp. salt
2 tbsp. sugar
1/4 tsp. baking powder
2 c. large curd cottage cheese
1/2 c. sugar
1 egg
1 c. sour cream

Combine first 7 ingredients in bowl. Beat with rotary beater until smooth. Spoon a small amount at a time into hot, lightly greased skillet, tilting to coat bottom. Bake until light brown on both sides. Repeat with remaining batter. Combine cottage cheese, 1/2 cup sugar and egg in bowl; mix well. Spread 1 1/2 tablespoons on each crepe; roll to enclose filling. Place in single layer in 9 x 13-inch baking pan. Spread sour cream over top. Bake at 350 degrees for 20 minutes. Yield: 6 servings.

My great-grandmother brought this recipe from Hungary over 75 years ago.

Approx per serv: Cal 425; Prot 19.9 g; T Fat 19.0 g; Chl 167.3 mg; Car 43.7 g; Sod 371.6 mg; Pot 265.4 mg.

Mary Sheidler, Cass

Breakfasts & Brunches

CHEESE SANDWICH SOUFFLE

16 slices bread, crusts trimmed
8 1-oz. slices sharp Cheddar cheese
1 c. sliced mushrooms (opt.)
1 c. crab meat (opt.)
1/4 c. (or more) butter, softened
6 eggs
1/4 tsp. paprika
3 c. milk

Arrange 8 bread slices in buttered baking dish. Place cheese slice on each. Sprinkle mushrooms and crab meat over cheese. Cover with remaining bread. Spread butter generously over bread. Beat eggs, paprika, milk and salt and pepper to taste in bowl. Pour over sandwiches. Let stand at room temperature for 1 hour or longer. Bake at 350 degrees for 1 hour. Yield: 8 servings.

NOTE: May be made ahead and chilled overnight in refrigerator. Bring to room temperature before baking. Serve for luncheons with green salad.

Approx per serv: Cal 457; Prot 23.3 g; T Fat 24.7 g; Chl 267.0 mg; Car 34.6 g; Sod 817.7 mg; Pot 319.5 mg.

Secretary and Mrs. John R. Block
United States Department of Agriculture
4-H Alumni

BROCCOLI AND HAM SOUFFLE

2 tbsp. chopped onion
3 tbsp. margarine
3 tbsp. flour
1/2 tsp. salt
1/8 tsp. pepper
1 c. milk
4 eggs, separated
1 10-oz. package frozen chopped broccoli, thawed, drained
1 c. finely chopped cooked ham
3 tbsp. Parmesan cheese
1 tsp. cream of tartar

Saute onion in margarine in saucepan until tender. Stir in flour, salt and pepper. Cook for 1 minute. Stir in milk gradually. Cook until thickened, stirring constantly. Stir a small amount of hot mixture into beaten egg yolks. Stir egg yolks into hot mixture. Cook over low heat for 2 minutes, stirring constantly. Squeeze excess moisture from broccoli. Stir into hot sauce with ham and cheese. Beat egg whites with cream of tartar until soft peaks form. Fold in broccoli

mixture gently. Spoon into lightly greased 1 1/2-quart souffle dish. Bake in preheated 350-degree oven for 30 minutes or until browned and puffed and knife inserted near edge comes out clean. Serve immediately. Yield: 4 servings.

Approx per serv: Cal 371; Prot 28.0 g; T Fat 23.3 g; Chl 316.6 mg; Car 12.4 g; Sod 1082.3 mg; Pot 535.4 mg.

Jean LaCross, Leelanau

JENNI'S STRATA

4 c. stale bread cubes
3/4 c. chopped ham
3/4 c. shredded Cheddar cheese
1/2 c. chopped green onions
1/2 c. chopped green pepper
1/2 c. sliced fresh mushrooms
2 eggs, beaten
2 c. milk

Place half the bread cubes in 9 x 13-inch baking dish. Layer ham, cheese, green onions, green pepper, mushrooms and remaining bread on top. Pour mixture of eggs and milk over all. Chill overnight. Bake at 375 degrees for 40 to 45 minutes or until set. Yield: 9 servings.

Approx per serv: Cal 165; Prot 9.0 g; T Fat 8.4 g; Chl 80.0 mg; Car 13.1 g; Sod 257.1 mg; Pot 171.2 mg.

Jennifer Coulson, Gratiot

BREAKFAST PIZZA

1 lb. pork sausage
1 8-count pkg. refrigerator crescent rolls
1 c. frozen hashed brown potatoes, thawed
1 c. shredded Cheddar cheese
5 eggs
1/4 c. milk
1/2 tsp. salt
1/8 tsp. pepper
2 tbsp. Parmesan cheese

Brown sausage in skillet, stirring until crumbly; drain. Separate rolls into 8 triangles. Press over bottom and up side of 12-inch pizza pan; seal perforations. Layer sausage, potatoes and Cheddar cheese over crust. Pour mixture of eggs, milk and seasonings over layers. Sprinkle with Parmesan cheese. Bake at 375 degrees for 25 to 30 minutes. Cut into wedges. Yield: 6 servings.

Jean Ellen Creyts, Eaton

BREAKFAST BRUNCH

1 lb. pork sausage
5 or 6 slices bread, cubed
1 c. shredded Cheddar cheese
6 eggs, slightly beaten
3/4 c. milk
1 can cream of mushroom soup
1/2 soup can milk
1   4-oz. can chopped mushrooms (opt.)

Brown sausage in skillet, stirring until crumbly; drain. Combine with bread in 9 x 13-inch baking dish. Sprinkle with cheese. Mix eggs and 3/4 cup milk. Pour over cheese. Chill, covered, overnight. Combine soup, 1/2 soup can milk and mushrooms in bowl; mix well. Pour over layers. Bake in preheated 350-degree oven for 40 to 50 minutes or until light brown. Yield: 6 servings.

Ina J. Golden, Oakland

FAMILY CHEESE AND EGG BAKE

1   12-oz. package pizza sausage
1 c. small curd cottage cheese
1/4 c. oil
1 3/4 c. pancake mix
3 c. cubed mozzarella cheese
6 eggs, well beaten

Brown sausage in skillet; drain. Add sausage, cottage cheese, oil, pancake mix and cheese to eggs; mix well. Pour into 9 x 13-inch baking pan. Bake at 350 degrees for 25 to 30 minutes or until set. Cut into squares. Serve warm with butter and syrup. Yield: 12 servings.

Approx per serv: Cal 227; Prot 11.8 g; T Fat 12.0 g; Chl 148.4 mg; Car 17.2 g; Sod 541.1 mg; Pot 125.5 mg.

Shirley Boudreau, Delta

OMELET ROLL

1/2 c. mayonnaise
2 tbsp. flour
1 c. milk
12 eggs, separated
1/2 tsp. salt
1/8 tsp. pepper
1 1/2 c. chopped ham
1 c. shredded Swiss cheese

1 c. mayonnaise
2 tbsp. prepared mustard
2 tbsp. chopped green onion

Blend 1/2 cup mayonnaise and flour in saucepan. Stir in milk and beaten egg yolks gradually. Cook over low heat until thickened, stirring constantly. Cool for 20 minutes, stirring occasionally. Fold in stiffly beaten egg whites, salt and pepper. Line 10 x 15-inch baking pan with waxed paper. Grease with mayonnaise. Spread batter in prepared pan. Bake at 425 degrees for 20 minutes. Invert onto towel; peel off waxed paper. Sprinkle with mixture of ham and cheese. Roll as for jelly roll from narrow end. Place on serving plate. Slice. Blend remaining ingredients in saucepan. Heat to serving temperature. Serve with Omelet Roll. Yield: 6 servings.

Approx per serv: Cal 777; Prot 28.0 g; T Fat 71.0 g; Chl 600.6 mg; Car 7.0 g; Sod 1113.5 mg; Pot 322.3 mg.

Barbara Gawron, Jackson

CRUSTLESS QUICHE

1 lb. sausage
2 tbsp. margarine
2 c. shredded Cheddar cheese
2 c. shredded Swiss cheese
12 eggs
8 oz. fresh mushrooms, finely chopped
1 onion, finely chopped
1 green pepper, finely chopped
1/4 tsp. salt
Pepper to taste
2/3 c. cream
1 sprig of parsley, finely chopped
Paprika to taste

Brown sausage in skillet, stirring until crumbly; drain. Grease 7 x 11-inch baking dish with margarine. Sprinkle half the cheeses in prepared baking pan. Add eggs, mushrooms, onion, green pepper and salt and pepper; mix lightly with fork. Sprinkle sausage over top. Drizzle cream over layers. Do not mix. Top with remaining cheeses, parsley and paprika. Bake at 350 degrees for 30 minutes. Cool for 5 to 10 minutes before serving. Yield: 6 servings.

Approx per serv: Cal 778; Prot 41.7 g; T Fat 64.0 g; Chl 647.6 mg; Car 8.5 g; Sod 1151.1 mg; Pot 601.9 mg.

Grace Deshaw Wilmer, Bay

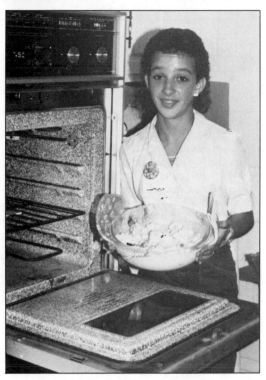

HEIRLOOM QUICK BREAD

1 c. shortening
1 c. sugar
1 c. packed brown sugar
4 eggs
1 tsp. almond extract
2 c. applesauce
4 c. flour
2 tsp. baking powder
1 1/2 tsp. soda
2 tsp. salt
1 tsp. cinnamon
1/2 tsp. nutmeg
1/2 c. ground walnuts
2 c. chopped cherries

Cream shortening, sugar and brown sugar in bowl. Add eggs, flavoring and applesauce; mix well. Add mixture of flour, baking powder, soda, salt and spices; mix well. Stir in walnuts and cherries. Pour into greased and floured 9 x 13-inch baking pan. Bake at 350 degrees for 55 to 60 minutes or until bread tests done. Yield: 16 servings.

Approx per serv: Cal 314; Prot 5.8 g; T Fat 4.3 g; Chl 63.2 mg; Car 64.5 g; Sod 405.7 mg; Pot 172.2 mg.

Veronica A. Dluzen, Monroe

CINNAMON BREAD

1/4 c. margarine, softened
1 c. sugar
1 egg
2 c. flour, sifted
1 tsp. soda
1 c. buttermilk
1/4 c. sugar
1 tsp. cinnamon

Cream margarine and 1 cup sugar in bowl. Add egg; mix well. Add mixture of flour and soda. Stir in buttermilk. Mix 1/4 cup sugar with cinnamon. Pour half the batter into greased loaf pan. Sprinkle with half the cinnamon sugar. Repeat layers. Bake at 350 degrees for 45 minutes. Yield: 10 servings.

Approx per serv: Cal 245; Prot 4.2 g; T Fat 5.5 g; Chl 25.8 mg; Car 45.2 g; Sod 176.9 mg; Pot 66.6 mg.

Shannon Kempf, Newaygo

APPLE PIZZA

1 loaf frozen bread dough, thawed
4 to 6 med. apples, peeled, sliced
2/3 c. sugar
1/2 c. flour
1/2 c. chopped pecans
1/4 c. butter
2 tsp. cinnamon
1 c. confectioners' sugar
1 tsp. vanilla extract

Stretch dough to fit 14-inch pizza pan. Let stand for 15 minutes. Arrange apple slices over dough. Mix sugar, flour, pecans, butter and cinnamon in bowl until crumbly. Sprinkle over apples. Let rise, in warm place, for about 1 hour or until doubled in bulk. Bake at 350 degrees for 45 minutes. Combine confectioners' sugar, vanilla and 1 tablespoon water in bowl; mix well. Spread over warm pizza. Yield: 8 servings.

Approx per serv: Cal 497; Prot 6.8 g; T Fat 13.8 g; Chl 19.5 mg; Car 90.3 g; Sod 359.6 mg; Pot 288.6 mg.

Sally Nebel, Macomb

WESLEE'S MONKEY BREAD

2 10-count pkg. refrigerator biscuits
1/2 c. sugar
1 tbsp. cinnamon
1/2 c. packed brown sugar

5 tbsp. butter
1 tbsp. cinnamon

Cut each biscuit into fourths. Coat with mixture of sugar and cinnamon. Arrange in greased loaf pan. Combine remaining ingredients in saucepan. Heat until blended. Pour over biscuits. Bake at 350 degrees for 35 minutes. Yield: 10 servings.

Approx per serv: Cal 315; Prot 4.1 g; T Fat 11.0 g; Chl 18.3 mg; Car 50.2 g; Sod 625.2 mg; Pot 105.5 mg.

Weslee Smith, Grand Traverse

FRUIT-FILLED COFFEE CAKE

1 c. margarine, softened
1 3/4 c. sugar
4 eggs
1 tsp. vanilla extract
3 c. flour
1/2 tsp. salt
2 tsp. baking powder
1 can blueberry pie filling
1 c. confectioners' sugar
2 tbsp. (about) milk

Cream margarine and sugar in bowl until light and fluffy. Beat in eggs 1 at a time. Add vanilla and sifted dry ingredients; beat well. Batter will be thick. Reserve 1 cup batter. Spread remaining batter in greased 11 x 16-inch baking pan. Spread pie filling over batter; dot with reserved batter. Bake at 350 degrees for 35 to 40 minutes. Cool slightly. Drizzle mixture of confectioners' sugar and milk over top. Yield: 16 servings.

NOTE: May substitute cherry, pineapple, strawberry or apple pie filling for blueberry.

Approx per serv: Cal 369; Prot 4.3 g; T Fat 13.2 g; Chl 63.5 mg; Car 58.8 g; Sod 264.9 mg; Pot 46.0 mg.

Carol Whittredge, Allegan

CINNAMON COFFEE CAKES

3/4 to 1 c. raisins
1 pkg. dry yeast
1 egg, beaten
3/4 c. lukewarm milk
1/3 c. sugar
1/4 c. shortening
1 tsp. salt
3 1/2 to 3 3/4 c. flour

1 tbsp. grated lemon rind
1 tbsp. (or more) butter, melted
2 tsp. cinnamon
1/2 c. sugar

Combine raisins with 1/2 cup water in saucepan. Cook for 10 minutes. Cool. Dissolve yeast in 1/4 cup warm water. Combine egg, milk, sugar, shortening and salt in bowl; mix well. Add with yeast to mixture of flour and lemon rind; mix well with wooden spoon. Add raisins; mix well. Place in greased bowl; grease top of dough. Cover with towel. Place in warm oven. Do not allow oven to become hot or yeast will be destroyed. Let rise for 1 hour. Divide dough into 2 portions. Roll each portion into rectangle on lightly floured surface; brush with butter. Sprinkle with mixture of cinnamon and sugar. Roll as for jelly roll; shape into loaf. Place in greased loaf pans. Sprinkle with additional cinnamon sugar. Let rise until doubled in bulk. Bake at 350 degrees for 30 to 35 minutes or until loaf sounds hollow when tapped. Yield: 24 servings.

Approx per serv: Cal 149; Prot 2.9 g; T Fat 3.5 g; Chl 13.1 mg; Car 26.9 g; Sod 103.2 mg; Pot 84.8 mg.

Marie Wieland, Bay

SOUR CREAM COFFEE CAKE

1 stick margarine, softened
1 c. sugar
2 eggs
1 tsp. vanilla extract
2 c. sifted flour
1 tsp. baking powder
1 c. sour cream
1 tsp. soda
1/4 c. sugar
1/2 c. chopped walnuts
1 tsp. cinnamon

Cream margarine, sugar, eggs and vanilla in mixer bowl until light and fluffy. Add flour and baking powder. Beat for 2 minutes. Add sour cream and soda; mix well. Mix 1/4 cup sugar, walnuts and cinnamon in small bowl. Alternate layers of batter and walnut mixture 1/2 at a time in greased tube pan. Bake at 350 degrees for 40 to 50 minutes or until coffee cake tests done. Cool in pan for 15 minutes. Invert on serving plate. Yield: 12 servings.

Approx per serv: Cal 306; Prot 4.5 g; T Fat 16.0 g; Chl 50.6 mg; Car 37.1 g; Sod 210.3 mg; Pot 82.3 mg.

Sue Devecsery, Wayne

RHUBARB COFFEE CAKE

1 pkg. yeast
1/3 c. milk, scalded
1/4 c. margarine
2 tbsp. brown sugar
1/4 tsp. salt
1 egg
2 1/2 to 3 1/2 c. flour
1 1/2 c. chopped rhubarb
3/4 c. packed brown sugar
1/2 tsp. grated lemon rind
1/8 tsp. allspice
1/2 c. raisins
1/2 c. coconut
1 egg white, beaten

Dissolve yeast in 1/4 cup warm water. Combine milk, margarine, 2 tablespoons brown sugar and salt in large bowl. Cool to lukewarm. Add yeast, egg and 2 1/2 cups flour; mix well. Knead on floured surface until smooth and elastic, adding flour as necessary. Place in greased bowl. Let rise, covered, until doubled in bulk. Combine rhubarb, 3/4 cup brown sugar, lemon rind, allspice and 1/3 cup water in saucepan. Cook for 30 minutes, stirring frequently. Stir in raisins and coconut. Cool. Roll dough into 10 x 15-inch rectangle on floured surface. Spread rhubarb mixture to within 1/2 inch of edges, roll as for jelly roll from long side, sealing edge. Shape into ring on greased baking sheet, sealing ends. Slice 2/3 through from outer edge at 1-inch intervals; twist each slice cut side down. Let rise, covered, for 45 minutes. Brush with egg white. Bake at 350 degrees for 20 to 25 minutes. Cool on wire rack. Garnish with confectioners' sugar. Yield: 16 servings.

Approx per serv: Cal 210; Prot 4.2 g; T Fat 5.1 g; Chl 16.5 mg; Car 37.3 g; Sod 84.5 mg; Pot 165.3 mg.

Cathy Kuehne, Bay

COFFEE CAKE MUFFINS

1 1/2 c. sifted flour
1/2 c. sugar
2 tsp. baking powder
1/2 tsp. salt
1/4 c. shortening
1 egg, beaten
1/2 c. milk
1/2 c. packed brown sugar
1/2 c. chopped pecans
2 tbsp. flour

2 tsp. cinnamon
2 tbsp. melted butter

Sift first 4 ingredients into bowl. Cut in shortening until crumbly. Stir in egg and milk. Combine brown sugar, pecans, 2 tablespoons flour, cinnamon and butter in bowl; mix well. Alternate layers of batter and pecan mixture in paper-lined muffin cups, filling 1/2 full. Bake at 375 degrees for 20 minutes. Yield: 12 servings.

Approx per serv: Cal 234; Prot 3.2 g; T Fat 11.1 g; Chl 28.4 mg; Car 31.4 g; Sod 180.2 mg; Pot 98.8 mg.

Jennifer Spoering, Monroe

FRENCH BREAKFAST MUFFINS

1/3 c. shortening
1/2 c. sugar
1 egg
1 1/2 c. flour
1 1/2 tsp. baking powder
1/2 tsp. salt
1/4 tsp. nutmeg
1/2 c. milk
1/2 c. melted butter
1/2 c. sugar
1 tsp. cinnamon

Cream shortening, 1/2 cup sugar and egg in bowl until light and fluffy. Add mixture of flour, baking powder, salt and nutmeg alternately with milk, blending after each addition. Fill greased muffin cups 2/3 full. Bake at 350 degrees for 20 to 25 minutes or until brown. Roll hot muffins in melted butter. Coat with mixture of 1/2 cup sugar and cinnamon. Serve hot. Yield: 12 servings.

Approx per serv: Cal 258; Prot 2.6 g; T Fat 14.9 g; Chl 46.2 mg; Car 29.2 g; Sod 234.0 mg; Pot 38.1 mg.

Alina Andersen, Menominee

CURRANT SCONES

1/2 c. butter, softened
1/2 c. sugar
1 egg
1 1/2 c. flour
1/4 tsp. salt
1 tsp. baking powder
1/4 c. currants

Cream butter and sugar in bowl. Beat in egg. Add mixture of flour, salt and baking powder;

mix well. Stir in currants. Knead lightly on floured surface. Pat into 6-inch circles 1/2 inch thick. Cut into wedges. Place on greased baking sheet. Bake at 325 degrees for 10 minutes. Do not overbake; bottoms brown before tops. Yield: 10 servings.

Approx per serv: Cal 207; Prot 2.8 g; T Fat 10.0 g; Chl 53.7 mg; Car 27.2 g; Sod 205.8 mg; Pot 55.1 mg.

Gail Gross, Livingston

PEACHES AND CREAM FRENCH TOAST

1 8-oz. package cream cheese, softened
3 peach slices, chopped
3 tbsp. peach Brandy
6 1-in. slices French bread
3 eggs
3 tbsp. peach preserves
3/4 c. half and half
2 tbsp. butter
1 1/2 tbsp. oil
1/3 c. peach preserves
1/4 c. butter, softened
2 peaches, sliced
1/4 c. confectioners' sugar
1/4 c. chopped toasted almonds

Combine cream cheese, chopped peaches and peach Brandy in bowl; mix well. Cut pockets in bread slices. Stuff with cream cheese mixture. Place in single layer in 7 x 11-inch dish. Mix eggs, 3 tablespoons preserves and half and half in bowl. Pour over bread. Chill overnight. Brown on both sides in mixture of 2 tablespoons butter and oil in skillet. Beat 1/3 cup preserves and 1/4 cup butter in mixer bowl until light and fluffy. Serve hot French toast with peach butter and sliced peaches. Sprinkle with confectioners' sugar and almonds. Serve with maple syrup if desired. Yield: 6 servings.

Approx per serv: Cal 601; Prot 11.8 g; T Fat 39.3 g; Chl 217.8 mg; Car 51.3 g; Sod 486.2 mg; Pot 275.5 mg.

Paula Bennett, Livingston

CREPES FRANGIPANE

1 1/2 c. milk
1 2/3 c. flour
2 tbsp. oil
3 eggs
1 c. sugar
1/4 c. flour
1 c. milk
2 eggs plus 2 egg yolks, beaten
3 tbsp. butter
1/2 c. ground toasted almonds
2 tsp. vanilla extract
1/2 tsp. almond extract
1/4 c. melted butter
1/2 c. confectioners' sugar
1 oz. grated unsweetened chocolate
1/4 c. sliced almonds

Combine first 4 ingredients in bowl. Beat until smooth. Pour 1/4 cup at a time into hot greased 7-inch crepe pan; tilt to coat bottom of pan. Bake until brown on both sides. Cool between pieces of waxed paper. Combine sugar and 1/4 cup flour in saucepan. Stir in 1 cup milk. Cook until thickened, stirring constantly. Cook for 2 minutes longer, stirring constantly. Stir a small amount of hot mixture into beaten eggs; stir eggs into hot mixture. Bring just to a boil; remove from heat. Stir in 3 tablespoons butter, almonds and flavorings. Cool. Spread 2 tablespoons filling on each crepe; roll up. Brush with melted butter. Coat with confectioners' sugar. Place on serving plate. Sprinkle grated chocolate and almonds over top. Yield: 8 servings.

Approx per serv: Cal 559; Prot 13.2 g; T Fat 29.8 g; Chl 262.6 mg; Car 62.6 g; Sod 202.8 mg; Pot 309.2 mg.

Katy Short, Monroe

POLACHETAS

5 eggs, beaten
1/2 c. sugar
1 tsp. vanilla extract
1/4 tsp. salt
3 c. milk
2 c. flour
Butter
2 to 3 c. cottage cheese
1/2 c. sugar

Combine first 6 ingredients in bowl. Mix with wire whisk until smooth. Pour a small amount of batter into butter in skillet; cook until brown on both sides. Spoon mixture of cottage cheese and sugar onto each pancake. Roll as for jelly roll.

Amy Sherman, Lenawee

RAISED DOUGHNUTS

2 pkg. dry yeast
1/2 c. milk, scalded
1/3 c. shortening
1/3 c. sugar
1 tsp. salt
1 c. sifted flour
2 eggs
2 1/2 to 3 c. sifted flour
Oil for deep frying

Dissolve yeast in 1/2 cup warm water in bowl. Combine milk, shortening, sugar and salt in bowl. Cool to lukewarm. Add 1 cup flour; mix well. Add yeast and eggs; beat well. Stir in enough remaining flour to make soft dough. Place in greased bowl, turning to grease surface. Chill for 3 hours to overnight. Punch dough down. Roll 1/3 inch thick on floured surface. Cut with doughnut cutter. Let rise for 30 to 40 minutes. Deep-fry for 2 minutes, turning once.

Ray Laura, Monroe

HOMEMADE PANCAKE SYRUP

2 c. sugar
1 tsp. maple flavoring

Combine sugar and 1 cup boiling water in saucepan. Cook for 5 minutes. Stir in flavoring. Serve hot. Store, tightly covered, in refrigerator. Yield: 32 one-tablespoon servings.

Approx per serv: Cal 48; Prot 0.0 g; T Fat 0.0 g; Chl 0.0 mg; Car 12.4 g; Sod 0.1 mg; Pot 0.4 mg.

Ada Huyck, Jackson

BUTTERMILK PANCAKES

1 egg, slightly beaten
2 c. buttermilk
2 c. flour
1 tsp. soda
2 tbsp. sugar
1 tsp. salt
6 tbsp. oil

Combine egg and buttermilk in bowl. Sift in dry ingredients. Stir in oil. Ladle desired amount of batter onto hot greased griddle. Bake until brown on both sides. Yield: 4 servings.

Approx per serv: Cal 496; Prot 12.6 g; T Fat 22.6 g; Chl 65.7 mg; Car 60.1 g; Sod 914.0 mg; Pot 247.3 mg.

Ada Huyck, Jackson

OVEN PANCAKE

3 eggs
1 c. milk
1/4 c. flour
2 tbsp. sugar
2 tbsp. margarine

Beat eggs in mixer bowl for about 5 minutes until light and thick. Add milk, flour and sugar gradually, beating constantly. Mixture will be consistency of heavy cream. Melt margarine in 9 x 13-inch pan in 425-degree oven. Pour batter into prepared pan. Bake for 15 to 20 minutes or until golden brown. Cut into squares. Serve hot with syrup or fruit. Yield: 4 servings.

Approx per serv: Cal 206; Prot 7.9 g; T Fat 12.3 g; Chl 198.1 mg; Car 15.8 g; Sod 146.7 mg; Pot 145.6 mg.

Karen Kangas, Gogebic

GINGERBREAD PANCAKES

1 egg
1 c. milk
1 14-oz. package gingerbread mix
2 tbsp. melted butter

Combine egg and milk in bowl; mix well. Add gingerbread mix and butter; mix well. Drop 2 or 3 tablespoonfuls per pancake onto hot lightly greased griddle. Bake until brown on both sides. Serve with honey or syrup. Yield: 20 servings.

Martha Wlodarski, Alpena

TEXAS PECAN WAFFLES

2 c. flour
4 tsp. baking powder
4 tsp. sugar
1 tsp. salt
2 eggs
1 3/4 c. milk
1/3 c. melted butter
1 c. coarsely chopped pecans

Combine first 4 ingredients in bowl. Add eggs and milk gradually; mix well. Stir in butter and pecans. Bake in hot waffle iron. Serve hot with butter and syrup. Yield: 5 servings.

Approx per serv: Cal 556; Prot 13.1 g; T Fat 34.9 g; Chl 150.9 mg; Car 49.9 g; Sod 906.8 mg; Pot 345.9 mg.

Christine Shore, Ogemaw

Quantity Cooking

Quantity Cooking

Kettunen Center is a complete conference facility for 4-H leader training owned and operated by the Michigan 4-H Foundation. Located in central Michigan in Tustin, Osceola County, on 140 rustic acres fronting on Center Lake, the Center is used by 4-H groups to train volunteer and teen leaders and provide summer and winter camping experiences. Kettunen Center serves as host to many non-profit organizations other than 4-H.

Named for A. G. Kettunen, director of State 4-H Youth Programs for 31 years, this facility was the culmination of a life-long dream.

One of the most enjoyable parts of a visit to Kettunen Center is the wonderful meals. Whether it be eating in the dining room, a barbecue under the trees, or dining in the gazebo overlooking the lake, the sound of the bell calls all to a marvelous feast. Many of the quantity recipes offered here are from Kettunen Center.

EASY PARTY PUNCH

2 pkg. fruit-flavored drink mix
2 c. sugar
1 46-oz. can pineapple juice
1 qt. ginger ale, chilled

Dissolve drink mix and sugar in 2 quarts water in large container. Add pineapple juice. Chill. Pour over ice in punch bowl. Add ginger ale. Serve immediately. Yield: 50 servings.

NOTE: An especially good punch is made from a combination of 1 package cherry and 1 package raspberry drink mix. For special occasions add 2 to 3 pints raspberry sherbet to red punch or lemon sherbet to green punch made from lemon-lime drink mix.

Approx per serv: Cal 51; Prot 0.1 g; T Fat 0.0 g; Chl 0.0 mg; Car 12.9 g; Sod 0.3 mg; Pot 37.5 mg.

Michele Zurface, Barry

HOT CHOCOLATE MIX

1 32-oz. jar chocolate instant drink mix
1 11-oz. jar nondairy coffee creamer
1 8-oz. package nonfat dry milk powder
1 c. confectioners' sugar

Combine all ingredients in large bowl; mix well. Store in airtight container. Combine 1 teaspoon mix with 1 cup hot water in mug; mix until dissolved. Yield: 50 servings.

Approx per serving: Cal 164; Prot 6.6 g; T Fat 5.8 g; Chl 13.5 mg; Car 22.9 g; Sod 151.8 mg; Pot 344.2 mg.

Margaret Purdy, Livingston

4-H — there's something in it for you!

CINNAMON ROLLS

1/2 c. dry yeast
2 tbsp. sugar
4 c. shortening, melted
1/2 c. salt
3 1/2 c. sugar
11 lb. (about) flour
15 eggs
12 lb. (about) brown sugar
6 tbsp. cinnamon
5 lb. butter, melted

Combine yeast and 2 tablespoons sugar in 2-quart bowl. Stir in 4 cups warm water until yeast and sugar dissolve. Combine shortening, salt and 3 1/2 cups sugar in large mixer container. Add 8 cups hot water and a small amount of flour; mix well. Add eggs; mix well. Add yeast; mix well. Add enough remaining flour 4 cups at a time to make medium dough, mixing well after each addition. Place in greased tub. Let rise until doubled in bulk. Divide into 6 portions on floured surface. Roll each portion into rectangle. Sprinkle with mixture of brown sugar and cinnamon. Drizzle with butter. Roll as for jelly roll; slice 1 to 1 1/2 inches thick. Arrange 40 slices on each of 3 large greased bun pans. Let rise until doubled in bulk. Bake at 425 degrees until golden. Remove from pans immediately. Yield: 120 servings.

Approx per serv: Cal 472; Prot 5.5 g; T Fat 8.5 g; Chl 31.0 mg; Car 94.6 g; Sod 440.0 mg; Pot 250.6 mg.

Mary Miller, Lenawee

CHEDDAR BREAD

1/3 c. sugar
1 tbsp. salt
1 c. butter, softened
1 pkg. dry yeast
7 c. flour
1/3 c. dry milk powder
1 c. butter, softened
2 tbsp. instant minced onion
1 tsp. dry mustard
1 tbsp. Worcestershire sauce
1 1/2 lb. Cheddar cheese, grated

Combine 4 cups warm water, sugar, salt and 1 cup butter in mixer bowl. Add yeast. Let stand for 10 minutes. Add flour and dry milk powder. Beat with dough hook until well mixed. Divide dough between three 13 x 18-inch baking sheets; pat in evenly. Combine 1 cup butter, onion, mustard and Worcestershire sauce in mixer bowl; beat until well blended. Spread over dough. Top with cheese. Bake at 400 degrees for 25 minutes. Cut into 3 1/2 to 4-inch squares. Yield: 50 servings.

NOTE: May substitute milk for water and omit dry milk powder.

Mary Miller, Lenawee

4-H is building on experience.

OVEN STEW

8 lb. stew beef
4 onions, sliced
10 stalks celery, sliced diagonally
24 carrots, coarsely chopped
2 c. mixed vegetable juice cocktail
1/2 c. tapioca
8 tsp. salt
1/4 c. sugar
8 potatoes, chopped (opt.)

Layer beef, onions, celery and carrots in large shallow baking pan. Combine vegetable juice with tapioca and seasonings in bowl; mix well. Pour over beef and vegetables. Cover tightly with heavy foil. Bake at 250 degrees for 2 1/2 hours. Stir from bottom with fork. Bake, covered, for 1 1/2 hours. Add potatoes. Bake, covered, for 1 hour longer or until potatoes are tender. Yield: 24 servings.

Approx per serv: Cal 503; Prot 31.1 g; T Fat 29.9 g; Chl 102.8 mg; Car 26.6 g; Sod 909.7 mg; Pot 1099.4 mg.

Hazel Noe, St. Joseph

EASY SWISS STEAK
FOR-A-CROWD

20 lb. round steak
2 50-oz. cans cream of mushroom soup

Cut round steak into serving pieces. Alternate layers of steak and soup in large baking pan. Bake, covered, at 350 degrees for several hours until tender. Yield: 40 servings.

Approx per serv: Cal 526; Prot 47.2 g; T Fat 33.6 g; Chl 160.0 mg; Car 6.0 g; Sod 729.6 mg; Pot 791.7 mg.

Patricia Bunyea, Wayne

SWISS STEAK WITH ONIONS

3 c. flour
2 tbsp. seasoned salt
75   5-oz. cube steaks
2 lg. onions, sliced
5 tbsp. beef bouillon
Cornstarch

Combine flour and seasoned salt in shallow dish. Coat each steak with seasoned flour. Brown on both sides on well-oiled grill. Layer 25 steaks in each of three 12 x 20-inch baking pans. Layer onions over top. Dissolve bouillon in 6 quarts water; pour over layers. Bake, covered with foil, at 325 degrees for 3 hours. Drain pan juices into saucepan about 30 minutes before serving time. Stir in enough cornstarch dissolved in a small amount of water to thicken to desired consistency. Cook until thickened, stirring constantly. Serve gravy with steaks.
Yield: 75 servings.
NOTE: Nutritional information does not include cornstarch.

Approx per serv: Cal 300; Prot 29.4 g; T Fat 17.5 g; Chl 97.0 mg; Car 4.2 g; Sod 367.6 mg; Pot 471.6 mg.

Kettunen Center

LASAGNA

5 lb. ground beef
1 No. 10 can spaghetti sauce
1/4 c. dried onion
2 1/2 lb. mozzarella cheese, shredded
23 oz. uncooked lasagna noodles

Brown ground beef in skillet, stirring until crumbly; drain. Add spaghetti sauce and onion; mix well. Reserve about 1/3 of the cheese. Alternate layers of sauce, noodles and remaining cheese in 12 x 20-inch baking pan ending with sauce. Refrigerate, tightly covered, overnight. Bake, uncovered, at 325 degrees for 1 1/4 hours. Top with reserved cheese. Let stand for 15 minutes. Cut into serving portions.
Yield: 30 servings.

Kettunen Center

BURGOO

4 1-lb. smoked ham hocks
1 3-lb. chicken
2 c. chopped potatoes
2 lg. onions, chopped
2 c. chopped carrots
1   10-oz. package frozen lima beans
1 tbsp. salt
1/2 tsp. cayenne pepper
2 c. shredded cabbage
2 c. corn
2 c. thinly sliced celery
2 c. chopped tomatoes
2 tbsp. Worcestershire sauce
1/2 c. chopped green pepper
1/2 c. chopped parsley

Combine ham hocks and chicken in stockpot. Add enough water to just cover. Simmer, covered, for 1 1/2 hours or until chicken is tender; remove chicken. Cook for 1 hour longer; remove ham hocks. Let broth stand; skim off fat. Combine 12 cups broth with potatoes, onions, carrots, lima beans and seasonings in stockpot. Simmer for 15 minutes. Add cabbage, corn, celery, tomatoes and Worcestershire sauce. Simmer for 15 minutes. Bone, trim and chop chicken and ham. Add to stockpot with green pepper and parsley. Heat to serving temperature. Ladle into soup bowls. Serve with bread or hot rolls. Yield: 20 servings.

Jane Wade, Muskegon

MICHIGAN FISH BOIL

20 lb. whitefish fillets
80 med. red potatoes
Salt
Bay leaves (opt.)
Whole peppercorns (opt.)
40 onions

Cut fish into serving pieces. Cut ends from potatoes. Do not peel. Fill large kettle with water, adding 1/2 cup salt per gallon and spices tied in cheesecloth bag. Bring to a full rolling boil over open fire. Place potatoes in wire basket. Place in boiling water. Cook for 12 minutes. Add onions. Cook for 5 minutes longer. Place fish in second wire basket. Add additional 1/2 cup salt per gallon of water to boiling kettle. Place fish basket in boiling water. Cook for 12 minutes. Increase fire until kettle boils over, removing scum and extinguishing fire. Remove fish and vegetables. Serve with butter, fresh bread, coleslaw and cherry pie. Yield: 40 servings.
NOTE: If prepared in kitchen, potatoes and onions may be cooked loose in kettle with fish in basket. Skim liquid. Remove basket; drain

vegetables. Nutritional information does not reflect sodium absorbed from salted cooking water.

Approx per serv: Cal 624; Prot 51.1 g; T Fat 19.0 g; Chl 124.7 mg; Car 61.5 g; Sod 143.1 mg; Pot 2056.1 mg.

Michigan State University
Cooperative Extension Service

FRUIT SALAD WITH PUDDING

1 No. 10 can pineapple chunks
1 24-oz. package vanilla instant pudding mix
10 unpeeled apples, chopped
1 No. 10 can mandarin oranges, drained

Pour pineapple with juice into large bowl. Sprinkle pudding mix over top; mix with spoon. Add apples and oranges; mix lightly. Add a small amount of water or mandarin orange juice if necessary to make of desired consistency. Yield: 50 servings.

Approx per serv: Cal 147; Prot 1.1 g; T Fat 0.7 g; Chl 0.0 mg; Car 37.7 g; Sod 63.7 mg; Pot 179.7 mg.

Kettunen Center

PISTACHIO SEAFOAM SALAD

1/2 No. 10 can crushed pineapple
1 3-oz. package pistachio instant pudding mix
4 c. whipped topping
3 c. miniature marshmallows

Mix pineapple and pudding mix in bowl. Fold in whipped topping and marshmallows. Yield: 25 servings.

Approx per serv: Cal 115; Prot 0.6 g; T Fat 2.7 g; Chl 0.1 mg; Car 23.5 g; Sod 26.0 mg; Pot 66.3 mg.

Kettunen Center

RHUBARB GELATIN

4 c. chopped rhubarb
2 c. sugar
1 6-oz. package raspberry gelatin

Cook rhubarb with 1 cup water and 2 cups sugar in saucepan until tender. Beat with electric mixer until well blended. Add gelatin; stir until dissolved. Pour into dish. Chill until firm. Yield: 20 servings.

Kettunen Center

THREE-BEAN SALAD

2 16-oz. cans green beans
2 16-oz. cans wax beans
3 16-oz. cans kidney beans
1 green pepper, chopped
1 onion, chopped
1 1/2 c. sugar
1 c. vinegar
1 c. oil

Drain canned vegetables. Combine with green pepper and onion in large bowl. Combine sugar, vinegar and oil in small bowl; mix well. Pour over vegetables; mix gently. Yield: 25 servings.

Approx per serv: Cal 202; Prot 4.7 g; T Fat 9.1 g; Chl 0.0 mg; Car 27.3 g; Sod 169.0 mg; Pot 271.3 mg.

Kettunen Center

FREEZER SLAW

16 c. shredded cabbage
1 tbsp. salt
1 green pepper, shredded
2 carrots, shredded
1 c. vinegar
2 c. sugar
1 tsp. celery seed

Sprinkle cabbage with salt; mix well. Let stand for 1 hour. Drain. Mix cabbage with green pepper and carrots. Combine vinegar, sugar and 1/2 cup water in saucepan. Boil for 1 minute. Cool. Pour over cabbage mixture. Add celery seed. Let stand for 30 minutes. Spoon into freezer containers. Store in freezer. Yield: 24 servings.

Approx per serv: Cal 80; Prot 0.7 g; T Fat 0.1 g; Chl 0.0 mg; Car 20.4 g; Sod 279.2 mg; Pot 144.3 mg.

Gus Zurface, Barry

PEA AND PEANUT SALAD

2 16-oz. packages frozen peas, thawed
1 c. Spanish peanuts
3 tbsp. salad dressing

Combine peas and peanuts in large bowl. Add salad dressing; mix gently. Chill until serving time. Yield: 25 servings.

Approx per serv: Cal 68; Prot 3.5 g; T Fat 3.7 g; Chl 0.9 mg; Car 6.0 g; Sod 81.5 mg; Pot 93.5 mg.

Kettunen Center

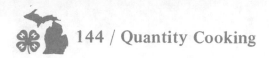

POTATO SALAD

15 lb. potatoes, peeled, cooked
12 hard-boiled eggs, chopped
1 1/2 lg. onions, finely chopped
1/2 bunch celery, chopped
2 c. salad dressing
3/4 c. mustard
3/4 c. sugar
1/2 c. vinegar

Cut potatoes into 1/4-inch cubes. Combine with eggs, onions and celery in large container. Combine salad dressing and remaining ingredients in bowl; blend well. Pour over potato mixture; mix well. Yield: 50 servings.

Approx per serv: Cal 173; Prot 4.5 g; T Fat 5.8 g; Chl 65.5 mg; Car 26.5 g; Sod 122.7 mg; Pot 537.1 mg.

Kettunen Center

TABOULEH

2 c. bulgur
1 c. chopped parsley
1/2 c. chopped onion
2 tbsp. chopped mint leaves
1 c. lemon juice
1 c. oil
2 tomatoes, chopped

Combine first 6 ingredients in large bowl; mix well. Refrigerate overnight. Stir in tomatoes just before serving. Yield: 25 servings.
NOTE: May soak bulgur in 1 cup warm water for 1 hour before mixing salad and chill until serving time if same day serving is desired.

Approx per serv: Cal 123; Prot 1.6 g; T Fat 7.6 g; Chl 0.0 mg; Car 12.9 g; Sod 92.1 mg; Pot 99.3 mg.

Kettunen Center

THOUSAND ISLAND DRESSING

4 c. mayonnaise
2 c. catsup
2 hard-boiled eggs, chopped
2 c. sweet relish
1 stalk celery, finely chopped
7 tbsp. steak sauce
1/2 tsp. garlic powder
1/4 tsp. hot sauce
1/2 tsp. Worcestershire sauce

Combine all ingredients in large bowl; mix well. Pour into jars. Store in refrigerator.

Diane Frost, Barry

BUCKEYE BALLS

1 lb. butter, melted
2 lb. peanut butter
3 16-oz. packages confectioners' sugar
4 6-oz. packages chocolate chips
1 stick paraffin

Combine butter, peanut butter and confectioners' sugar in large bowl; mix well. Shape into walnut-sized balls; place on baking sheets. Let stand until firm. Melt chocolate chips and paraffin in double boiler. Keep warm over hot water. Dip each ball in chocolate with toothpick; coat with chocolate leaving a small portion uncovered to resemble buckeye.
Yield: 100 servings.

Approx per serv: Cal 185; Prot 2.9 g; T Fat 11.4 g; Chl 11.5 mg; Car 20.4 g; Sod 108.2 mg; Pot 88.7 mg.

Betty Kolcz, Branch

CRANBERRY-RASPBERRY WHIP

4 c. pear juice
14 oz. raspberry gelatin
4 c. whipping cream
3 16-oz. cans jellied cranberry sauce
1 No. 10 can pears, drained, chopped

Heat pear juice in saucepan. Add gelatin; stir until dissolved. Chill until partially set. Whip cream in large mixer bowl at medium speed. Reduce speed to low. Add cranberry sauce; beat until blended. Stir in gelatin. Fold in pears. Pour into large pan. Chill until firm. Cut into serving portions. Yield: 30 servings.

Approx per serv: Cal 227; Prot 1.8 g; T Fat 0.3 g; Chl 0.0 mg; Car 57.2 g; Sod 62.7 mg; Pot 249.4 mg.

Kettunen Center

PUNCH BOWL CAKE

1 2-layer pkg. yellow cake mix
3 lg. packages vanilla instant
pudding mix
2 20-oz. cans crushed pineapple
2 cans cherry pie filling
2 16-oz. cartons whipped topping

Bake cake according to package directions; cool and crumble. Prepare pudding mix. Layer half the cake, pudding, and remaining ingredients in punch bowl. Repeat layers; garnish with nuts.

Shirley Merriman, Calhoun

PAM'S TEXAS SHEET CAKE

2 c. sugar
2 eggs
1/2 c. sour cream
2 sticks margarine
1/4 c. cocoa
2 c. flour
1 tsp. soda
1 stick margarine
1/4 c. cocoa
6 tbsp. milk
1 16-oz. package confectioners' sugar
1 tsp. vanilla extract

Combine sugar, eggs and sour cream in bowl; mix well. Combine 2 sticks margarine, 1/4 cup cocoa and 1 cup water in saucepan. Bring to a boil. Pour over mixture of flour and soda in large bowl; mix well. Add sour cream mixture; mix well. Pour into ungreased 12 x 18-inch baking pan. Bake at 350 degrees for 15 to 20 minutes or until cake tests done. Combine 1 stick margarine, 1/4 cup cocoa and 6 tablespoons milk in saucepan. Bring to a boil; remove from heat. Add confectioners' sugar and vanilla; mix well. Spread hot icing over hot cake. Yield: 54 servings.

Approx per serv: Cal 136; Prot 1.0 g; T Fat 6.0 g; Chl 10.5 mg; Car 20.4 g; Sod 82.1 mg; Pot 26.5 mg;

Pam Babbitt, Muskegon

LEBKUCHEN

4 c. sour cream
2 tbsp. soda
8 oz. seedless raisins
8 oz. golden raisins
8 oz. currants
8 oz. prunes, chopped
8 oz. figs, chopped
8 oz. candied cherries and
  pineapple, chopped
8 oz. almonds, chopped
5 lb. flour
2 tsp. salt
1 tbsp. each cinnamon, cloves and nutmeg
1 1/2 c. shortening
1 16-oz. package brown sugar
4 c. molasses

Mix sour cream and soda. Combine fruits and almonds in large bowl. Add a small amount of flour; mix until coated. Mix remaining flour with salt and spices. Cream shortening and brown sugar in large bowl. Add flour mixture alternately with sour cream and molasses, mixing well after each addition. Add fruit mixture; mix well with hands. Let stand, covered, in cool place for 6 hours to overnight. Drop by spoonfuls onto baking sheet. Bake at 350 degrees for 10 to 12 minutes. Yield: 300 servings.

Approx per serv: Cal 80; Prot 1.2 g; T Fat 2.2 g; Chl 1.4 mg; Car 14.0 g; Sod 27.2 mg; Pot 30.0 mg.

Janelle Eisele, Livingston

MONSTER COOKIES

1 lb. margarine, softened
2 16-oz. packages brown sugar
4 c. sugar
12 eggs
1/4 c. vanilla extract
3 lb. peanut butter
8 tsp. baking powder
18 c. quick-cooking oats
2 lb. chocolate chips
1 12-oz. package butterscotch chips
1 lb. M and M candies
1 lb. chopped pecans (opt.)

Cream first 4 ingredients in bowl. Add vanilla, peanut butter, baking powder and oats; mix well. Fold in remaining ingredients. Drop by tablespoonfuls onto cookie sheet. Bake at 350 degrees for 8 to 10 minutes. Cookies are ugly but taste great. Yield: 200 servings.

Approx per serv: Cal 289; Prot 5.5 g; T Fat 18.9 g; Chl 30.6 mg; Car 28.4 g; Sod 216.7 mg; Pot 205.7 mg.

David Dostaler, Houghton, Melissa Elliot, Delta
Eric Smith, Muskegon

NO-FAIL PIE CRUSTS

5 c. flour
1 tbsp. salt
2 c. lard
1 egg, beaten
1 tbsp. vinegar

Mix flour and salt in bowl. Cut in lard until crumbly. Beat egg with vinegar and 1/2 cup cold water. Sprinkle over flour mixture; mix well. Divide into 5 portions. Roll out on lightly floured surface; fit into 9-inch pie plates. Prick with fork. Bake at 375 degrees until golden. Yield: 5 crusts.

Sandy Hilts, Ogemaw

Nutrients for Good Health

Food is important for health and growth. It is made up of many different nutrients, each of which has a certain job to do in the body. Most foods contain more than one nutrient but no one food provides all the different nutrients needed. So, it is important to eat a variety of foods every day to supply your body with the various nutrients it requires. Nutrition labels on food products can be used as a guide to the amounts of nutrients in the foods you choose to buy.

Following is information on why you need some of these nutrients and the types of foods in which they are found.

Important Nutrients Your Diet Requires

PROTEIN
Why?   Absolutely essential in building, repairing and renewing of all body tissue. Helps body resist infection. Builds enzymes and hormones, helps form and maintain body fluids.
Where?   Milk, eggs, lean meats, poultry, fish, soybeans, peanuts, dried peas and beans, grains and cereals.

CARBOHYDRATES
Why?   Provide needed energy for bodily functions, provide warmth, as well as fuel for brain and nerve tissues. Lack of carbohydrates will cause body to use protein for energy rather than for repair and building.
Where?   Sugars: Sugar, table syrups, jellies, jams, etc., as well as dried and fresh fruits. Starches: cereals, pasta, rice, corn, dried beans and peas, potatoes, stem and leafy vegetables, and milk.

FATS
Why?   Essential in the use of fat soluble vitamins (A,D,E,K) and fatty acids. Have more than twice the concentrated energy than equal amount of carbohydrate for body energy and warmth.
Where?   Margarine, butter, cooking oil, mayonnaise, lard, bacon, vegetable shortening, whole milk, cream, ice cream, cheese, meat, fish eggs, poultry, chocolate, coconut, nuts.

VITAMIN A
Why?   Needed for healthy skin and hair, as well as for healthy, infection resistent mucous membranes.
Where?   Dark green, leafy and yellow vegetables, liver. Deep yellow fruits, such as apricots and cantaloupe. Milk, cheese, eggs, as well as butter and fortified margarine.

THIAMIN (VITAMIN B_1)
Why?   Aids in the release of energy of foods, as well as in normal appetite and digestion. Promotes healthy nervous system.
Where?   Pork, liver, kidney. Dried peas and beans. Whole grain and enriched breads and cereals.

RIBOFLAVIN (VITAMIN B_2)
Why?   Helps to oxidize foods. Promotes healthy eyes and skin, especially around mouth and eyes. Prevents pellagra.
Where?   Meats, especially liver and kidney, as well as milk, cheese, eggs. Dark green leafy vegetables. Enriched bread and cereal products. Almonds, dried peas and beans.

VITAMIN B_6
Why?   Helps protein in building body tissues. Needed for healthy nerves, skin and digestion. Also helps body to use fats and carbohydrates for energy.
Where?   Milk, wheat germ, whole grain and fortified cereals. Liver, kidney, pork and beef.

VITAMIN B$_{12}$
Why? Aids body in formation of red blood cells, as well as in regular work of all body cells.
Where? Lean meats, milk, eggs, fish, cheese, as well as liver and kidney.

VITAMIN C (ASCORBIC ACID)
Why? Promotes proper bone and tooth formation. Helps body utilize iron and resist infection. Strengthens blood vessels. Lack of it causes bones to heal slowly, failure of wounds to heal and fragile vessels to bleed easily.
Where? Citrus fruits, cantaloupe and strawberries. Broccoli, kale, green peppers, raw cabbage, sweet potatoes, cauliflower, tomatoes.

VITAMIN D
Why? Builds strong bones and teeth by aiding utilization of calcium and phosphorus.
Where? Fortified milk, fish liver oils, as well as salmon, tuna and sardines. Also eggs.

VITAMIN E
Why? Needed in maintaining red blood cells.
Where? Whole grain cereals, wheat germ, beans and peas, lettuce and eggs.

IRON
Why? Used with protein for hemoglobin production. Forms nucleus of each cell, and helps them to use oxygen.
Where? Kidney and liver, as well as shellfish, lean meats, and eggs. Deep yellow and dark green leafy vegetables. Dried peas, beans and fruits. Potatoes, whole grain cereals and bread. Enriched flour and bread. Dark molasses.

CALCIUM
Why? Builds and renews bones, teeth and other tissues, as well as aids in the proper function of muscles, nerves and heart. Controls normal blood clotting. With protein, aids in oxidation of foods.
Where? Milk and milk products, excluding butter. Dark green vegetables, oysters, clams and sardines.

NIACIN
Why? Helps body to oxidize food. Aids in digestion, and helps to keep nervous system and skin healthy.
Where? Peanuts, liver, tuna, as well as fish, poultry and lean meats. Enriched breads, cereals and peas.

MAGNESIUM
Why? Aids nervous system and sleep.
Where? Almonds, peanuts, raisins and prunes. Vegetables, fruits, milk, fish and meats.

ZINC
Why? Needed for cell formation.
Where? Nuts and leafy green vegetables. Shellfish and meats.

PHOSPHORUS
Why? Maintains normal blood clotting function, as well as builds bones, teeth and nerve tissue. Aids in utilization of sugar and fats.
Where? Oatmeal and whole wheat products. Eggs, milk and cheese, dried beans and peas. Nuts, lean meats, and fish and poultry.

IODINE
Why? Enables thyroid gland to maintain proper body metabolism.
Where? Iodized salt. Saltwater fish and seafood. Milk and vegetables grown in iodine-rich soil.

Microwave Tips

- Always choose the minimum cooking time given in a recipe. Remember, food continues to cook after it is removed from the microwave.
- Keep your microwave clean. Built-up grease or spatters can slow cooking times.
- Do not try to hard-cook eggs in the shell in a microwave. They will build up pressure and burst.
- When cooking an egg in the microwave, always pierce the center of the yolk with a fork to keep the egg from exploding.
- To prevent soggy rolls, elevate rolls on roasting rack and wrap in paper towels while heating. Heat on 30 percent power if available.
- Do not use metal dishes or aluminum foil except as specifically recommended by the manufacturer of your microwave.
- Be sure to prick potatoes before baking to allow steam to escape.
- Cut a small slit in pouch-packed frozen foods before heating to allow steam to escape.
- When placing more than one food item in microwave, arrange foods in a circle.
- Arrange large pieces of meat and poultry with the thickest parts to the outside.
- Be sure to have pot holders handy. Microwave utensils can become hot from the heat in cooked food.
- Carefully take off coverings. Always remove plastic wrap or lid away from your face to prevent burns from built-up steam.
- Stir foods from the outside edge of the dish to the center; edges cook faster in microwave ovens and this will help to equalize the temperature.
- Use your microwave oven to melt chocolate or soften cream cheese and butter.
- Roast shelled nuts for 6 to 10 minutes on 100 percent power, stirring frequently.
- Plump dried fruit by placing in a dish with 1 to 2 teaspoons water. Cover tightly with vented plastic wrap. Heat for 1/2 to 1 1/2 minutes on 100 percent power.
- Precook barbecued ribs or chicken until almost done then place on the grill to sear and add a charcoal flavor.

Substitution Chart

	INSTEAD OF . . .	USE . . .
BAKING	1 teaspoon baking powder	1/4 teaspoon soda plus 1/2 teaspoon cream of tartar
	1 tablespoon cornstarch (for thickening)	2 tablespoons flour or 1 tablespoon tapioca
	1 cup sifted all-purpose flour	1 cup plus 2 tablespoons sifted cake flour
	1 cup sifted cake flour	1 cup minus 2 tablespoons sifted all-purpose flour
	1 cup fine dry bread crumbs	3/4 cup fine cracker crumbs
DAIRY	1 cup buttermilk	1 cup sour milk or 1 cup yogurt
	1 cup heavy cream	3/4 cup skim milk plus 1/3 cup butter
	1 cup light cream	7/8 cup skim milk plus 3 tablespoons butter
	1 cup sour cream	7/8 cup sour milk plus 3 tablespoons butter
	1 cup sour milk	1 cup sweet milk plus 1 tablespoon vinegar or lemon juice or 1 cup buttermilk
SEASONINGS	1 teaspoon allspice	1/2 teaspoon cinnamon plus 1/8 teaspoon cloves
	1 cup catsup	1 cup tomato sauce plus 1/2 cup sugar plus 2 tablespoons vinegar
	1 clove of garlic	1/8 teaspoon garlic powder or 1/8 teaspoon instant minced garlic or 3/4 teaspoon garlic salt or 5 drops of liquid garlic
	1 teaspoon Italian spice	1/4 teaspoon each oregano, basil, thyme, rosemary plus dash of cayenne
	1 teaspoon lemon juice	1/2 teaspoon vinegar
	1 tablespoon prepared mustard	1 teaspoon dry mustard
	1 medium onion	1 tablespoon dried minced onion or 1 teaspoon onion powder
SWEET	1 1-ounce square chocolate	3 to 4 tablespoons cocoa plus 1 teaspoon shortening
	1 2/3 ounces semisweet chocolate	1 ounce unsweetened chocolate plus 4 teaspoons sugar
	1 cup honey	1 to 1 1/4 cups sugar plus 1/4 cup liquid or 1 cup molasses or corn syrup
	1 cup granulated sugar	1 cup packed brown sugar or 1 cup corn syrup, molasses or honey minus 1/4 cup liquid

Equivalent Chart

WHEN RECIPE CALLS FOR . . .	YOU NEED . . .
BAKING ESSENTIALS	
1/2 cup butter	1 stick
2 cups butter	1 pound
4 cups all-purpose flour	1 pound
4 1/2 to 5 cups sifted cake flour	1 pound
1 square chocolate	1 ounce
1 cup semisweet chocolate pieces	1 6-ounce package
4 cups marshmallows	1 pound
2 1/4 cups packed brown sugar	1 pound
4 cups confectioners' sugar	1 pound
2 cups granulated sugar	1 pound
3 cups tapioca	1 pound
CEREAL AND BREAD	
1 cup fine dry bread crumbs	4 to 5 slices
1 cup soft bread crumbs	2 slices
1 cup small bread cubes	2 slices
1 cup fine cracker crumbs	28 saltines
1 cup fine graham cracker crumbs	15 crackers
1 cup vanilla wafer crumbs	22 wafers
1 cup crushed cornflakes	3 cups uncrushed
3 1/2 cups cooked rice	1 cup uncooked
DAIRY	
1 cup freshly grated cheese	1/4 pound
1 cup cottage cheese	1 8-ounce carton
1 cup sour cream	1 8-ounce carton
1 cup whipped cream	1/2 cup heavy cream
2/3 cup evaporated milk	1 small can
1 2/3 cups evaporated milk	1 13-ounce can
FRUIT	
4 cups sliced or chopped apples	4 medium
1 cup mashed banana	3 medium
2 cups pitted cherries	4 cups unpitted
3 cups shredded coconut	1/2 pound
4 cups cranberries	1 pound
1 cup pitted dates	1 8-ounce package
1 cup candied fruit	1 8-ounce package
3 to 4 tablespoons lemon juice plus 1 teaspoon grated rind	1 lemon
1/3 cup orange juice plus 2 teaspoons grated rind	1 orange
4 cups sliced peaches	8 medium
2 cups pitted prunes	1 12-ounce package
3 cups raisins	1 15-ounce package

WHEN RECIPE CALLS FOR . . .		YOU NEED . . .
MEATS	4 cups diced cooked chicken 3 cups diced cooked meat 2 cups ground cooked meat	1 5-pound chicken 1 pound, cooked 1 pound, cooked
NUTS	1 cup chopped nuts	4 ounces, shelled 1 pound, unshelled
VEGETABLES	2 cups cooked green beans 2 1/2 cups lima beans or red beans 4 cups shredded cabbage 1 cup grated carrot 1 4-ounce can mushrooms 1 cup chopped onion 4 cups sliced or diced raw potatoes 2 cups canned tomatoes	1/2 pound fresh or 1 16-ounce can 1 cup dried, cooked 1 pound 1 large 1/2 pound, fresh 1 large 4 medium 1 16-ounce can

COMMON EQUIVALENTS

1 tablespoon = 3 teaspoons
2 tablespoons = 1 ounce
4 tablespoons = 1/4 cup
5 tablespoons + 1 teaspoon = 1/3 cup
8 tablespoons = 1/2 cup
12 tablespoons = 3/4 cup
16 tablespoons = 1 cup
1 cup = 8 ounces or 1/2 pint
4 cups = 1 quart
4 quarts = 1 gallon

6 1/2 to 8-ounce can = 1 cup
10 1/2 to 12-ounce can = 1 1/4 cups
14 to 16-ounce can (No. 300) = 1 3/4 cups
16 to 17-ounce can (No. 303) = 2 cups
1-pound 4-ounce can or 1-pint 2-ounce can (No. 2)
   = 2 1/2 cups
1-pound 13-ounce can (No. 2 1/2) = 3 1/2 cups
3-pound 3-ounce can or 46-ounce can = 5 3/4 cups
6 1/2-pound or 7-pound 5-ounce can (No. 10)
   = 12 to 13 cups

Metric Chart

1 teaspoon = 5 milliliters
1 tablespoon = 15 milliliters
1 fluid ounce = 30 milliliters
1 cup = 250 milliliters
1 pint = 500 milliliters

1 quart = 1 liter
1 ounce = 30 grams
1 pound = 450 grams
2.2 pounds = 1 kilogram

NOTE: The metric measures are approximate benchmarks for purposes of home food preparation.

Index

158 / Index

Savor it!

COMPLETE YOUR COOKBOOK LIBRARY
OR GIVE AS PERFECT GIFTS

FOR ORDER INFORMATION
WRITE TO:

MICHIGAN 4-H FOUNDATION
220 Nisbet Building
1407 South Harrison Road
East Lansing, Michigan 48823

FAVORITE RECIPES® OF
THE MICHIGAN 4-H FAMILY